Translated from the Czech
by Sir Cecil Parrott

THE GOOD SOLDIER ŠVEJK
AND HIS FORTUNES IN THE WORLD WAR
by Jaroslav Hašek

The Tightrope

CECIL PARROTT

FABER AND FABER

LONDON

First published in 1975
by Faber and Faber Limited
3 Queen Square London WC1
Printed in Great Britain by
Western Printing Services Ltd
Bristol

ISBN 0 571 10256 5

CONTENTS

ILLUSTRATIONS

Between pages 96 and 97

MAPS

TO SMATZO

YUGOSLAVIA

Scale 1cm=57km

CHAPTER ONE ◇ A SINISTER POSTAGE STAMP

◇ As a child, I remember a lady once showing me a stamp and telling me an exciting story about it. It bore the heads of two rulers in profile, one beside the other. They came from a faraway country: one of them was the founder of a royal dynasty, and the other his grandson and a king.

I saw nothing unusual in the stamp until the lady turned it upside down and asked me to have another look. I peered closer. The outlines and shadings of the inverted noses and mouths of the two rulers revealed – a ghastly mutilated head. She then began to trace the outline of what could have been the plot of a Renaissance drama. It was the story of two dynasties and the blood feud between them.

I cannot remember the details as they were told to me at the time, but I learned afterwards that the stamp was issued in Serbia in 1904. One night a year earlier, conspirators had burst into the palace of King Alexander Obrenović and his Queen, Draga, at Belgrade, brutally murdered them, and thrown their savagely mutilated bodies out of the window. Prince Peter Karageorgević of the rival dynasty, who was living in exile, returned to Serbia and ascended the throne. The regicides were given leading positions in the state.

The new régime issued a stamp to celebrate the centenary of the founding of the Karageorgević dynasty. This was the one the lady had shown me. The two heads it depicted were those of the new ruler, King Peter, and Kara or 'Black' George, his grandfather, who had led the first Serbian rising against the Turks. The blood feud between the families had started with an 'original sin', the murder of Kara George by his rival and fellow Serb, Miloš Obrenović, in 1817. What made the crime even more heinous was that it was carried out by Kara George's godfather.

Although the 1903 murder wiped out the Obrenović family, they still had supporters in the country, who were only too ready to blame the crime on the Karageorgević dynasty. Hostile elements surreptitiously introduced the head of the murdered king into the stamp in the contours of the two rulers' features. It was like a horrible children's puzzle: find the head of the King.

This little incident captured my imagination and remained with me long after. I recalled it vividly when I was offered the post of tutor to the last reigning Karageorgević, then Crown Prince and later King Peter II of Yugoslavia.

✧ Many people have asked me how I came to be appointed. Even by that time the number of European crowned heads had diminished so much that there were only a few who would be likely to want an Englishman to educate their sons. The process of appointment was a great deal more conventional than one might have supposed.

In 1934 I suddenly received a letter from my former Cambridge tutor, Paul Vellacott, asking me whether I would be interested in taking on the job of tutor to the Crown Prince of Yugoslavia. 'I think you would do well seriously offering yourself for this job,' he wrote. 'It would give you a new experience and might lead to something else very interesting and more permanent.' He told me I should receive more information if I wrote to Miss Ida Marr, the ex-governess of the Queen's sister, Princess Ileana of Romania, who lived near Cambridge. I accordingly did so, and received back a nice letter with some entrancing photographs of the royal children and the palace, one of which will be found in plate 1. They conquered me. Although I really wanted to make myself a German specialist and had no particular interest in the Balkans, I felt I could not reject this opportunity. It seemed the chance of a lifetime.

The next development was the arrival of a letter from the Minister of the Court, Mr. Milan Antić, offering me the appointment and proposing the princely salary of £250 a year. I showed the letter to Lionel Smith, the Rector of Edinburgh Academy where I had been teaching, and himself a former tutor to the Prince of Wales, who commented drily: 'If they want an Englishman they've got to pay him an Englishman's salary.' And so, taking my courage in my hands, I wrote back and asked for £450. The Minister replied, more in sorrow than in anger, that £250 was perfectly adequate in view of 'the privileges and perquisites which you will receive *on* your post.' However, in the last paragraph of the letter he increased the offer to £350, and I accepted it.

✧ One morning in April of that year, I found myself looking out over the undulating Serbian countryside at breakfast time as the Simplon Orient Express sped towards Belgrade. Sitting opposite me was an Englishman, and when the waiter asked him whether he would like bacon and eggs, he replied, 'No thanks! Not after I've seen their pigs.' I looked out of the window. There were indeed lots of dark brown and hirsute creatures, not at all like our English pigs, to be seen on both sides of the track and my travelling companion might easily have mistaken them for bears. But like many Englishmen he was quite ignorant of the history of the country he was travelling through. He did not know that in the old days Serbia had exported large quantities of pork to Vienna and that the discriminating inhabitants of that city had prized it highly. In fact, in the so-called 'Pig War' the Austrian government had had to abandon all attempts to coerce Serbia by boycotting her exports because the Monarchy could not exist without Serbian pork. What is more, the hero in the struggle for Serbian independence – Kara George – had himself driven his pigs and cattle through these very tracts. In Yugoslavia it was hardly decent to speak deprecatingly of pigs!

I arrived at Belgrade railway station with my heart in my mouth. No one met me, so I took a taxi and drove off to the British Legation for guidance. Here I was breezily received by the Second Secretary, Mr. Cowan, who drove me in his Riley car to the Old Palace. He introduced me there to a young Serb attaché by the name of Botorić. Mr. Botorić spoke English perfectly and seemed very Western in his habits.

I was immediately ushered into the presence of the Minister himself who informed me with grave dignity that the Queen and the young princes were staying at a place called Hercegnovi on the Dalmatian coast between Dubrovnik and Kotor. Tomorrow I should travel there by train. Meanwhile, Mr. Botorić would show me something of Belgrade. The same afternoon the attaché called at my hotel in one of the palace cars and drove me to Dedinje, the newly built palace of the King and Queen. It lay on top of a hill a few miles out of the town and commanded a wonderful view of the Serbian countryside. The royal couple had the main palace to themselves, and the little princes and their governesses lived in a small English cottage with a thatched roof in the middle of the grounds.

My visit was brief and I did not have time to take much in, but my attention was at once caught by a remarkable sculpture of a Dalmatian woman in front of an azure blue *bassin* with a floor of mosaics. Near it were two urns bearing a frieze of peasants and warriors in relief. They were powerful and noble, and typical of the work of the Croat sculptor, Ivan Mestrović.

A friendly officer from the Palace Guard took me round the

foundations of a new building which was being constructed for the Crown Prince. It filled me with self-importance. A special house under construction for my charge! Later he pointed out the foundations of a room which was designed for the Crown Prince's tutor. This was greatness indeed!

The following day, which happened to be May Day, Mr. Botorić and I were rattling and jolting along in a train towards Bosnia and Herzegovina, those provinces which became famous after their annexation by Austria in 1908 followed by the murder of the Archduke Franz Ferdinand at Sarajevo in 1914. We shared a first-class carriage, which could be converted into a sleeper for the night. In the next compartment travelled a gendarme with a rifle and the royal mail.

The journey took some thirty hours with a stop at Sarajevo, the Bosnian capital, where we had to change trains and proceed by small gauge railway to Hercegnovi. It was evening when we arrived at Sarajevo, and as we had about an hour to wait for the connection, my companion engaged a taxi and drove me round the town. In the dusk I could just make out fascinating old Turkish houses with upper storeys jutting out over the ground floor rooms, and catch fleeting glimpses of veiled women and men with fezes. Bosnia was then more Turkish than Turkey itself. At my request Mr. Botorić took me to the spot where the Archduke Franz Ferdinand had been assassinated. On the embankment before one crossed the bridge over the Miljacka River, a black marble plaque had been set up in commemoration of the two revolver shots which 'murdered seven million men'. The inscription on it read: 'Here in this historic place, Gavrilo Princip was the harbinger of liberty on the day of Vidovdan (St. Vitus' day) on 15th (28th) June 1914.' As the assassin was only twenty years old at the time, he was spared capital punishment – only to die of tuberculosis on 28th April 1918 in the Austrian prison of Terezín or Theresienstadt in Bohemia, later notorious as one of Himmler's ghettos. It was just too soon for him to see the liberation of his country. I was told that his body lay with those of eleven of his comrades in the Orthodox cemetery under a simple monument with the stark alliteration 'SAMO SLOGA SERBINA SPASAVA' – 'Only Unity saves the Serb.'

When we at last arrived at Hercegnovi it was a hot summer day and the Adriatic sparkled so brilliantly that I was blinded. A Court car driven by a chauffeur in royal livery was waiting to collect us, and we drove up the narrow, steep and winding high street of this small fishing town to the Hotel Boka, my home for the next few months. The Packard slid down the short drive to the hotel entrance and within a few minutes I was sitting at a table beneath orange and lemon trees, drinking Turkish coffee with officers in gay uniforms, under the powerful glare of the Dalmatian sun and the azure blue of the Adriatic.

Hercegnovi was a townlet of some 1,500 inhabitants perched on the terraces of the mountains of Montenegro and looking out over the Boka Kotorska (the Bay of Cattaro). Founded by a Bosnian king in the fourteenth century, it has passed under Turkish and then Venetian rule. It was dominated by a fortress which bore an inscription in Arabic. The hotel, famous for its garden and exotic arboretum, was situated high above the sea, and to reach the beach one had to thread one's way down a labyrinth of steep terraces, its so-called 'park'.

Two giant Serbian guards standing in resplendent uniforms before the hotel door were an intimidating obstacle. The spectacle of the officers off duty as they sat drinking coffee for at least the twentieth time that morning was less impressive, with their white tunics soiled and creased in the hot weather, and their collars open. But the sense of grandeur was restored when to the strains of loud martial music the royal guard appeared marching up the short drive of the hotel. They were a remarkable sight in their scarlet, blue and white uniforms in the setting of orange and lemon trees, magnolias, and semi-tropical flowers.

◇ Once installed in the Hotel Boka, I seemed to lose all concept of time. I cannot remember how long it was before I was presented to my royal pupil. I had all meals with the Queen's adjutants and orderly officers except breakfast, which I had by myself in the big room that had obviously been the hotel dining-room. The order of the day was as follows. I got up and had my breakfast at a reasonable hour and called in at the adjutants' room to find out whether I would be needed, the answer always being the same: 'We must wait until Her Majesty comes downstairs.' Thereupon I was offered a cup of Turkish coffee and sat down and relaxed with the officers. The peace and tranquillity was regularly broken by the strident sounding of a gong, at which the adjutant and orderly officers on duty at once put out their cigarettes, sprang up, did up their collars, fastened their swords and dashed out into the hall. From there I could hear the sound of feet and children's voices, followed by the loud and boisterous voice of someone speaking Serbian with a German accent, whom I took to be the Queen. The clicking of heels, kissing of hands and clinking of spurs would have been audible a mile off. Presently there was a banging of doors, children's laughter and finally the noise of a car driving away, after which silence returned. The door of the room opened and the adjutants came in, undid their collars, took off their belts, resumed their comfortable attitudes in their armchairs, lit new cigarettes and ordered another round of coffee. Then they began to talk. They talked incessantly the whole day long except when they were interrupted by duty, settled down to an interminable game of chess, or sipped their countless cups of coffee.

The day was divided up by two events, the moment when the Royal Family came down that staircase and went out, and the moment when they returned in the evening and went upstairs again. In between I was completely free, since they were on the other side of the bay and as good as incommunicado, and I attempted to create some kind of pleasurable existence for myself.

The meals in the adjutants' quarters were attended by the Captain of the Guard and his junior officer as well as by visiting minor court functionaries from Belgrade. I was attracted by a fine, upstanding, handsome Bosnian lieutenant with whom I tried to strike up a conversation in my bad Serbian. It was difficult for me to grasp his sentiments; what he seemed to be conveying was that without question he would lay down his life for his King. Once he told me that the next day would be St. George's day – a national holiday. Would I like to attend it as his guest? Of course I would, I said. To my consternation he added that we should have to get up at five o'clock. I obediently did so. We strolled along the road in the early hours and soon found ourselves in a field bordered by gorgeous wild lilies and shaded in part by olive trees. Even at this hour it was swelteringly hot, and I suffered as I stood for hours watching the endless processions of boys and men in Sokol uniforms, military uniforms, scout dress and national costumes, which were the inevitable feature of such celebrations in Yugoslavia during that period. To dispel the tedium I tried from time to time to carry on a conversation with my host, but without success. In the meantime, I was becoming extremely eager for my breakfast. To my relief I saw that a table was being set out and spread with all sorts of good things. But however much my stomach groaned for sustinence my friend never gave me the sign to come and eat. At one point I ventured to suggest to him that we might move in the direction of the table, but from his answer I assumed that it was reserved for special guests or high officials. In the end, I returned to the hotel at about ten o'clock in a ravenous state and tried to beg some breakfast. The adjutant kindly arranged this but he looked at me curiously. 'There was a very good breakfast to be had there,' he said. 'Why didn't you want to have it?' His version of the incident was that the lieutenant had offered me food but I had for some unknown reason declined it. It was a glowing tribute to my knowledge of Serbian! I resolved that it would be a matter of life and death for me to be able to speak and understand the Slav languages.

I got to know a Slovenian naval lieutenant in command of one of the royal motor boats that carried the Queen and her family to other parts of the bay who spoke excellent Serbo-Croat, Russian and German and had a Russian wife. I spent long hours in their friendly company, either sailing alone with him in the Bay of Kotor in a small boat or spending evenings with them both trying to talk Russian. By this time I had decided that if I was going to make the effort required to learn Serbian I might as well learn the language of the big Slav brother with its world literature, too. I had halcyon days with Lieutenant Stiglic sailing over the wide reaches of the Boka and picnicking in various delightful creeks. Sometimes we got becalmed in these treacherous waters and wearily had to row our way back to the shore. Sometimes we made expeditions by night spearing fish by lamplight. Afterwards we lit a camp fire, and cooked and ate what we had caught.

The evenings brought magical Russian lessons with Mrs. Stiglic – Elizaveta Georgevna. For endless hours the three of us joked in Russian, laughed at my mistakes and saw each other home, only to return and repeat the operation once more, to the accompaniment of nightingales answering one another from grove to grove and of fireflies guiding our steps with their tiny beacon lights. The Russian manual the lieutenant had lent me was an old-fashioned German one, which contained innumerable sentences about monks with beehives being attacked by swarms of bees, these words apparently having in Russian some mystical grammatical connection. In that carefree atmosphere even the complexities of Russian grammar lost their importance for me. We laughed at everything. It did not matter that I had not yet been presented to my pupil. I was living in lotus land.

The first member of the Royal Family I caught a glimpse of was the youngest, Prince Andrej (Andy). He was about four. I was having a late breakfast by myself in the big dining-room at the hotel when all at once I heard gay laughter and a child's voice saying, 'Who's that man?', after which a girl's voice quickly hushed him up. I looked round and saw a golden apparition. A girl with a fairness of hair and skin which suggested that she was neither Yugoslav nor English was passing through the dining-room at the other end, holding a child by the hand. Fortunately I did not have to get up. The hall was big enough for me to be able to regard myself as invisible, and anyhow I had not been presented to the Prince or introduced to the girl.

In this exotic Ruritanian atmosphere I had forgotten what it felt like to be at home. Such feelings came surging back to me when I saw this domestic scene. Andy was all the time turning his head round to have a good stare as he was being led out, and I was conscious only of two enormous ears, but the girl did not allow me to see her face.

◇ One day a shadow fell. The senior adjutant on duty warned me that 'any day now' Her Majesty might wish to see me. From that moment I had to be constantly on the alert. Someone had told me that when I was presented to the Queen I should have to wear a morning coat and striped trousers. As at any hour my time might come, I now had to get up and put on these awful garments in the hottest of summers. I could only take them off when it was clear that the Royal Family had gone away for the day. Sometimes the weather changed and they were kept indoors, and then I had to go on suffering in this outfit until I received permission to shed it. However, at last the order came. 'Her Majesty will receive you this afternoon in her apartments.'

Her Majesty was Queen 'Mignon' of Yugoslavia, daughter of King Ferdinand of Romania and of his wife Marie, who was in turn daughter of the Duke of Edinburgh, second son of Queen Victoria. The room to which I was ushered was a small one, more typical of a fifth floor bedroom in an English seaside hotel than a Queen's sitting-room. It was sparely furnished – desk, sofa and chairs but no books. There was a marvellous view of the sea from the balcony.

The Queen was thirty-five years old. She was handsome and of large build and simply, almost primitively dressed in a blouse and skirt, and she had bright blue eyes, a pretty mouth and a marked German accent. In her animated conversation, she laid a heavy guttural stress on every word. She had an attractive, trusting approach, free from any trace of standoffishness.

She kept me for about an hour talking about my pupil. She told me that he was eventually to go to school in Belgrade and would learn most of the stock subjects there. I was to teach him English, tutor him and be his companion. She did not conceal his shortcomings: although quite intelligent he was dreamy and slow and had 'no grasp'. He had no ambition to improve but was inordinately sensitive if his brothers did something better than he did, so that instead of being spurred to greater achievements by their successes he was piqued by it. He was physically underdeveloped and needed to be encouraged to take part in outdoor sports. Here fear was a great deterrent, particularly in riding. The Queen asked me if I rode, and when I said with the minimum of truth that I did, she was pleased. 'Good, you can go with him.' She was particularly keen for him to be a good rider, as she herself and her family had always ridden since they were babies.

Then she took me outside and presented me to him. My first impression as he stood in the garden in front of the Hotel Boka was of a very pale, thin and stiff little child, but his face was attractive and his small hazel eyes revealed humour and good will. Not for the first time I felt there was something pathetic about him. It was hardly fair to judge him on this first meeting, though, because he had been in bed for a fortnight. To start with, he was rather wary of me and uncertain how he should react. The next day I went over to the other side of the bay with him – to Njivica, the strip of beach where the Royal Family had been spending their days. He fished most of the time and talked to me in what seemed a childishly frank and friendly way. He was then not quite eleven years old.

Going across the bay every day to bathe, which was what we did, was a dull, lazy and monotonous existence in the Dalmatian heat. I soon felt I must vary the programme and take him on expeditions to get him out of the nursery atmosphere. Moreover, I wanted anyhow to see more of the country and not be thrown together too much with the Queen, the younger children and the nurses, the senior of whom was an Englishwoman. The golden-haired one was attractive, but duty called.

One day the Queen took me round to the front of the hotel where her Packard car was standing ready for an excursion. 'Do you drive?' she asked. 'A little,' I said. 'Good,' she replied, 'then you can drive him.' Later she showed me a Ford roadster, which she christened the 'bone-shaker'. 'This is his car,' she said, 'I put it at your disposal and you can use it when you like.' Evidently there would be no trouble about excursions.

I had driven cars since the age of thirteen, when I had filled up a form saying that I was 'in my fourteenth year' and thus obtained a motor cycle licence which I then used for driving a car. But it was some time since I had last driven and the prospect of being responsible for the life of the Crown Prince of a Balkan country made me hesitate. I asked Boža, the chauffeur, if I could begin by taking the car out with him alone. We drove together down the narrow streets of Hercegnovi.

I was not familiar with the car or the geography of the place. The streets were full of pot-holes and there were jay-walking trippers everywhere. In striving to avoid a boulder on one side I nearly ran into some tourists on the other. The chauffeur looked as if he was going to have a fit but the tourists escaped unscathed.

This contretemps was to have its consequences. The next day the adjutant on duty came up and said in a mysterious tone. 'I have been asked to make a request of you.' 'Really,' I replied. 'What's that?' 'I have been asked,' he went on, 'to persuade you not to drive the Crown Prince in the car.' 'Who asked you?' I enquired. 'After all the Queen herself said she wanted me to drive and especially authorized me to do so.' 'Nonetheless, I have been asked to persuade you not to,' he continued stonily.

I swallowed my pride and took the hint. From that day on I never drove the Crown Prince in his car outside the grounds. And it was good advice. By wisely submitting to what was a galling request I spared myself much unpleasantness. I knew the move had not emanated from the Queen herself.

✧ I have mentioned that during all this time the King was away. I believe he was hunting somewhere in the north of the country. All of a sudden, the news was announced that he was coming to stay. As if by magic, everything improved: the service became more efficient, the menus better, and various higher-ranking officers appeared to prepare for his arrival. I was warned that I would probably be presented to the King, and once again I had to put on my morning coat and be in a state of alert. Now I had no respite whatsoever, since no one had any idea what the King might be doing or where he would be going. All they knew was that when he wanted something it had to be ready at once.

I was impatient to have this audience. I had made up my mind that the conditions in which the Crown Prince was living were not really conducive to the proper education of an heir to a throne, especially a Balkan one. He was too much in the company of the younger children and the nurses, when at his age he should have been in the society of boys, or at least of males. Because he was slow in going to bed, the English head nurse used to send him up before his younger brothers, and this was not only a humiliation, but provided no cure. Devoid of ambition, how would he ever escape from such a vicious circle? And there were other problems, too. No one could have behaved more obsequiously to him than the servants – and even the higher officers. If his shoe laces were undone, generals with clinking medals and epaulettes would flop down on the floor and do them up for him. When the servants tried to do this, I could stop them, but how could I tell the Marshal of the Court not to be an idiotic toady? I realized that the only thing to do was to get the child away altogether and send him to a school abroad. As things were, the odds were against his getting an adequate education in his own country. On the other hand, if I suggested a foreign school to the King I should become redundant, and I was beginning to enjoy life in Yugoslavia and growing more and more interested in the country. Already I could hardly bear the thought of leaving.

CHAPTER TWO ◇ SERBS, CROATS AND THE FATHER-IN-LAW OF EUROPE

◇ What kind of a monarch was Yugoslavia's King, and what kind of a country was it? Yugoslavia, in Serbo-Croat 'South Slavia', had only recently changed its name from 'the Kingdom of Serbs, Croats and Slovenes'. It was made up of parts of the former Austro-Hungarian monarchy – Slovenia, Croatia, Slavonia, the Vojvodina, Dalmatia, Bosnia and Herzegovina – and two formerly independent Kingdoms, Serbia and Montenegro. Part of the much disputed territory of Macedonia was thrown in, too, for good measure, mainly to the detriment of Bulgaria.

There were some countries that thought Yugoslavia should never have existed at all. Among these were Hungary, who had lost much of her former territory under the Peace Treaties after the First World War, Italy, who had joined the war on the Allied side on the secret understanding that she would receive the Dalmatian coast lands, and Bulgaria, who regarded all Macedonians as fellow-nationals and the land they inhabited as Bulgarian soil. It was an inauspicious start for a new country.

More serious was the fact that the 'Yugoslavs' themselves did not see eye to eye. The South Slavs in the Austro-Hungarian monarchy regarded themselves as a cut above the Balkan Serbs and their brother Montenegrins. Indeed, some thought they were joining a very different state from what they eventually found it to be. But the nub of the matter was that the two largest groups – the Serbs and Croats – were soon plunged into a power struggle. Which was to be the dominating 'race' in the new kingdom? It would be the Serbs, and the Croats and Slovenians did not relish the prospect.

King Alexander Karageorgević, the Crown Prince's father, was the great grandson of Kara George and son of King Peter I. He was a ruler of ability and determination who stood out among the heads of state of his time. But his background was uncompromisingly Montenegrin and Serb, and he had no experience whatsoever of the Croats, Slovenians, Dalmatians and the rest. He had been so much identified with Serb politics since he was a stripling that he was regarded almost as a foreigner by those Yugoslavs who were proud to have lived in a more civilized and cultured part of the world than the Balkans.

We have seen how the Karageorgević family returned to the throne of Serbia in 1903 after the murder of King Alexander Obrenović by their supporters. King Peter I, generally lauded in English history books as a 'democratic and constitutional ruler' may have known about the murder, though there is no proof that he did or that he instigated it. One of the best friends of his son Alexander Karageorgević was Pera Živković, the young captain of the Guard who opened the gate to the murderers. When I came to Yugoslavia he was Commander of the Royal Guard, having twice been Prime Minister in King Alexander's governments.

Alexander Karageorgević, who was the second son, had become heir to the throne six years after the murder. His elder brother, George, who was mentally unbalanced and violently anti-Austrian, made himself unacceptable after the annexation of Bosnia and Herzegovina in 1908 and was forced to renounce his right of succession. The immediate cause, however, had been the savage and mortal kick in the stomach he had given his old and already ruptured valet.

King Peter I had received his military training in France, where he passed through St. Cyr and served in the French army. In the Franco-Prussian War he had been captured by the Germans but had managed to escape by swimming across the Loire and rejoining his regiment. He was forced to stand for a long time up to his neck in icy water and contracted bad rheumatic fever which affected him all his life. In 1875 he raised an insurrection in Bosnia against the Turks, assuming the name of the famous Serb hero, Petar Mrkonjić. He then went back to Paris to lead a gay life there. In 1883 he married Zorka, the eldest daughter of Prince Nikola of Montenegro and settled down in its capital Cetinje to a quiet and happy family life. After his wife's death he moved to Geneva. Both he and Alexander were imbued with French culture and French was the language spoken in the family.

Coming to the throne at the age of fifty-nine after an adventurous and battle-scarred life, in which he had proved his great personal valour and ardent Serbian patriotism, he was already suffering from softening of the brain when the First World War broke out, and was then induced to hand over royal power to Alexander, who became Prince Regent of Serbia at the age of twenty-six. In his old age, Peter had become a churlish misanthrope who hated everybody except his unbalanced elder son, George, on whom he doted. Alexander inherited his father's valour but added charm and polish. As Commander-in-Chief of the Serb army, he shared with his people the fearful calvary of the retreat through Serbia, and emerged in 1918 as the ruler of a much larger and more important country – in time to be called Yugoslavia. He quickly showed a great capacity for statecraft, and he certainly needed it.

He could only with difficulty live down his reputation as a Serb nationalist and become a leader acceptable to all the Yugoslav peoples. He had himself been a member of the Black Hand, that sinister Serb patriotic secret society which had inspired the assassination of the Archduke Franz Ferdinand, and had allowed it to continue until 1916 when, after an alleged attempt on his life in Salonika, he had had 'Apis', Colonel Dragutin Dimitrijević, its leader, tried and executed. He was still surrounded by Serbian generals of the most reactionary kind.

In the new Yugoslavia, two forces stood opposed to each other – King Alexander, now unchallenged leader of the Orthodox Serbs, and Stjepan Radić, the spokesman for the overwhelming majority of the Catholic Croats. Radić demanded for his people at least the autonomy they had been accustomed to under the Austro-Hungarian monarchy. However, no one could agree on a line dividing Croat from Serb territory, especially in Bosnia. Radić boycotted the parliament, but just as the moment was reached when Alexander was persuading him to co-operate, the Croat leader was shot in the parliament building by a Montenegrin deputy. Some weeks later he died of his wounds.

Faced with the severest crisis the new state had yet encountered, Alexander suspended the constitution, inaugurated personal rule, changed the name of the country to 'Yugoslavia' and did what he could to give it a Yugoslav rather than a Serb, Croat or Slovene identity. However, to the Croats, Alexander's rule still meant Serb rule, and the country remained tragically divided. After attempts on the life of the royal pair, Croatia and Zagreb, its capital, became unsafe for them to visit. Police control was tightened still further and the leading opposition politicians including Dr. Maček, the successor to Radić, and Father Korošec, the leader of the Slovenes, were interned.

Two years before I arrived in 1934, King Alexander had revoked his 'personal rule', but the Croats and Slovenes together with some of the Serb parties continued to oppose his régime. He was in considerable personal danger, because he was the target not only of Croat terrorism but of the Macedonian Secret Society IMRO as well. And both organizations were receiving help from the governments of countries which coveted Yugoslav territory – Italy, Hungary and Bulgaria.

No wonder that the monarchy in Yugoslavia was by no means stable, as Professor Harold Temperly had warned me when I went to see him before leaving England. 'But I support the King's efforts,' he had gone on to say. 'Robert Seton-Watson thinks the opposite. He is firmly opposed to his policies. Indeed,' and he lowered his voice, 'I am sorry to say that I have heard him remark that if by chance the king were assassinated, it would be no bad thing for the country.'

◇ I looked forward with considerable interest and anticipation to my approaching interview with this remarkable ruler. When it came, it was something of a disappointment. I had hoped to see him alone so that I could broach with him the question of his son's education, because it would have been awkward to do so in the presence of the Queen: it might have sounded like criticism of her methods. And now, here she was standing with him. However, as I had had little experience of my pupil as yet, it was perhaps for the best that I was inhibited from saying to his father all I had planned to tell him.

The audience was brief. King Alexander, who was forty-six, was very much the soldier and commander. He had great charm of manner and distinction, much more than had appeared in his photographs, and I felt more at ease in speaking with him than I had with the Queen. He at once started by asking me in French if I had got to know my pupil. Most of my answers were 'Oui, Sire,' or 'Non, Sire.' Had I been in the Balkans before? Were any of my English compatriots here? Did I know the British Ambassador, Sir Nevile Henderson? He was *un grand chasseur*. Did I know how to ride? 'Oh yes,' the Queen interpolated, 'and he is very fond of sport.' 'Tennis?' asked the King. 'Yes.' 'Have you seen much of the surroundings?' 'Yes. I have made a few car trips.' '*Enchanté de faire votre connaissance*.' And with that, it was over. As can be imagined, this did not relieve me of my worries about the future education of the Crown Prince.

I used to give him lessons in his room in the mornings and during the first days they were badly interrupted by the band of the Palace

Guard which regularly played selections from *Trovatore* and *Rigoletto* under our window. I summoned up courage to ask that this should be dispensed with during lesson times. It was a daring thing to do to the Royal Guard – like asking a barrel organist to go to the next street – but happily it worked. Our lessons continued undisturbed.

The Prince was backward. He wrote badly, was hopelessly weak in mathematics and terribly slow in all subjects. It was difficult to make progress because it took such a long time to extract answers, let alone get any work out of him. He wrote at a snail's pace, painting his letters like a little child. He was neither lazy nor apathetic, but simply the victim of a neglected education.

The King went off on his travels again and, still brooding on his future, I decided to take the bull by the horns and write a report of a relatively alarmist kind which I would give to the Queen to send to him if she saw fit. In it I recommended that the Crown Prince should be sent to school abroad. It was a somewhat audacious step, but to my surprise and relief the Queen received it with good grace. I had already noticed a slight tendency on her part to be pleased if I confirmed her opinion of her son's shortcomings. It disturbed me, but on this occasion it served the boy's interests. When King Alexander came back later, he sent for me and discussed my report. He wanted to know in what country I thought his son would get the best education. I replied that it did not matter much provided he left his own country and his present environment. I said that as an Englishman I might naturally be prejudiced in favour of an English school, but a Swiss school, of which the King himself would have had experience, would do as well. The King said that he thought an English school would be good and instructed me to make the necessary arrangements. I asked how long he wished the Crown Prince to remain at school abroad.

'Well, not so very long. Only for a year or two. I don't want my son to become an Englishman.'

The Queen was overjoyed at the idea of him going to England as she was very fond of our country. She had herself been for a short time in an English school and had happy memories of it. It had been her idea in the first place to get hold of an English tutor for him and it seemed only logical that he should end up in an English school. Much later she was to leave Yugoslavia and settle permanently in England.

◇ Among the excursions we made while we were staying in Dalmatia, a particularly interesting one was to Cetinje, which was the capital of the extinct Kingdom of Montenegro. The 'Black Mountains' (Crna Gora), which were dominated by the 6,000 foot Lovćen massif, provided the hinterland to the Dalmatian coastal strip where we were staying. Before the First World War, when Montenegro was a small independent Kingdom, it only touched the sea at a little strip round Bar and Ulcinj, the last Yugoslav port before Albania. Today, the Federal Republic of Montenegro with its new capital of Titograd has swallowed up many coastal Dalmatian towns including Hercegnovi itself.

The old palace of the princes of Montenegro was already a museum and nearby stood the house which King Peter of Serbia had built for his family, and where his sons had been born. I looked with interest at the family pictures of the Montenegrin rulers and the war trophies of their heroic race. I was shown, too, the legendary oak tree, under which Nikola, the patriarchal last King of Montenegro, had dispensed arbitrary justice.

◇ The King had been a gifted poet, and an astute ruler as well. He unjustly lost his throne in the general reshuffle which took place in the Balkans at the end of the War. While the Obrenović dynasty were on the throne in Belgrade and the Karageorgević family were in exile, Prince Peter lived for some time in Cetinje with his father-in-law. The memories he and his sons had from their time in this small court must have been curious. King Nikola had been most successful in enhancing the prestige of his obscure dynasty. He had a large number of daughters and married them all off into influential foreign dynasties. In addition to Zorka, the wife of the future King of Serbia, two of them, Milica and Stana, were married to Russian grand-dukes (one of them being responsible for introducing Rasputin to the Russian court); another, Eko, became the wife of King Victor Emmanuel of Italy; and the youngest, Ana, who died only recently in Switzerland, married of all people a Mountbatten – Prince Franz-Joseph of Battenberg. And so the King of little Montenegro became known as 'the father-in-law of Europe'.

The youngest daughter's wedding laid the foundation for what might have been a close friendship between Prince Nikola as he then was and Queen Victoria. It was held at Cannes, and Queen Victoria, who was very fond of Prince Franz-Joseph, her daughter's brother-in-law, attended it in person, although she was at an advanced age. At the wedding, she saw King Nikola, who was dressed in his striking Montenegrin national costume for the first time, fell for him, and invited him to come and stay at Windsor. In May 1898, the King (then still called Prince) travelled by cross-Channel ferry to Britain and on to London accompanied by the British Chargé d'Affaires. Afterwards the British diplomat recorded in a privately printed book the experiences of that trip.

The King had not travelled much outside his Crna Gora, his 'eagle's nest', of which Tennyson wrote:

> Great Tzernagora! Never since thine own
> Black ridges drew the cloud and brake the storm
> Has breathed a race of mightier mountaineers.

The King of the 'mighty mountaineers' knew France, Austria and parts of Germany, but he had never been to England. He was a roguish man and it could not have been much fun for him staying alone with our ageing Queen. When he was sitting in the special steamer sent by the Queen to fetch him from Calais to Dover, he whispered to our Chargé d'Affaires: 'I must now compose my face and assume that expression of serious solemnity which, I understand, is considered "correct" in England.' On his way back, he travelled by ordinary channel steamer to Ostend without his English guide and told him afterwards how he had helped a middle-aged lady move her deck-chair to a more sheltered spot out of the reach of the spray. The Chargé d'Affaires asked if he knew who she was. 'No,' he replied, 'I know nothing about her except that she was English.' 'But how did she betray her nationality?' 'By not thanking me,' was the laughing but sarcastic reply. 'After all from an English point of view she was quite right. How could she speak to me when we had not been introduced?'

How did King Nikola get this impression of Englishwomen? Could it have been from Miss Everard, his Karageorgević grandchildren's English governess at Cetinje? If so, the influence of English governesses can be traced even in rocky fastnesses where Turks have not been able to find a footing! But she does not appear to have had much success with her English lessons, since King Peter and his sons always conversed in French.

The Windsor visit was a resounding success for the Prince's ambitious diplomacy and it put him one up on Serbia, his rival. Just at this time the King of Serbia, Alexander Obrenović, had also been making every effort to improve relations with Britain. The Serbian Minister was instructed to go and see the British Foreign Secretary,

Lord Salisbury, and try and persuade him to advise the Queen to invite King Alexander over to London for a visit. Lord Salisbury was embarrassed: the Queen was now getting very old and did not like new faces. It was hard, he pleaded, to persuade her to meet someone she did not know and he did not feel able to recommend it to the Queen with any hope of success. The Serbian Minister left the Foreign Office in a gloomy frame of mind. His gloom soon turned to fury when he passed a newsvendor's stand at a street corner and heard him shouting out the latest news: 'Prince of Montenegro invited to Windsor.'

Prince George, King Alexander and their sister Princess Jelena (who was later married to a Russian prince) were all born at the Montenegrin Court. But when Alexander became king of a country which was much larger than the original Serbia – the Kingdom of Serbs, Croats and Slovenes – he let the little principality of Montenegro be engulfed. King Nikola and his sons were edged out of their heritage.

In addition to his many daughters, King Nikola had two sons. One of them, Prince Danilo, was at first very pro-Austrian and he figures in the famous Lehar operetta *The Merry Widow*. In it, the name 'Montenegro' is diplomatically disguised as 'Pontevedrino', but Danilo's name remains unchanged. Even when I was in Yugoslavia, *The Merry Widow* was still not allowed to be put on, in case it might exacerbate the feelings of the Montenegrins, almost all of whom seemed to be related to their Royal Family. The younger son, Prince Mirko, was ostensibly pro-Russian. That seems to have been a carefully contrived move by his father to keep the two great powers at bay. If the Austrians complained that Montenegro was too pro-Russian, Nikola would point to Danilo. If the Russians complained that it was too pro-Austrian, he would point to Mirko. The King was almost completely dependent on Russian subsidies. The Montenegrin army, for instance, was financed *in toto* this way and every month the Montenegrin Minister of Defence called personally for the money at the Russian Legation and took it away with him. At the same time he fetched the much smaller Austrian subsidy as well, as for some technical reason it had to be paid out through the Russian Legation too. King Nikola had no shame in referring to this openly. One thing he loved doing was playing cards, which he was very bad at, and when a diplomat said: 'Careful, Your Majesty! You will lose a lot of money,' the King winked at the Russian Minister and said, 'Solovyov will pay!'

Thus it was that the Montenegrins lost their dynasty and had to play second fiddle to Serbia within monarchical Yugoslavia. However, no Montenegrin likes to play second fiddle. It was actually impossible to persuade Montenegrin troops to number 'one', and 'two'. . . . It had to be 'one' and 'next to number one'. In Yugoslavia I often ran into proud Montenegrins who were very much aware of their former independence. There was an orderly officer at the court called Vukotić (a Montenegrin name) who of course claimed to be related to the former ruling house. He was extremely proud and sat apart from his brother officers like a Byronic hero overcome by *Weltschmerz*. And an interesting experience for me was an invitation from a Montenegrin 'millionaire' to go on an evening's cruise with him in his luxury yacht. As we danced and sang in the moonlight, I had my first taste of caviare. It was indeed the Viennese operetta coming to the shores of the Adriatic.

The Montenegrins took their revenge for all the humiliations that had been inflicted on them by playing an important role in Tito's Yugoslavia. Many of the leading partisans during the Second World War were Montenegrin, the most eminent being Djilas. And many Montenegrins or Serb husbands of Montenegrin wives became leading diplomats in Federal Yugoslavia.

CHAPTER THREE ◇ A CULTURED PRINCE

◇ As the Dalmatian summer wore on it became unpleasantly hot, and in accordance with a pre-arranged plan the Queen began our move to the royal villa in Slovenia near the Julian Alps. We all embarked in the pride of the Yugoslav navy, the destroyer *Dubrovnik*, which had been recently delivered from Jarrow shipyard, and sailed up the coast to Split past the islands of Korčula, Hvar and Brač. There we got into the royal train and after a night's journey found ourselves next morning in the cooler and fresher mountain air of Bled, where 'Suvobor' was situated. This was an Austrian-type villa which had once belonged to Prince Otto Windischgraetz, husband of a grand-daughter of the Emperor Franz-Joseph, and its small garden, heavily shaded by trees and full of mosquitoes, led down to the very edge of the lake of Bled. From its upper rooms, and above all from the balcony of the royal apartments, there was a magnificent view of the whole lake, the magic island in the middle and the Julian Alps beyond – their highest peak, the Triglav, peeping up above the rest.

Now I was to come into contact with another of the many fascinating peoples that make up Yugoslavia, the Slovenes. Having but recently been Austrian subjects they spoke German well, which was a comfort since their own language was sufficiently different from Serbo-Croat to be incomprehensible for me, except for reading purposes. Most of them went about in Tyrolean-type jackets and *Lederhosen*, the scenery and their costume combined giving me the feeling that I was not in Yugoslavia at all but some part of Austria. This suited me, because I was fond of Austria and was happy for the moment to have a change from more southern climes and Balkan conditions. The Slovenes appeared to have a higher standard of living and culture than the Serbs and even the Croats as well, who were on a level somewhere between the other two. Books published in Ljubljana, the capital of Slovenia, were much better got up than those in Belgrade, and rather better than those published in Zagreb, the Croatian capital. Since the Slovenes living in Yugoslavia only amounted to a little more than a million people it was remarkable that they had managed to preserve their individuality and their language, particularly when one considers the difficulties the more numerous Czechs experienced in preserving theirs. But they were eyed somewhat jealously by the other peoples in Yugoslavia; they had something of the reputation the Scots have in Britain. It was said that there were no Jews in Slovenia because they could not hope to make a livelihood among the Slovenes. The Croats, who did not love them, used to complain: 'They are our Jews, for they have all the jobs.' The truth was that they had the ability.

When we arrived in Slovenia the 'natives' came into their own in the Court. The Queen's adjutant, Colonel Pogačnik, was a Slovene; the Slovenes among the other adjutants and orderly officers had a spell of duty at Bled, as you would expect; and the only Slovene lady-in-waiting, the charming, persuasive and strong-willed Madam Šverljuga, wife of a Croat ex-minister, was on duty all the time. She made full use of the opportunity she had to press the claims of both Croats and Slovenes. They did not have many chances as the Royal Family tended otherwise to be surrounded by Serbs, who watched her closely.

With the move to Bled my daily life changed. The Crown Prince had come to the end of his school 'term' and was now on holiday. But as it was planned that he should leave for school in England in September, I had to prepare him for this and our lessons had to continue, if at a more relaxed tempo.

Pleasant as it was at Hercegnovi to have the Adriatic Sea at our doorstep, it meant getting into a motor launch and crossing to the other side of the bay whenever we wanted to swim. At Bled the lake was at the bottom of the garden, as I have said, and the Royal Family had their own private bathing establishment complete with springboards for diving, and so on. We spent a lot of time bathing and boating and also for a change went on mountain trips and fishing excursions. There were times, however, when I felt I simply had to get away on my own, and one day I decided I would just leave the villa by myself and climb to the top of the Triglav, Yugoslavia's highest mountain (9,400 feet).

I received permission to do this and was able to obtain transport by car to the foot of the mountain. Unfortunately, what with my casualness and a certain amount of delay on the part of the court transport, I was not able to start my climb until the late afternoon. As a consequence I was nowhere near the top when darkness fell. I had no idea what to do. I was extremely badly equipped; I had gone on the expedition with a very light heart – a thing one should never do when one is in the mountains. When some real mountaineers met me on the way up they told me that I would never get to the top in the shoes I was wearing. They proved in fact to be wrong, but had I been in their place with my present wisdom I would have said the same.

Though the weather was fine, I began to feel rather cold as the evening went on: I determined to take shelter under a stone and try and have a bit of sleep until dawn broke, when I would hope to proceed further on my climb. Then ruefully I came to realize that I should be completely frozen when I woke up, if indeed I managed to sleep at all.

I remained like this for about an hour, feeling increasingly convinced I had got myself into a dangerous mess. But it was pitch dark and I had no light, so I could neither go up nor down. Presently, however, I saw far below me some lights slowly approaching and gradually I identified these as a party of climbers going to the mountain top by night. It was my salvation. I could attach myself to them.

They proved to be a group of young people from a climbing club in Ljubljana and were very competent mountaineers. Under their guidance and protection I proceeded upwards, crossing and jumping hair-raising crevices which I am sure I would never have risked in daylight. It was not long before we reached the hut that lay about an hour or two's climb beneath the summit. It had started raining very early in the morning, so it is clear what I would have felt like if I had had to stay under that stone all night. But the downpour was not sufficient to prevent me from getting to the top, although I was disappointed when I reached the summit to find that there was nothing whatsoever to see as everything was covered in mist. Since I was getting pretty cold and wet, I decided to dash down as quickly as I could.

It was on my return that I realized how fantastic it was I had managed to cover the terrain safely by night. By this time the rain was pelting down and the ground had become dangerously slippery. I was extremely lucky to get to the bottom and back to the royal villa without breaking my leg or catching pneumonia. But I had acquired some prestige. I could tell the Slovenes that an Englishman had set out just as he was and climbed their 'Everest' by night!

✧ During that summer I met some interesting people. First, I was presented to King Alexander's cousins, Prince Paul and Princess

Olga, who had come to spend their summer holiday in a villa about an hour's drive away at Bohinj. This was another lakeside villa in a more secluded part of the Slovenian Alps near the source of the river Sava. Since these were the two with whom I was in closest *rapport* during the five years I was to spend in Yugoslavia, I should like to say something about them.

Prince Paul was born in St. Petersburg in 1893 but he left it before he was one year old and never returned to Russia. He was the son of Prince Arsene Karageorgević, old King Peter's brother, and the beautiful Princess Avrora Pavlovna Demidov. She was a member of a wealthy Russian family, which could trace its origins back to Nikita Demidov, a gunsmith from Tula, who, rather like the hero of Leskov's famous story *The Left-handed Smith from Tula*, won the favour of Peter the Great by copying and improving a pistol of foreign make. Eventually the Tsar sent him to the Urals to study large-scale iron production and, from the foundries he set up there and at Tula, he and his descendants acquired a considerable fortune, which was however much dispersed in later generations. Princess Avrora's brother, Elime Demidov, was a leading Russian diplomat. He accompanied Izvolsky to the famous talks at Buchlov in 1908 just before the Austrian annexation of Bosnia and Herzegovina.

Prince Arsene, who was born in 1859, probably at Temešvar, where his father, Alexander, was living in exile, studied at the Lycée Louis le Grand and served eight years in the Foreign Legion. He fought in the eighties at Tonkin, where he caught yellow fever, and in Monaco. Subsequently he joined the Russian Horse Guards, fought in the Russo-Japanese War of 1905 and was promoted General. During the Balkan Wars he came to Serbia and commanded a cavalry division there. In the First World War he was not offered a post and went back to Russia, where he remained until the outbreak of the Revolution.

He treated his young and beautiful wife very badly and she divorced him in 1896 at the age of twenty-three. A year earlier she had taken her two-year old son, Paul, to Geneva and left him in the charge of her brother-in-law, the then Prince Peter Karageorgević. As her great-uncle had been made Prince of San Donato by the Grand Duke of Tuscany and later by the King of Italy, the family had property in Italy as well. She moved to Italy, remarried and died in Turin in 1904, when Prince Paul was only eleven years old. Prince Arsene settled in Paris, and he lived there until his death in 1938.

Staying with his uncle in Geneva, Prince Paul had been too young to have a Swiss and Russian education like his elder cousins, George and Alexander, who after going to school in Geneva completed their education in St. Petersburg. When Prince Peter became King of Serbia in 1903 and moved to Belgrade, Prince Paul was sent to a leading school in the capital. He had a miserable childhood. His father took no interest in him and he hardly caught a glimpse of his mother; and his uncle, King Peter, was on the whole a hard man to the children, including his own. The young prince was brought up in a house where there was no feminine influence at all, no tenderness, no affection; he never knew what it was to see a Christmas tree even.

Fortunately destiny was then kind to him. He had shown marked intelligence at school and in 1912 asked to be sent to Oxford, to Christ Church. These must have been happy years and he would have found it difficult to go back to Belgrade after experiencing the new world which opened up for him in England, where he made many friends. But as a result of the Balkan Wars in 1912 and 1913 and the ensuing outbreak of the First World War in 1914 he had to return to Serbia. He took his degree after the war.

In 1923, he married the beautiful Princess Olga of Greece, who was ten years his junior. She was the daughter of Prince Nicholas of Greece and the Grand Duchess Helen Vladimirovna, granddaughter of the Emperor Alexander II of Russia and sister of Grand Duke Kiril, regarded by Russian emigrés after the death of the last Tsar as heir to the Imperial throne.

After their marriage Prince Paul and Princess Olga settled permanently in Belgrade and lived in a small and unsatisfactory apartment in the Old Palace in the centre of the town. They relieved the tedium of their existence by regular visits to England, where their two elder children, Alexander and Nicholas, were born. Apart from having inadequate accommodation, Prince Paul was given very little of importance to do. The British Legation reported that King Alexander was jealous of him because of his superior education and greater intellectual gifts, and for that reason kept him out of public life. Later, however, he was made President of the Yugoslav Red Cross and a few weeks before King Alexander's death he was promoted to the rank of Lieutenant Colonel. As a great art lover he devoted himself to the creation of a gallery in Belgrade, which was called the Prince Paul Museum. Serbia remained culturally backward and this modest collection, to which he devoted much care and energy, did a lot to raise the cultural prestige of the capital.

At one time King Alexander had apparently thought of giving Prince Paul some political responsibilities, and there was the possibility of his going to live permanently in Zagreb as representative of the Crown. Since he was the type of man likely to appeal to the more cultured Croats, it might have been politically beneficial, and Prince Paul himself would have welcomed it. But nothing came of the idea. Nonetheless, the personal relationship between King Alexander and his cousin was good and they were fond of each other. During the last year of his reign, as though by intuition, King Alexander seems to have drawn closer to him and to have discussed political questions with him more frequently. Prince Paul was then suffering from indifferent health, which was no doubt partly due to the frustrating circumstances in which he lived.

I immediately felt at home with him because he reminded me of an Oxford or Cambridge don. Considering that later when I asked him what he would really have liked to be, if he had had the choice, he answered 'Curator of the Ashmolean', my feelings seem not to have been unfounded. Although I got on very well with Yugoslav people, particularly those who could speak English or German, the Balkans were initially a strange world for me and I was glad to come into such a haven of western homeliness. Princess Olga was kind and helpful, and showed much sympathy with some of the difficulties I had in my task of educating the Crown Prince.

Once when I paid a visit to Bohinj, the Crown Prince went off to play with his cousin Alexander, Prince Paul's eldest son, and I was able to relax indoors in the company of my hosts. The relaxation took the form of my playing Chopin on Prince Paul's piano, while Princess Olga's sister Princess Marina lay on a sofa and did some sketching. She said it helped her when I played. As she was making sketches of an El Greco painting, which Prince Paul possessed, the *Laocoon*, now in Washington, I am not sure that my rendering of Chopin fitted in too well.

Prince Paul's father-in-law, the Danish born Prince Nicholas of Greece, was tall, lean, fair and very Scandinavian to look at. His wife, the Grand Duchess, was a true Russian princess with dark eyes of incredible beauty and unbelievable sadness. My passionate interest in Russian that I had acquired from my nightly promenades along the Adriatic in the company of Lieutenant Stiglic and his wife formed a bond between us. I must admit, however, that at our first meeting I had not expected to get on so well with her.

One day I found myself placed next to her at lunch. There were members of various royal families present and they all seemed to be speaking English. Occasionally they would lapse into French when they wanted to say something that 'the children shouldn't hear'. It rather amused me to notice how they began to slip into French involuntarily if they thought they were saying anything which might possibly be regarded as *risqué*. They would sometimes do this in my presence, as though establishing the fiction that I did not understand the language! It was of course a tacit hint that I was not to listen.

When I heard all this international royalty speaking English and French I could be excused for wondering whether any of them spoke the languages of their own countries at all. Consequently, when I started a conversation with the Grand Duchess and inevitably got on to my hobby-horse – the Russian language – I asked her innocently whether she spoke Russian. To my alarm, she suddenly clapped her hands and called for silence. 'Do you know what Mr. Parrott has just asked me?' she said. 'He has asked *me* (understand here "me, a Romanov") if I speak Russian!' There was a tremendous peal of good-natured laughter, and I felt rather a fool. Afterwards some of the younger royalty round the table came up and looked as if they wanted to pat me on the back. They probably thought that I had scored a point over their Romanov relative. But the Grand Duchess was extremely helpful in teaching me Russian: she helped me to read letters written to me by Elizaveta Georgevna without asking any questions, and she even succeeded in making me carry on a conversation with her in Russian while I was engaged in a game of mixed doubles at tennis. It was a big test for my Russian, my sportsmanship and my diplomacy.

I could not imagine that a beautiful girl like Princess Marina could remain unmarried for long. She was by then twenty-eight and both her elder sisters had been married for some time. When I learned that Prince George, Duke of Kent, was coming to stay with Prince Paul and Princess Olga I had no idea what the event portended. Then it suddenly burst upon the world that he was to marry Princess Marina, and Bohinj and Bled immediately became centres of attention for the world press.

◇ In the absence of King Alexander, most of my life was still being spent in the company of the Queen, the royal children and the nurses. It was a happy party, because the Queen seemed to be simple and good-natured and to like simple things, but it was at the same time a glorified nursery existence which might have palled, if it had not been for the originality of the circumstances and the spontaneous friendliness of all around me. The Queen permitted a remarkable degree of freedom to those whom she employed and I felt an obligation not to abuse it. Nonetheless it was an easy and perhaps too comfortable life. I had almost all my meals with the Queen and her children, I played the piano in her drawing-room whenever I wanted to, I had one of her cars and chauffeurs always at my disposal and I was always able to rope her in to take part in the various games I improvised for the children. I think it is a good experience for anyone to be back in the nursery, yes, even a young man of twenty-five who considers he left it too long ago to be identified with it in any way. I could claim of course to be a tutor by profession and looking after children was one of the things I loved and thought I could do. And the Queen was like one of the biggest of the children.

But when the King appeared everything changed. Not only, as in Hercegnovi, did things become efficient and the food improve overnight; an entirely different spirit immediately pervaded the whole villa. This had really nothing to do with his personality. The King was always courteous and charming. It proceeded from the 'knights' and 'squires' who attended him. To the existing adjutants and orderly officers who looked after the Queen were added the King's more senior adjutants and even the First Adjutant himself. My initial impression of these dignitaries was that, like the Generals in *The Good Soldier Švejk*, the more senior they were the more senile they became.

One of the younger officers once confided to me that he had come out into the garden and seen the First Adjutant standing behind a tree like a naughty child who had been punished by his governess. On making enquiries he found out that the King was walking about in the garden and the First Adjutant had considered it imperative to demonstrate his complete unimportance by effacing himself completely in front of him. That was the way he had chosen to do it. Was it an oriental trait – a vestige of over four hundred years of Turkish occupation? Perhaps. Otherwise the senior officials of the Court – both military and civil – were most *un*-self-effacing. In relation to me and the officers they seemed set on making themselves appear as important as possible.

When the King was there, the guards on the villa were strengthened and I no longer had the free run of the Queen's salon or indeed of the house, and if I came anywhere near the King's room, I ran into an enormous Cerberus in the shape of a burly peasant sitting on a chair in front of his door, ready to bark at me if I made the slightest noise. It was so different from the way I was usually treated that it made me most circumspect. The latter-day Cerberus was Zečević, the King's *momak* or manservant.

I had already noticed that the Serbs were an independent and democratic people and I continued to wonder how it had come about that they were the most loyal element in the monarchy, whereas the Croats and the Slovenes, who in their time had served the Habsburgs with unusual devotion, were the least loyal. There were national reasons for this, as we have seen, since King Alexander was a Serb and the Serbs were not liked in Croatia or Slovenia. However, as an illustration of how a Serb peasant reacts in the face of royalty I will quote a story which the Queen herself told me about Zečević. When she was first married, Zečević would come suddenly into her room, point his finger at her and say 'Er will dich'. Zečević did not of course say this in German. He said it in Serbian. But the Queen translated it into German to convey the full force of what in English would have been: 'He (the King) wants thee.'

I found the behaviour of the guards disquieting because at night they closed in and came inside the palace. One night there was a violent thunderstorm (there were plenty of them in this mountain region) and all the lights fused. When one is living in the Balkans one has to be sure that a short circuit is caused by a mere thunderstorm: it may be the preparation for a palace revolution. I jumped out of bed, took my torch in my hand, shone it around and slowly walked out of my room into the corridor to see if anything was up. I could not see very well where I was going because my torch was not bright, but suddenly to my horror I found the point of a bayonet at my chest. The guard had been just as alarmed by the short circuit as I had, and, seeing someone stealing out of the room with a torch, had feared the worst. Considering that at that time Yugoslav soldiers were like Russians and took no chances, choosing to be trigger-happy rather than risking being shot for not shooting, I was lucky to escape being fired at.

The arrival of the King was important for me, because my plan for the Crown Prince's journey and his schooling in England needed his final sanction. I also had the delicate task of trying to find out what was going to happen to me when the Crown Prince was at school. I realized that I had been a trifle unwise to go and propose a course of action which would inevitably make me redundant. And in my conversation with the Queen I had observed uneasily that she made no reference to the possibility of my existing after this date. Clearly I could not say to either of them: 'What about me?' I was far too insignificant.

Because the atmosphere in the villa had changed so much, it would not have been at all easy for me to find a propitious moment to gain the King's ear in these circumstances, if by a freak of chance the Queen had not all of a sudden allotted me a special room where I was to give lessons to the Crown Prince each day. The room happened to be a link room between the Queen's and King's apartments, and so when the King came to see the Queen in the morning he had to pass through it on his way to her. This always happened at least once a day and at the moment of the King's entry we both had to stand up like ramrods, and my teaching words froze on my lips. The King, who was always very busy and had little time for anything except his immediate duties, normally confined himself to patting his son on his head and asking me in a perfunctory tone whether he was doing well at his lessons.

One day when he put this question I surprised him by answering him in Serbian. It evidently impressed him and it led to a conversation about my interest in the language. When, emboldened by his response, I asked if I might speak to him about plans for England, he suggested that I should do so at once. We withdrew into another room and I confided to him that when the Crown Prince was in England I should very much like to stay on with him and be at hand to take him out for excursions so as to supplement his school education. I could spend the rest of my time studying Serbo-Croat at the University of London. It seemed to the King a reasonable suggestion and he at once gave it his blessing. Nothing was said about whether my salary would continue to be paid or what it would be, but I left it at that.

While I was making preparations for the departure we had some alarming news. We were told that the Hungarians, who had long been working against the Yugoslav government because of their claim to parts of Yugoslav territory such as the formerly Hungarian Bácska, Barânya and Banat, and had gone so far as to organize terrorist camps at Janka Puszta, had recently infiltrated nine agents across the frontier with the aim of murdering the Royal Family. We were all put on the alert and I was told that I ought to carry a revolver. I did not think this spoke highly of Yugoslav security methods, as I had never handled a revolver in my life and was not likely to be much of a success with it. However, I had to obey instructions, and it was left to me to buy my defensive weapon at my own expense. Owing to the difficulty of getting licences for revolvers in England I ordered a Browning from Brussels and took lessons from the guard officers. After some weeks' target practice I satisfied them that I could pull my revolver out of its holster, bring it across my arm and aim reasonably accurately. But having a revolver is one thing; using it is another. There were many occasions when I was going out with the Crown Prince in an open car and someone could easily have shot him or me or both of us before anything could have been done to stop it. Wherever we went, people used to stand in crowds and throw flowers into the car. Sometimes these flowers had thorns in them and could draw blood if they hit us in the face. A few times it happened that they concealed something more solid. I can well remember once when someone put his hand up and nearly knocked my hat off. But I must say that on none of these occasions did I instinctively feel for my revolver. Somehow in conditions like these you forget fear. You realize there is nothing you can do and that you are in God's hands, and after that you relax.

However, it was plainly going to be different when the Crown Prince left the country. To begin with, it was the first time he had gone abroad since he had been a baby. And, in addition, he would have to cross potentially unfriendly country on his way to England. The King told me that the best security was complete secrecy and that he did not intend to send a guard with the Prince or even a private detective. That of course imposed an extra burden on me, but I had to accept it. The planned route was by car through Austria to Salzburg, where we were to step into the Orient Express and arrive in Paris. In Paris, the Crown Prince would have lunch with Princess Olga's father, Prince Nicholas of Greece, at his apartment. After that we would leave for London and stay at Claridge's until the time came for the Prince to go down to his school. Since his cousin, Prince Alexander, was already at an English school and was going back too, he was to accompany us. The party consisted therefore of one young man and two boys without any protection whatsoever.

CHAPTER FOUR ◇ IN THE SHADOW OF THE ASSASSIN

◇ When the day arrived for me to take my charges to England we set off in a fleet of cars to the Austrian frontier accompanied by the King, who had decided to take leave of his son there. Other members of the family came, too. To my surprise, the King decided at the last minute to take his nephew, Prince Alexander, in his own car rather than his son, with the result that the Crown Prince was left to go alone with me. The boy was probably rather hurt, and justifiably so, for the journey to the frontier was quite a long one and the time spent by his father in actually saying goodbye to him was very short indeed. I can remember clearly the last words King Alexander spoke to me. He told me first not to eat food in the train because it was not very good. Next, he said it was important to make sure that there was a protection over the seat before using the lavatory in the train. And finally, he turned to me and said: 'This is my son. I entrust him to your hands.' After that he spoke a word or two to the Crown Prince, kissed him, and the three of us left by open car for Salzburg. I was the only witness within earshot of this parting, and suggestions that the King, like Boris Godunov, gave his son a talk about his future responsibilities are a romantic figment.

It was a fine morning and a beautiful drive. The royal chauffeur took the Packard at a good lick, but I was conscious nonetheless of unusual activity around us. It was either motor-cyclists or else people awaiting us *en route*. It becomes difficult under conditions when one is already suspicious and on one's guard to tell who the police are and who might be a possible assailant. When we eventually arrived in Salzburg 'incognito', we were met by an operetta-like chief of police who escorted us round the town followed by a number of conspicuous detectives. We then had tea in the Mozart café, our new escorts sitting at the next table. Later, after walking about a bit longer, we saw that the crowds of followers were assuming considerable proportions, so we felt it was time to go to the hotel and have dinner before getting on to the train.

I remembered the King's warning words about not having dinner in a restaurant car. They were now to lose us a meal altogether, because unfortunately this particular hotel appeared to be overwhelmed by the honour paid to it by the unexpected appearance of a Crown Prince, and when we ordered what was in effect a very simple meal, that boys of eleven years old would like, the chef, wishing to excel himself, took such an unconscionable time in preparing it that as soon as it was served we had to fly. We were informed that the Simplon Express had already been held up at Salzburg for several minutes waiting for us to get on board. The boys swallowed as much as they could in a few minutes, and we rushed off to the train and boarded it at the very last moment. Standing on the platform was the Yugoslav Minister in Vienna, who whispered to me that he had thought he had better come up, in spite of the fact that the Crown Prince was travelling incognito, because he had heard that the Hungarian Minister had suddenly left Vienna for an unknown destination. 'You understand me?' he said. The atmosphere was heavy with intrigue.

If the journey was to be completely secret, it was certainly strange that so many people knew who was travelling and why. It was clear that everybody in Salzburg knew. King Alexander had been right when he had said that the best security is secrecy. But who can keep a secret – or at any rate a secret of that kind – in the Balkans? The Crown Prince was travelling under the name of the Count of Rudnik, a mountain in Serbia. However, some security had to be arranged with the authorities of the countries we were passing through and, at that time at any rate, once the security of a royal personage was under discussion, the secret would be sure to get out. I sighed with relief when the train pulled away and my two charges could soon be safely 'put to bed'. I stayed up myself until the stop at Munich, where a tailor was to hand me a suit made for the Crown Prince to wear in England. It was no time or place for a fitting.

It was pleasant when we reached Paris the next day to be met by a trusted friend of the household, M. Szirmai, who swept us off to Prince Nicholas's apartment where we had an enjoyable lunch. But there was not much time and we had to dash away to the Gare du Nord to catch the train for London. We found our places in the train, and just before getting in I seized the opportunity to buy one or two English illustrated dailies at the bookstall. To my consternation, though not my surprise, I saw that the papers were splashed with the headlines: 'The Crown Prince of Yugoslavia on a visit to England'. Indeed, the *Daily Mirror* and the *Daily Sketch* had the whole of their front pages taken up by pictures of my royal charge.

Our arrival at Victoria on that historic day, 19th September

1934, was most extraordinary. We faced a battery of cameras and flashlights, more reminiscent of what takes place today than what was usual forty years ago. My biggest shock was the appearance of a railway porter who addressed me in fluent Serbian. I might have been suspicious about this, but I was so bedazzled by everything that I had nothing to say. On the platform was Miss Fox, Princess Olga's former nurse, who had come to relieve me of Prince Alexander. The Crown Prince and I went on to Claridge's where again we were conscious of clicking cameras on all sides as we got out of the car and moved into the hall. Finally, we got up into the palatial suite which had been prepared for us.

When we came down for dinner and sat in a room where there was an orchestra, the players, who seemed to be mainly Hungarian, started to play a *kolo* – a Serbian dance. The Crown Prince had to make an acknowledgement. By that time there was not much left of his incognito. Luckily we were both tired and we quickly retired to bed.

The next day I had to take the Crown Prince to Harrods to buy him some shirts and other necessities for school. As we entered the hotel hall we immediately found ourselves surrounded by journalists. I had a taxi called at once and jumped into it with my charge. On the way I saw that there were several taxis following us at breakneck speed. Since I was alone with the heir to the Yugoslav throne in what was to him a foreign city, and since I knew that there was a plot to take his life, I felt anxious. Eventually I stopped the taxi, jumped out of it swiftly and grabbed a taxi going in the opposite direction. I thought we had escaped our pursuers, but I found that I was wrong. A taxi with a journalist and a camera in it was tailing us. As we were turning a corner we stopped the taxi, dashed out and jumped up on to the top of a bus which was about to go off. When we alighted from this, we passed a man with a full load of photographic equipment sitting downstairs. Many will think that such rash manoeuvres in the midst of heavy London traffic were almost as dangerous to the Crown Prince's life as possible assaults by hostile secret agents. However, I thought it my duty to try and protect my pupil from the attentions of journalists as well as from the risk of attack. Luckily, as is generally the case with the press, the whole thing quietened down after a day or two, when the visit of the Crown Prince had ceased to become front page news.

What was the Yugoslav Minister in London doing in the meantime? Why had he not come to the station to meet the Crown

Prince? And why did he not come and talk to me about his security? The reason was a perfectly logical one. King Alexander's orders were that the Crown Prince's anonymity was to be preserved. The Yugoslav Minister must therefore not show any sign of being aware that he was in the country. Apart from that, the Minister was at this time paying his annual visit to Holland, where he was accredited as Minister, too. I decided that when he came back I should have to have a talk with him.

My main objective was to consult Scotland Yard, which without the Minister's sanction I would have no authority to do. My predicament can be imagined. I had no contact at all with King Alexander or the Court. No one had given me any address to which I might turn in difficulty. Although I was overwhelmed by the trust which the King had reposed in me, I would have felt happier if the Yugoslav government had been carrying the can rather than myself.

Meanwhile, there was someone to whom I might possibly have turned – the Crown Prince's grandmother, Queen Marie of Romania, who happened to be staying at that moment at the Ritz. I did not know her, but a Romanian legation official got in touch with me by telephone, and it was arranged that I should bring her grandson to lunch with her at her hotel the next day. Perhaps it was not the best of ideas to bring the Crown Prince into contact with Queen Marie at this particular moment, because she was a personality who always attracted publicity wherever she went. A famous beauty, a glamorous figure in a very Ruritanian court, the mother of the wild, headstrong King Carol and herself the author of many books of fantastic fairy tales and of her extensive memoirs, she focused attention on herself wherever she went and thoroughly enjoyed it. She had but recently aroused controversy by accepting an invitation to lunch from the Soviet Ambassador in Washington, she being the cousin of the last Tsar. I will have more to say about her later on in the book, but for the moment the most important fact about her for me was that clearly she was genuinely devoted to her grandson. By now I had the impression that within the family the Crown Prince did not command a great deal of affection. Both the King and the Queen took more interest in his younger brothers who, as children, were calculated to steal anyone's heart. It was also partly due to the Crown Prince's mismanaged upbringing, which had caused his backwardness, and backward children can sometimes make more demands on their parents than parents are inclined to grant.

However, finding someone who had the boy's interests at heart was a different matter from finding a suitable person to discuss questions of security. After meeting the Queen of Romania I did not feel any useful purpose would be served by going into that kind of detail with her. It seemed best to preserve the fiction that everything was all right.

The Queen was enormously vivacious and full of humour and bonhomie, and it was agreed that the happy lunch we had at the Ritz should be followed up by a return lunch at Claridge's where the Crown Prince would be host. I had to arrange it.

The meal took place, and I was amused to note that in the same dining-room there were a number of royalty or ex-royalty - chiefly 'ex' – including King Amanulla of Afghanistan, the King and Queen of Siam and King George of Greece. I explained to Queen Marie the purpose of my remaining in England while her grandson was at school, and told her I was planning some visits for him to undertake during the weekends. The Queen was very ready to co-operate, and two visits were soon decided upon for the future. The first was a visit to the Zoo, which the Queen apparently liked taking people to. And the second a stay at Cliveden, the home of Lord Astor, the Queen's great friend since her girlhood days. This programme was to begin after the Crown Prince had gone to school, since I had secured the headmaster's agreement to a slightly different timetable than would have been imposed on the average boy. One of the things I had insisted on was that he should be taught as much as possible by men! I was not anti-feminist, but I felt it necessary to seek a quick antidote to the highly charged feminine atmosphere prevailing in the Court. Queen Marie later introduced me to her even more vivacious sister, the Infanta Beatrice of Bourbon Orleans, known in the family as 'Aunt B'. Her husband, the Infante Alfonso, was the cousin of the King of Spain, Alfonso XIII. I was to see more of these delightfully human people in Yugoslavia.

At a cocktail party to which the Infanta invited me, I was told that the Crown Prince had been invited to lunch at Buckingham Palace by his godfather, King George V. The Infanta conveyed it to me in a tactful manner that I was to bring the Crown Prince to the Palace, not stay to lunch, and collect him afterwards.

The Crown Prince was frightened to death by George V. He told me that when the monarch said the simplest thing, like 'pass the mustard' (assuming that he did say this), it was like a depth-charge and he was afraid he was going to blow off the roof. I explained that the King had been a naval officer and this was probably what remained of 'the quarter-deck manner'. The Crown Prince confirmed that the King became excited when talking about the Navy as, for instance, about the loss of a submarine which had failed to re-emerge after diving. Since the boy was very interested in 'his' navy, I was glad to think that the two – young and old – had at least something in common to blow their tops about.

The day was now swiftly approaching when I would have to take the Crown Prince to his school, Sandroyd, at Cobham in Surrey. I had picked it out of a lot of school prospectuses and had been predisposed in its favour because the Headmaster, Mr. Ozanne, had been a schoolmaster at Edinburgh Academy (before I joined the staff there) and was well spoken of by my friends. The Queen was excited about it when she heard, because by chance it was the school where 'Aunt B' had sent her sons. Not only did my choice meet with general royal approval, but I was happy myself because Mr. Ozanne was a helpful and understanding person to deal with. Of course, it suited him to have more royalty at his school, but he did not adopt towards foreign pupils the arrogant attitude of 'take it or leave it', so common in our schools at that time.

In the last days before he went away to school, I tried to console the Crown Prince by buying for him (out of his own money) a model stationary steam-engine which he was able to play with in his hotel suite. Here, an episode took place which has been inaccurately reported by the only witness – the Prince himself. I often thought that I might one day write a book about my pupil, when he had become King, but I never imagined that he would get in first and write something about me. (He did not, as it happens, write it himself.) He published his own memoirs some twenty years ago, and in them he or his ghost writer describes how I bought him a steam-engine and then went out after tea, giving him strict orders to use it in the bathroom only, in case it fell over, made a mess or caught fire. When I returned, I found that he had disobeyed my instructions. He had taken the 'infernal machine' out of the bathroom and had been fiddling with it on his dressing table, when it suddenly blew up and scorched the varnish on the table.

In the memoirs King Peter, as he had by then become, put the blame on the valet at Claridge's who, when asked for methylated spirits, so he claims, brought him a bottle of brandy. I am not sure that I credit this alibi, but at any rate I must protest against the King's allegation that I ordered him to bed without supper when his grandmother was coming. First, his grandmother never came to supper; and also I would never have sent him to bed *without supper*.*

At last the moment came for me to escort my charge down to his school. We obtained an antique car for the purpose. It was what I believe used to be called a *cabriolet*, which meant that while we sat shut in comfortably in the back, the unhappy chauffeur in front sat in the open air, exposed to the elements. But as he was a legation chauffeur he had a kind of awning over his head which kept him dry. This contraption made such a noise in the wind that we could hardly hear ourselves speak, and once or twice it blew off completely, so that he had to stop and pick it up. We certainly travelled in royal style.

I did not spend much time handing over my charge to the Headmaster. I had already briefed him about the boy *ad nauseum* and there was no sense in saying more. I felt that he understood the situation – better than the matron did! The Crown Prince was incensed to find himself dragged off at once to have a bath, although he had had one that same morning. It was 'prison regulations'. Poor good matron, her comfortable illusions must have since been shattered. The continent is no longer necessarily dirty and England and the English are no longer necessarily clean.

On my return to London I obviously could not go on staying at Claridge's. I still did not know how much money I was going to get, if any. I should have to settle that in correspondence with the Minister of the Court no doubt, and so I moved first to a cheaper hotel, and then to some extremely cheap digs. Meanwhile, the Yugoslav Minister had returned and at my request asked for a representative from Scotland Yard to call and discuss the Crown Prince's security. When the inspector came, he took a complacent view of the matter: foreign royalty were always coming to London and none of them ever came to any harm. The Yugoslav Minister pleaded that some security arrangements might be made at the school. 'It won't be difficult. The British have a nose for a foreigner and any suspicious intruder in the neighbourhood would at once be detected by the locals.' The gentleman from Scotland Yard objected that security at Sandroyd was not his concern; it was in the hands of the Chief Constable of Surrey. At length it was agreed that I should write to the Chief Constable to discuss arrangements. Why

* If anyone would like to read *his* alleged personal account of our five years together he should read *A King's Heritage* published in London in 1955. It is full of romantic inexactitudes.

I had to do it, I cannot think. Looking subsequently at the official record of the interview, I see that I stressed the danger to the Crown Prince's life from possible letter and parcel bombs. This was far-sighted in 1934.

At the same time, following my plan, which had the consent of the King, I began my studies in Serbo-Croat at the University of London. It presented no difficulties as the only lecturer in the language at the time was Dr. Subotić, the Cultural Attaché at the Yugoslav Legation. He was a charming, cultivated man – the author of a book in English on Serbian folk poetry – and I could see that I was going to enjoy myself.

The first weekend came, and the Queen of Romania and I drove down to Sandroyd, picked up the Crown Prince and took him to the Zoo. It was not a particularly exciting day for me, but the Crown Prince and his grandmother were delighted. What I looked forward to was the next 'political' weekend, which we should be spending at Cliveden, the famous seat of Lord Astor and 'the appeasers'. Alas, this weekend never materialized for tragic reasons.

It may not seem ideal from the educational point of view that a boy should be taken away from his boarding school every weekend, even before he had got used to school life. This was my idea and I should perhaps defend it. I remembered only too well the narrowing and frustrating weekends which English schoolboys were forced to spend at their prep schools. In some respects the Prince at the age of eleven was more mature than other boys. In other respects he was less so. In any case he responded much better to what he was shown and saw himself, than what he was told or had to read from books. I felt that these visits could play an important part in his education and I hoped they could be followed up on his return to Yugoslavia by educative tours of his country.

CHAPTER FIVE ✧ THE ASSASSIN STRIKES

✧ Let us now take a look at what was happening in Yugoslavia itself. King Alexander had just returned from a state visit to Bulgaria. The trip was fraught with danger as relations had long been tense between the two countries because of the Bulgarian claim to the part of Macedonia which was in Yugoslavia. The Macedonian frontier was one of the most strongly fortified frontiers in Europe, being protected against the Comitadji or Macedonian revolutionaries whose activities against Yugoslavia resembled those of the I.R.A. in Northern Ireland. Everyone heaved a sigh of relief when he returned safely from this visit.

Immediately afterwards the King and Queen were to make a state visit to France. They were to leave the Yugoslav port of Split in the destroyer *Dubrovnik*. As I was afterwards to learn, the weather on the Mediterranean was stormy and the Queen, who had not been well and was planning to have an operation for gallstones in Paris, decided to go by train and join up with the King in France. Thus the King sailed alone and was scheduled to arrive in Marseilles on 9th October.

I shall never forget the events of that day. I had lunch in London with the Yugoslav Minister and afterwards we walked back together across the park. I remember saying to him: 'There is one question which worries me. Here am I all alone with your Crown Prince in England. What do you think I ought to do in the event of his father's falling victim to an assassin?' The Minister replied: 'I could not possibly even contemplate such a calamity.' We did not discuss the matter further.

In the afternoon I visited Dr. Subotić in his flat and had a Serbian lesson. I returned by bus and along Oxford Street and even in those days traffic was very bad and I was held up in innumerable blocks. While I waited in the bus my eye caught the sinister headline on a newspaper placard: 'Shots at a King in France'.

Fearing the worst I jumped up to get out, but, as luck would have it, the bus gave a spurt forward and carried me far beyond the place where the placard had been. It was obviously stop-press news, since it did not appear on the other placards.

I got out as soon as the bus stopped and ran back along Oxford Street to look for the placard with the horrifying report. At last I found it, bought a paper, searched through it and found on the back page the brief message that an attempt had been made to assassinate King Alexander at Marseilles and that he was severely wounded.

I immediately hailed a taxi and drove back to Dr. Subotić's flat. He was very shaken by the news and at once rang up the Yugoslav Minister, who told him that he had had contradictory reports but feared the worst. We rushed to the Legation, only to be told that the King was already dead.

What had actually happened at Marseilles? On 9th October, the Yugoslav destroyer *Dubrovnik* had sailed into the harbour carrying the King in the uniform of a Yugoslav admiral. He was received on the quay by the French Foreign Minister, Louis Barthou. After some delay at the beginning, due to a change of cars and the withdrawal of the motor-cycle police guard – to permit the public to have a better view of the royal guest – the King drove off seated next to Louis Barthou with General Georges sitting opposite him. Initial photographs showed the King smiling and talking animatedly with his hosts.

Three factors were of importance: first, the running boards of the car were extremely wide; next, the design of the car may have enabled the crowds to see him at close range, but made him an easy target for an assassin; finally, there were no police outriders to deal with potential assailants in the crowd. The Yugoslav government had offered to send their own protective force but the French had declined the offer on the grounds that their own police were fully able to cope with the situation.

Suddenly a man had rushed out of the crowd, shouting 'Vive le Roi', leapt on to the running board and fired first at the King, then at Minister Barthou and finally at General Georges. The chauffeur swung round to push the assailant away and an officer of the mounted escort cut him down with his sabre as he shot wildly into the crowd.

For the King death was almost instantaneous: he was hit four times. Louis Barthou expired shortly after him. The murderer died two hours later at the police station.

Meanwhile the Queen was travelling by train on the way to Marseilles to join her husband. The news was broken to her at Lyons. She went on to Marseilles and was taken to a small chapel where the King's body lay in state next to that of the French Foreign Minister. The Queen said: 'I have one small compensation. The

King died in France, the country he loved best of all after his own.' On the old fortress of Kalemegdan in Belgrade there is a giant statue pointing with an enormous finger to the West. It was sculpted by Mestrović in 1929 and bears the inscription 'Gratitude to France'. Under some bas-reliefs stand the words: 'Let us love France as she has loved us'.

The assassination was the work of Anton Pavelić, the leader of the Croat Ustaši movement, acting in conjunction with Mihajlov, the head of I.M.R.O., the Macedonian Revolutionary Organization. The murderer was a Bulgarian member of Mihajlov's body guard. The object of the *attentat* was the overthrow of the Yugoslav régime and the dismemberment of the country, and the Italian and Hungarian governments were deeply involved in it.

The situation was extremely tense and the Minister was so emotional that he could give us no directive. My first thought was for the Crown Prince, now King, and I said that we must at once get into touch with his Headmaster. It was agreed that nothing should be said to the boy for the time being and that I should go down by car the next morning and take him away from the school before the other boys got up to avoid the risk of his hearing the tragic news before we had prepared him for it. The Yugoslav Minister kindly invited me to stay the night at the Legation so that we could be in constant touch. He was all the time awaiting instructions from Belgrade and receiving conflicting messages from there and Marseilles.

I telephoned the Headmaster and set out alone the next day at a very early hour to reach the school before breakfast. This time the Legation had ordered a better car from the Daimler Hire Company and the journey was quick. The police guarded the route all through London. When I arrived, the house was ringed round with a wall of 'bobbies'. The Headmaster woke the Prince up but did not tell him the reason for his imminent departure.

The Prince was not normally inquisitive in matters of this kind. He submitted passively to anything which was asked of him. It was therefore a little time before he enquired why I had come to fetch him. I explained that his father had had a bad accident in France. He immediately asked: 'Was it in a car?' and I said, 'Yes.' He was obviously turning over in his mind *which* car it might have happened in and what kind of an accident it had been.

The car sped on back to London and at every stationer's shop en route the tell-tale placards blazoned forth the facts which I had not been able to break to him. Not content with the headlines, some of the placards carried a huge polychrome photo of the body of the dying King lying on the floor of the car in a pool of blood.

I do not think the Prince had time to take these in, but I felt I had to tell him the full truth there and then. He took it phlegmatically, as I had expected he would. There had been no great affection between father and son. If anything the boy had been scared of him. In any case King Alexander had had scant time for his children and, as I have already mentioned, he barely concealed his preference for his second son, Tomislav.

The new King was taken first to his Legation and looked after there, while I rushed out to Hamleys, the toy shop, and bought him a new engine to absorb himself in. I went by taxi to my digs to pack my things and pick up the post. There I found a letter addressed to me from the Chief Constable of Surrey. 'I understand you would like to see me about the safety of the Crown Prince of Yugoslavia,' he wrote; 'I should be glad to receive you any day in the latter part of next week – not on Wednesday, as it is my bench day. . . .'

When I came back, I learnt from the Minister that instructions had come that the King was to proceed to Paris that afternoon and join his mother who was waiting there. We regretted this decision but understood that it was inevitable. The Foreign Secretary, Sir John Simon, when calling at the Legation to express his sympathy, said he thought it would be much better for the boy to remain a little longer in the peace and quiet of his school. But his grandmother sent word that I was to take him at once to the Ritz. It was a sad and agitated time, interrupted by visits of condolence from members of various royal families. All the Yugoslav and Romanian legation officials were in a 'flap' – in contrast to the stoic calm of the royalty. I remember having a friendly chat with the ex-King George of Greece, whose life had been full of tragedy. He preserved his debonair manner even on this occasion, and said to me: 'This is going to give *you* a lot more trouble than you bargained for.' Only the Queen of Romania was dramatic, as always. I was grateful to her. Some outward demonstration of grief was required and none could have been more fitting than hers.

By this time the plans were made. The Queen of Romania was to accompany the young King to Paris, and after a quick lunch we all left for Victoria Station. As we went down the steps of the Ritz, the Queen holding her pale and forlorn grandson by the hand, a crowd had gathered, and a man took off his hat and called out to him: 'Good luck, sir!'

In the reserved Pullman carriage the Infante Alfonso and Lord Astor were waiting to accompany the Queen. The latter had been her friend from girlhood days, as I have recounted, when, a beautiful and bored young lady, she had languished at the Bucharest court, at that time a Hohenzollern encampment. Lord Astor was a first-class entertainer and kept the young King amused with his conjuring tricks the whole journey to Dover. He must have entertained me too, because I cannot remember anything more about the journey until we were approaching Paris. We were supposed to alight at the Gare du Nord, but some quarter of an hour before our scheduled arrival the train suddenly stopped in the middle of the countryside. We got out and saw before us a whole line of flares and masses of detectives behind them. In ghostly silence we stumbled over the roughest of paths beside the track – over rocks and mud. The Queen went first, holding her grandson by the hand, and I felt impelled to keep as close to him as possible since we were now in the country where his father had been murdered. It was also so dark that it was impossible to identify anybody. We could have lost him. It was a nightmare. In time we were hustled into a car and I saw that the only passengers were Monsieur Flandin, the French Prime Minister, the Queen of Romania, the King and myself. We then rushed in a long cavalcade with motor cycle escort towards Paris. When we reached the centre the traffic seemed to have been stopped in all the side roads and there were gendarmes everywhere on our route. Paris at midnight is not generally so quiet and it looked as if the great city of night life had been struck dead. Our destination was the residence of the Yugoslav Minister in France, Mr. Spalajković. There, we were received by the Minister's wife and another woman, possibly her sister, both very beautiful but in a terrible state of grief. They had been personal friends of the late King. They wept on the shoulders of his son, and I then took him to his room and got him to bed. I withdrew and was soon asleep after the events of this disturbed day.

It was quiet and peaceful at the Residence. Next morning, after breakfast the Minister's pretty daughter came to help entertain the King and we played silly games. The conversation was in Serbian and the King kept on saying: 'If I win this trick, I'll eat my hat.' When translated into Serbian it sounded frightfully funny and we were convulsed with laughter. Miss Spalajković was charming and the atmosphere was very homely – a striking contrast with the tense but formal reception the young King had faced when he got out of the train. It had been a mixture of cloak and dagger and diplomatic protocol.

At about midday the King came down and his widowed mother came forward heavily draped in black and kissed him. My feelings were so intense that I could hardly bear to look at her. She said to me calmly: 'It's a difficult meeting, isn't it?' A funereal lunch followed at which it was impossible to talk, let alone eat. But the Queen made jokes and went out of her way to describe the presents she would give the young King. Among the people there was our Ambassador in Paris, Sir George Clarke, who had earlier been one of my predecessors in the British Embassy at Prague. He spoke to me with sympathy and fellow feeling and I was grateful for it. I needed some moral support myself.

Towards the evening, the King and his mother left the Legation for the station to catch the Arlberg Express, to which the Yugoslav royal carriages had been attached. I very nearly failed to make it, encountering a situation which was often to re-occur in the course of my stay in Yugoslavia – that is, until I took firm measures against it. No transport had been laid on for me to get to the station. Nobody had even thought of me. I scarcely existed for them. This was only understandable in the terrible emotion and excitement that possessed everybody, but I resented it because after all I had been making the arrangements for the King while he was in London, even to the point of looking after his security, which the Yugoslav government seemed to have neglected. I felt I deserved a seat in some car on its way to the station. I finally had to beg a place in one of the Romanian Legation cars and arrived at the station just in time to scramble on to the train.

There an extraordinary sight met my eyes. The train had moved two or three yards when, as sometimes happens, it stopped all at once with a jolt and there was an embarrassed moment for those on board and the spectators. I saw the Queen looking out of her window and giving a restrained farewell bow to the assembled French government on the platform. They all stood there like waxworks, frozen in this last unexpected moment that never seemed to come to an end. I could recognize the enormously broad figure of Monsieur Herriot and I believe that President Lebrun was there too. The royal passengers in the train stared at the whole French government, and the whole French government stared back. There was no movement, nothing. It was like a movie which has been brought to an abrupt stop.

The train eventually moved off and I noticed that various other people seemed to have attached themselves to the party, including the Queen Mother's younger sister, Princess Ileana of Romania. I soon made the acquaintance of this charming young princess who had a most exhilarating personality.

Somehow new feelings had come over me. When I had been in Yugoslavia I had found it strange and exotic to be living in the Court. Now in France it was a great relief to get away from the diplomats and French politicians and rejoin the family circle of the Queen. By getting into the train I had come home. It was as well for me that I did feel this because I was to live in that 'home' for the next five years.

CHAPTER SIX ◇ CHILD KING

◇ As we approached Belgrade I was worried about what my life would be like in the Royal Palace. I had no experience of living in the city and I knew I would shortly come into contact with a lot of strange people – generals and court functionaries. The arrival of the new King at the station in Belgrade would be a historic occasion. Under King Alexander's will three regents had been appointed to govern during his minority. One of them was Prince Paul, and the other two were Mr. Perović and Mr. Stanković, whom the King and I were later to call 'Tweedledum and Tweedledee'. They were both of them short and rather alike, and they contrasted with the tall slim figure of Prince Paul, who was the *Prince* Regent.

The immediate problem for me was a practical one – one of transport. How was I to get to the palace? It was quite far from the station and I did not want to suffer the fate I had suffered at the Yugoslav Legation in Paris. I therefore asked Mr. Antić, the Minister of the Court, who was responsible for all arrangements, what transport I should take to get to the palace. He told me to wait until the royal party had got out and then appropriate arrangements would be made for me. I thought no more about it and blindly obeyed his instructions – but for the last time! The royal party left the train, the Minister of the Court left the train, the troops left the train, the servants left the train. I remained on it until the cleaners came and drove me out.

I then wandered about the platform and at length found a military car standing in the yard and persuaded the officer in it to take me up to the palace. I was consequently debarred from witnessing two historic occasions: the new King's arrival in his capital and his entry into his palace.

The next few days, indeed the next few weeks, were difficult though memorable times. King Alexander's palace was at the top of the hill of Dedinje, as I have said, and was built in a neo-Byzantine style. It had been completed comparatively recently and the garden and parks still showed signs of being not entirely finished. The front upper windows of the palace commanded a magnificent view of the Danube flowing past the old fortress of Smederevo towards the

Romanian frontier. In the old days this was the frontier between the giant Austro-Hungarian Empire and the little kingdom of Serbia. At the back and to the south one looked at the vast spaces of Serbia.

The autumns in Belgrade were beautiful and sometimes lasted until Christmas. It was only October and it was like late summer. The young King's joy at being home again and finding his brothers was irrepressible. The children chased each other harum-scarum all around the garden, shrieking at the tops of their voices. This was hardly in harmony with the mood of universal grief apparent everywhere, but I suppressed an instinct to hush them. I realized that they had to let off steam and that the King himself needed this escape valve after being cooped up for so long in trains and experiencing the full force of ceremonial visits and leave-takings.

The first event of consequence was the King's funeral. His body was brought from France by ship and train, and the cortège accompanied it from Belgrade station to the cathedral. It was a tiring walk and we were not sure whether it might not be too much for the young King. And so I took part in the procession, walking just behind him and preparing myself, should it be necessary, to signal to his car which was driving slowly at the side. As it turned out, he coped admirably with the walk, the immensely long Orthodox church service, the journey by train to the family mausoleum at Oplenac, the exhausting ceremony there, and the return to Dedinje. It was an unnerving experience for me to be in the procession and hear the oriental wail of the population bemoaning the loss of their King. It was something one does not hear in our part of Europe and would have been more in place in the Middle East. It was another of those traces of Turkish dominion which one stumbled upon in Serbia. Everyone was in tears, even the gendarmes who were controlling the crowds. The Duke of Kent's detective, who had been at all royal funerals for the last twenty years, told me he had never seen any like it, nor wished to again. He mentioned that the police arrangements were magnificent and said the assassination could not have happened here.

The question of who should represent Britain at the funeral led to complications. For some unexplained reason, King George V rejected the suggestion of the Foreign Office that one of the royal princes should attend. He seems to have dug in his toes until our Minister, Sir Nevile Henderson, sent two telegrams deploring the decision. King Alexander had been our ally in the last war, he wrote, and was known for his friendliness to the West. What would the reaction be in Yugoslavia if, when France sent her President and Germany Field-Marshal Goering, the British Royal Family were unrepresented? In the meantime reports came in of more and more countries sending high representatives. The King at last gave in, and the Duke of Kent was selected.

There were many other important foreign guests. France was represented by President Lebrun and Marshal Petain, Germany by Field-Marshal Goering and Italy by the Duke of Spoleto. And of course King Carol of Romania, the Queen's brother, was there, as well as one of the Greek princes. At one moment Marshal Goering and I walked together through a doorway. It was still just possible for us to do so. Later, when he got even fatter, there might have been some congestion. He brought with him a wonderful electric model railway as a present for the King. Due to the technical perfection of this model the King was able to stand at the controls and run several trains over the various tracks at the same time, varying their routes and avoiding collisions. I spent many hours in the room where it was installed, since it was a favourite occupation of his. I was afraid that Goering would act like most grown-ups do, when they give children presents of trains, and sprawl on the floor playing with them. But fortunately he was in no shape to do so. It amused me to see how foreign countries were beginning to vie with each other in courting the young King's favour. Earlier on, the Czechoslovak government had presented the Crown Prince with an outside miniature railway, which was big enough for the children to ride in. Later, they gave him a small model Škoda car, and the Germans countered with a miniature Adler. King Peter preferred the Škoda, not, I fear, out of solidarity with the Little Entente, but because he liked the whiffs of petrol it always emitted when it went round corners.

If Goering went out of his way to ingratiate himself with the government and the public, he was not popular. It was said that while driving in his car he had two S.S. men on each side of him with revolvers in their hands. But the inability of the French to protect the life of a King as Francophile as Alexander had undermined Yugoslav trust in France and the Germans were alive to the fact that it was time for them to try and exploit the situation.

The young King moved into his father's bedroom and I had all meals with him in the sitting-room adjoining. As a result of the large number of guests staying in the palace, which was in any case rather small, I could only be found a bedroom in the attic. It was a bit far away from the King, so I improvised a bed in the bathroom next door to him and slept there the first few nights in case he should need me. But the attic which was the *mansard* or servants' quarters and thus had access to all the bedrooms had its uses.

The Queen of Romania was living in one of the bedrooms near the King and she was naturally worried about how her daughter was going to get on under the new conditions after her husband's death. She wanted to consult me about the people around the King and asked me to come and see her in her room. At the appointed hour (I think it was about 10 a.m. in the morning) I knocked at her door and found her – in bed! She was looking very beautiful and reading her own memoirs! Though I sympathized with her concern for her daughter and grandson, and wanted to be helpful, I did not want to be party to any intrigues. Speaking of the royal children, she said that the English governess would be leaving and we must try and persuade the 'little Swede' to stay. Then she began to tell me of her fears about 'Mignon'. Would she be strong enough to stand up for herself? I could not very well express an opinion on this, but just at that moment I heard the sound of voices in the hall and, as luck would have it, some of the royal relatives had arrived. 'I don't think they had better find you here,' the Queen said. 'I think you should go.' But where could I go? The voices and footsteps were coming nearer. The Queen whispered: 'There is a side door there which leads upstairs. You can go out there.' So I left through a 'secret' door, which led to my attic. It reminded me more and more of a Renaissance drama, but Queen Marie loved drama of course. It was as well that I was not concealed 'behind the arras', although in that civilized family there was little likelihood of my sharing Polonius' fate.

My first Christmas in Belgrade was a remarkable one. I shall always remember how I received Christmas presents from three queens – the Queens of Romania, Yugoslavia and Greece, all of whom were in the palace at the time. The Queen of Romania was always kind and good-tempered, and charmingly vain. She had just completed her memoirs by then, and when she told stories about her childhood, which were fascinating to listen to, she nearly always referred to her book. I once asked her about Queen Victoria and she answered: 'She was so —. How did I put it in my book? I put it so well there. Zwiedineck! Go and fetch my book and read the passage aloud for me.' The last order was spoken in German to her adjutant, who was obviously a Romanian German and was translating her book into German. The general conversation then shifted into

German, but it soon righted itself again in English when the Queen went off on another tack. Zwiedineck was an elderly A.D.C. with a good sense of humour. Once the whole party, including King Carol of Romania, came down to the little pavilion to see where the King had his lessons. There was more to it than that, because Queen Mignon, who was fond of sculpturing and painting, had also made an atelier there for herself. I arranged tea for them and acted as host on behalf of my pupil. Afterwards, as they all went out followed by Zwiedineck and me, the former turned to me and said in German: 'And here come the two Rasputins!'

Another side to the 'Three Queens' was less romantic and more down to earth. When I say 'three' I must put in something about the third – the Queen of Greece, formerly Princess Elizabeth of Romania. I called her 'Pique Dame'. She looked like a witch but a handsome and striking one. (It seemed impossible for any of the Queen of Romania's daughters to be plain!) When she got out of the train on her arrival she was a figure which imprinted itself indelibly on my memory. She was tall with an aquiline nose and red hair and walked with a stick. And when I was introduced to her, she said at once, 'Ah, I am so glad to meet you. I have heard so much about you, Mr. Parrott' – which was most flattering. She had been married to King George of Greece but had left him and was living with a Romanian on an estate near the Romanian frontier.

In the evenings I made a four with the 'three queens' when they played their own variety of the game 'word making and word taking'. The liberties the ladies took in spelling the words convulsed me with laughter. They were very unsound at it, but to make up for that they had a peculiarly rich vocabulary – particularly in 'four-lettered words'. Sometimes it seemed that every word they began must inevitably finish in a certain direction, the Queen of Greece being especially enterprising in this respect. The point was that the letters they added must not form a word and in order to challenge their intentions I had to name the word, which was exactly what they wanted, since it was great fun for them to try to embarrass me. They must have had a good laugh about it among themselves afterwards.

Of course the King had to have his official Yugoslav schooling and soon a whole staff of teachers arrived complete with a Governor. At first I was not quite sure what the functions of this Governor would be, since he marched in with the air of an invading general taking over the government of a country he had conquered. However, I was soon able to draw up lines of demarcation between his functions and mine. He was responsible for organizing lessons (which I found he did not do too well) while I looked after the King's general upbringing and organized his daily life.

Whenever the King went out he was accompanied by one of his adjutants. *The Good Soldier Švejk* gives an amusing picture of some of the officers of the Austro-Hungarian army, who included Czechs, Hungarians, Poles, Serbs, Croats and Slovenes as well as Austrians. Some of them were stupid, cranky or senile. It was not surprising, therefore, that the Yugoslav army, which was made up of officers drawn partly from the Austro-Hungarian army and partly from the Serbian army, had its quota of them, as I have said.

One of these was Colonel Petrović, whom we soon christened 'Russian boots'. I think he must have served in Russia because he seemed to ape the characteristics of a Tsarist officer, though he may have been a Montenegrin. He always addressed the King as 'Gospodar' (Lord). This corresponds to the Russian 'Gosudar', which was the name given to the Tsar in old Russia. He was a great talker and boaster and at the same time rather stupid, but we never any of us imagined he could be quite such a fathead as he showed himself to be when we were once staying in Bled and the young King and his cousin Prince Alexander were playing on the banks of the Sava River in the company of one or two of the boys the King had invited to spend some of his holiday with him.

The King had got a boomerang. I do not know whether it was I who bought it for him or whether he had received it as a present, but at any rate we had gone out to a suitable wide stretch of terrain to experiment with it and see if it really came back to the spot from which it was thrown. At one point, one of the boys stood on the rather high bank over the river and threw the boomerang. Instead of returning to the bank it got caught in a wind and fell on a small island in the middle of the river. We had no boats and as the river there was somewhat rapid, it was risky to try and ford it. Nevertheless, we all started to wade out to see if we could reach it. In the rear of the column was Colonel 'Russian boots' who followed us bravely, although he was dressed in full uniform. We had taken off our shoes and socks, but he could not do so because he was on duty. As we went on ahead, we got to some rapids and the water got deeper and deeper. I had long trousers on and rolled them up. The boys had shorts, but even so the water was becoming pretty high for them. Moreover, the current was strong and the river bed was covered with very slippery round boulders. To avoid any unfortunate accidents I called the expedition off. But the colonel continued to advance, roaring out at the top of his voice 'Samo napred!' in Serbian–literally 'Only forwards', but perhaps best translated by something like 'No retreat!' or 'Excelsior!'

We had got back to the bank and we climbed up to a position on a comfortable grassy promontory from which we looked down on the river below and watched how the drama would proceed. The adjutant, still shouting out and singing to himself, went on and on. His slogan remained 'Samo napred' and certainly it was only forwards that he went. Oblivious of everything – his uniform, his boots, the slipperiness of the stones, the force of the current – he was determined to reach that island and win his laurels by returning the boomerang to the King. We were howling with laughter when suddenly he eclipsed himself by tripping up and falling headlong into the water.

It now became embarrassing and we turned away as he battled with the few yards that separated him from the island. We saw him later stripping off his uniform piece by piece and lighting a fire, over which he slowly dried everything. Out of sympathy for his predicament we determined to remain around, because he would have been in trouble if we had returned home and left him. There would have been questions about why he had not accompanied the King. His misadventure was due partly to bravado and anxiety to show off before the King and partly also to the fixed idea all these officers had that they must be near the King at any cost (quite superfluously since there were detectives there who could easily have rushed into the water in case of an emergency). It was carried so far that I am sure that if the King had all at once gone up in a balloon and he had not been invited to accompany him, the adjutant would have gone on a cross-country run following the balloon up hill and down dale until he received orders to the contrary.

Once we all of us made an expedition to the Triglav mountain and spent the night in the hut near the summit where I had been before on my ill-prepared journey. But this time we had superb conditions. When we rose early in the morning there was a very fine *Alpenglühe* – that glorious pink glow which, if one is lucky, one sometimes sees illuminating the tops of the highest mountains. We had decided to climb the last stretch and reach the summit, when the Serbian adjutant attached to us, who had accompanied us all the way in military uniform without making any concessions to the requirements of mountaineering, unexpectedly declared that he could not get to the top since he was not equipped for it and therefore refused to allow the King to go without him. We pleaded with him, and I told him that I had done it myself under much less favourable conditions and that I was no mountaineer and found it a simple climb. There was absolutely no danger this time because we were accompanied by mountain guides and the director of the royal hunt. The colonel replied that if I took the King to the top he would at once telephone the Prime Minister. And so with great sadness we gave it up. When one considers that this was the highest mountain in Yugoslavia and the effect it would have had if people had read the next day that the young King, aged twelve, had scaled it, it was a tragedy that we had to turn back. It was undoubtedly a great disappointment to the King.

Some of the adjutants did become unnecessarily fussy on the tours we made. However, I must admit that the situation was a difficult one for them. They were not really in charge of the King's movements, because it was I who planned what he should do and where he should go. On the other hand, they knew that if anything happened the authorities would immediately pick on them and make them the scapegoats. And I must also concede that these were exceptional cases and in general the officers were good sports and made our expeditions much more enjoyable than they would have been had we gone alone. Most of them had a marvellous sense of humour and could often also contribute something to the King's experiences by their observations and reminiscences.

Sometimes they were uneasy since they felt that I was driving the King too hard or making him do dangerous things. This was nonsense, because no one was more conscious than I was of the awful responsibility which devolved on me. It was not only a responsibility to the nation but particularly to the late King, the Queen Mother and the Prince Regent who had placed so much trust in me. And there were occasions too when they thought that I offended against national traditions. On the day of the royal 'Slava', I arranged a football match for the young King and some of the adjutants looked at me askance for doing so. The Slava is the day of the saint protector of a Serb family. What normally happens in Yugoslavia when anybody has a Slava is that he stays at home and receives the congratulations of all his friends. He has to fill them (and himself) up with drink and he must serve countless cups of coffee too. The host is drunk quite early in the day and at the end of it all his guests are as well.

In the case of the Royal Family's Slava of course nothing like this occurred. The day started with a church service and after that there was nothing at all for the children to do. There could not be any lessons because it was a holiday. It seemed to me that a football match was a good idea. However, as we went down I noticed grumblings going on behind my back from our escorts.

All the same, football is very popular in Yugoslavia and the Yugoslavs – as we all know today – are great football players. There was therefore some sympathetic interest in my programme. Indeed, on one occasion the Minister of the Court came down solemnly to watch a match to make sure that the King was being properly treated. After observing the game for about ten minutes he remarked to me reproachfully that the King was not being given opportunities to get at the ball. I suppose he expected me to tell the other boys never on any account to kick the ball themselves until the King had missed it at least three times!

I was less sensible when I tried to introduce cricket. First of all, 'my sportsmaster', Mr. Kovač from the Sokol, who was such a splendid help in everything, was completely at sea with cricket, which is always mixed up in foreigners' minds with croquet. When I started introducing it (and I had to get the equipment from England), some of the boys thought that it must be baseball, of which they had vaguely heard. Soon after we started playing, one of the boys was hit on the head by a ball and so the idea soon caught on that cricket was 'rough'. It did in fact tend to become rough when played in the Balkans. Boys were apt to throw the ball at the players instead of at the stumps, but a more or less good time was had by all nonetheless.

Imagine my excitement when the Prince Regent came to me one day and asked me whether I would arrange for a squash court to be built in the grounds, since he thought he would like to play the game. Maybe he regarded it as an occupation for his guests, for he himself was not a great sports-lover.

Trying to build a squash court in a foreign country where they have no idea of the game is no easy task. I ordered all the instructions from Prince's club in London and had to negotiate with a local Russian architect to get it put up. There were many misunderstandings between us and these resulted in some peculiar malformations in the court. In the first place, they put on the *service line* the material they should have put on the *play line*, so that whenever the ball hit the service line in the course of the game it jumped up just as it always does when it hits the play line in a normal court. Another thing was that the architect did not like to have flush joints between the walls and the floor, and bevelled the edges instead, with the result that whenever the ball touched the edge it sprang up again as if it had touched the play line, like a Rugby football in fact. However, with patience we gradually eliminated these faults and the day dawned when the court was ready for inauguration. The first game in it was between the Prince Regent and myself. Unfortunately, in the course of it I inadvertently hit him sharply in the neck with the ball which damped his pleasure and spoilt mine. I did not have much opportunity of playing in it myself, because I did not stay long after it had been completed. But I hope that it was put to good use. It was then the only squash court in that part of Europe.

Now that Tito has this palace I wonder whether 'my' squash court has survived. Even if it has, which I doubt, I cannot imagine that the new rulers in Yugoslavia would ever invite me to play with them on it. I am sure I am recorded somewhere in the state archives as a dangerous player, capable of assassination on (or in) a court.

The King was supposed to have riding lessons three times a week and I always took part in them with him. For about three years I did this without a break, riding in a manege when it was not possible to ride outside. I went through all the gambits of a military riding school – riding without stirrups, jumping without stirrups, in fact going through everything which is supposed to make you a good rider. And I had the benefit of being instructed by the King's riding master, who was a very good teacher. But sadly his efforts met with no success at all, for not only did the King himself hate riding but his tutor was unenthusiastic about it too. Neither of us were any credit to him.

However, there was a time when I enjoyed it. At one period during the King's morning school hours I used to take a horse out and ride all over the country, and this was splendid. I noticed sometimes when I rode through villages and met peasants that they shook their fists at me or gave me hostile glances. No, they were not members of the Communist Party. I learnt later that this was another of the things about the Turks which the Serbs had never forgotten. In the old days before Kara George liberated them, anybody who came riding on horseback into a village could be taken for a Turkish oppressor. Christians were not allowed to ride on horseback. A donkey was good enough for them.

The horse I used to ride was the Queen of Romania's horse, 'Montana'. She was a lovely mount and just made for an enchanting rider like the Queen of Romania herself. But when I went out in the cavalcade with the King, the riding instructor and his adjutant, it was essential for me to keep in the rear. As it happened, Montana had never been used to being anywhere but in the lead and I had a terrible business trying to keep her back. In the end I found it so embarrassing that I decided to change horses and take a less dominant one. Princess Olga allowed me to ride hers, which was less ambitious. I could then take a back seat.

CHAPTER SEVEN ◇ ANGLO-NORWEGIAN AFFAIRS

◇ I must now say something about my own private life which ran parallel to that of the great ones but on a different plane, and developed in a far from normal fashion. When in Hercegnovi I caught a fleeting glimpse of a golden-haired girl, I had, as I have already said, a sudden awareness of feeling at home. She turned out to be a Norwegian nurse to the royal children and her name was Ellen Matzow affectionately called 'Smatzo' by them. We met for the first time in the Queen's company on one of the picnics we used to have when the Crown Prince joined his brothers after bathing. Her hair really was the pure gold of fairy tales – *une pluie d'or* as the French put it – and she had a very fair skin and a sunny, happy look. There are few people I have met of whom it can be truthfully said that they were radiant. She had that quality.

She was two years younger than I was and we were thrown together quite a lot. It was good to have someone to talk to, and she did a great deal to make me feel welcome in that somewhat exotic milieu. Now when the cat's away the mice will play, especially when the mice are being smiled upon by a benevolent queen, who was almost another mouse herself. In the autumn of 1934, when we went to Bled in Slovenia, the English nurse went home on leave for a short period. From that time on, expeditions mostly consisted of nobody but the Queen, Smatzo and me.

After lunch, when the children always *had* to rest (as prescribed by the English nurse), I used to go up to her room and laugh and joke with her. When the now eminent Slovenian artist, Božidar Jakac, came to sketch the young King he offered to sketch me too. Smatzo came and joined in the fun, and her presence ensured that both artist and subject were in a good mood. Later, when Mr. Jakac offered to sketch her, I tried to reciprocate.

Once the Queen decided to go away for a weekend to the King's hunting lodge which lay right in the midst of the Kamnik Alps with their high and jagged peaks. It was an unusual building, designed by the Slovenian architect Plečnik, who was much sought after in the twenties and was given the task of cleaning up and restoring the Prague Hradčany. The massive granite obelisque in the courtyard there is his design as well as the modern church at Vinohrady. In his own country, Plečnik was commissioned to restore the city of Ljubljana, the capital of Slovenia, and regulate the river Sava which flowed through it. But if his heavy and massive geometrical forms were appropriate for castles, churches and town planning, they were less in place in a small chalet. The features of his interior ornamentation were ingenious and I spent my time staring at them (because I dined not with the Queen and Smatzo but less interestingly with two of the suite). But in a hunting lodge one wants simplicity and *Gemütlichkeit*, not ingenious architectural quirks. It was the best excursion I ever had in Yugoslavia, perhaps because I was so close to Smatzo – and yet so far! When I came back to Bled, I realized I had fallen in love with her.

The affair was finally settled one night when I asked her to come out and have dinner with me at a hotel in Bled. It was by the lakeside, and we went out in a boat and afterwards walked all round the lake. By the time we had completed the circle and were almost dropping with fatigue, a proposal was made by one party or the other – it has long been a matter of dispute which – and it was mutually accepted.

Great difficulties had to be overcome. Even on that starlit night of beauty we were talking serious business. I told her I felt I had a duty to stay with the Crown Prince until he was able to stand on his own feet. He had just celebrated his eleventh birthday. I thought I should remain with him at least another five years until he was sixteen.

Smatzo had already been three years at the Court and had wanted to leave before I came. The Queen had continually asked her to postpone her departure. She knew that she really must get home, see her parents again and find a proper job. Moreover, by that point she was aware that I was going to England with the Crown Prince and would be staying most of the year there. We talked of how we might meet in England or Norway. We little knew then that we had no need to worry. Fate itself would solve our problems. But as we returned that night to the villa of Suvobor my fiancée had generously promised to wait five years before we were united.

Our engagement was kept a strict secret. Although we were together so often we were good actors and played our self-appointed parts. It was excruciatingly hard of course when I had to leave for England because in all the leave-taking there was almost nothing I could do to express the real anguish I felt. However, once I was there

I was soon cheered by regular letters from Yugoslavia. Yes, from Yugoslavia, because Smatzo was still unable to tear herself away from the embraces of the Court.

When after the King's murder I returned to Belgrade, I immediately found myself in a much more problematical situation. I was overjoyed to be with her again, but it was clearly not possible to keep it dark any longer. We were reduced to placing notes for each other behind the clock in the drawing-room of the little thatched pavilion. At all costs the English nurse must not find out, or else Smatzo would get into hot water. I was compelled to break the news to the Queen, whom we regarded as an ally or even a fellow conspirator. She was very sympathetic and pretended that she had long suspected it. And I told the Prince Regent and his wife, who were particularly warm in their congratulations. They were genuinely fond of Smatzo and I felt that they whole-heartedly approved.

Smatzo managed after a while to get back home to Norway, notwithstanding renewed attempts to prevail upon her to stay, particularly when it had been decided to change the English nurse. At such a tragic time for the Royal Family she naturally felt anxious to help, but she declined the pressing requests not only from the Queen but also from some of the visiting royal relations to stay on and take over. She modestly said that the children no longer needed a nurse, which was what she was, but a governess, which was what she was not.

Before we let the secret out I had a lot of amusement hearing comments about my fiancée. Once I was looking out of the window with the Duke of Kent and he said, 'By George, who is that girl? What fantastic hair!' The Court doctor once asked me what kind of impression I had formed of Miss Matzow. 'I have a rather positive impression,' he said. 'Do you?' Another time the Queen of Romania said to me, 'We must all work to see that the "little Swede" (as she erroneously called her) stays here, because she will be good with the children.' It was not to be. The 'little Swede' was wise not to yield to any of the royal blandishments, affectionate and flattering as they were, but go back to her lovely Norway.

We talked gaily about our five years' separation without meaning a word of it. I cannot remember whether it was she or I who first weakened, but eventually we agreed that we must get married in a year's time. Her parents knew little about me – to them I was nothing more than 'a tutor' in a land of brigands – and they were justifiably anxious that we should not hurry the proceedings. But in the end they gave their consent. Twice I made the journey third class all the way to Trondheim to see Smatzo and my future in-laws. It took me three days and three nights in the train each time. I have no space here to describe the marvellous impression I had from my first contact with Norway and the Norwegian people. They were so kind and charitable to each other and there seemed to me to be none of that family bickering and 'barging' which went on among relatives in England. I had come to Yugoslavia as a Crown Prince's tutor. I was welcomed in Norway as a Crown Prince himself.

My troubles now began in earnest. As my bride was a Norwegian, the Norwegian state required evidence that I was not already married before they would issue the necessary documents. And so one day when I was in the palace in Belgrade I rang up the British Minister, Sir Nevile Henderson, and asked him if I might come and see him. 'I am going to get married,' I added. 'The devil you are,' he replied encouragingly. I told him that the Norwegian government required a certificate to prove that I was not a bigamist and I wondered whether he could advise me on how I could obtain it. He told me to go and see the Consul.

Early one morning I went down and called upon the Consul, who was a Scotsman too, but a very different kind from Henderson – kindly and helpful. He told me regretfully that there was no consular document to attest that a British subject was not already married and that, since I knew Sir Nevile personally, the only way I could solve my problem quickly would be to go and ask him whether, as British Minister, he would write me a personal attest.

'I suggest,' he continued, 'you go up and see him and I'm sure he'll do it for you.' Having telephoned and satisfied himself that the Minister would receive me, he led me upstairs and left me outside his door. I knocked. A gruff voice called out 'Come in', and as I did so I could hardly take the scene in before two enormous dogs leapt at my throat and nearly pushed me over, barking deafeningly. The Minister was having breakfast with his First Secretary. They were both in pyjamas and dressing gowns.

In time, Henderson and his First Secretary Jock (afterwards Sir John) Balfour quietened the dogs down and the Minister asked me what I wanted. I explained falteringly that I wanted his help in providing me with a document to confirm that I was not already married. He interrupted me testily: 'But I told you it was a Consular matter.' It was useless telling him what the Consul had said. I was at once marched out of the room and sent downstairs again. The

Consul tried to calm me down and said in his suave, fatherly way: 'The Minister is not right, when he says it is a Consular matter. We have no provision for this. Why not go back to him again and ask him *very nicely* if he will take a sheet of notepaper and just write that to the best of his knowledge you are not already married?' It was a pretty game of buck-passing between Minister and Consul, reflecting the strained relations existing at that time between members of the Diplomatic and Consular Services. Once again I returned upstairs; once more the dogs sprang at my throat; and finally, feeling a good deal weaker and expressing myself no doubt very much less confidently, I explained what the Consul had said and I asked him timidly whether he would not take a piece of notepaper and . . . I had hardly got so far when he shouted at me: 'I'm not going to write anything on any bit of paper. I tell you, it's a Consular matter.' Here the gentler of the two, Jock Balfour, intervened. I got the letter, but it is not to be wondered at that afterwards I had small desire to return to the British Legation.

The wedding took place on 12th June 1935 at Trondheim in the most northerly cathedral in Europe, at the time of the 'midnight sun'. The previous night we had walked round the church at midnight and it had been bright as day. The wedding was a big one (indeed it was the talk of the town for many a day) and the church was already packed full when I was still feverishly sitting in a hotel room with the best man, my brother-in-law, waiting for my trousers. They had not come back from the tailor who was pressing them. In the end, everything went off successfully, and as the wedding took place at five p.m. in accordance with Norwegian custom and was followed by an enormous banquet and dance with speeches, we were lucky to get home before the dawn. Early next morning, before we were awake, my father-in-law came to the hotel, where we were spending what was left of the night, and paid the bill. It was so like him. We then set off in a hired car, but we were both feeling so ill that we had to get out from time to time and walk about to recover our equilibrium. After a short honeymoon up in the mountains among the goats at Kongsvold we travelled back to Belgrade via Berlin and Munich. When we reached Belgrade we had no accommodation and stayed the night at the Hotel Excelsior, which still exists today. At that point it was the haunt of Croat politicians, and maybe it remains so now. A few days later, we went down to Dalmatia to join the royal party on holiday.

When we returned to Belgrade I should have moved out of the

palace but the young King had contracted malaria followed by jaundice and I had leg trouble. My wife had been similarly afflicted with boils on her leg and had had to have her leg cut. Then to cap everything I contracted tonsilitis. We were thus not able to move into the flat we had found and the Queen kindly allowed us to stay in the small thatched cottage in the garden of the palace until we got better. When the Court doctor came to see the twin patients he christened them 'Papagei' and 'Mamagei'.

Though the flat we had found for our permanent abode was a little outside the centre of the town, it was very near the Royal Palace. It was a five- or six-storey building and we were on the fifth floor. We had two rooms, bathroom and kitchen and a balcony, and the heating was by what the Austrians call *Kachelofen*, i.e. tiled stoves which consumed wood and were quite warm except when the notorious *košava* blew. This fearsome wind, which comes from the plains of Russia, brings glacial temperatures and tears tiles and chimney-pots off Belgrade houses. It was one of the least attractive features of the city.

The flat belonged to an emigré Russian of whom there were many living in Belgrade. His name was Elfenbein, which means 'ivory' in German. A meal to which they invited us was my first experience of Russian hospitality. Unfortunately we misunderstood the invitation. We were asked to 'spend the evening' with them and thought we were meant to come *after* supper. Consequently I came down from the palace having had dinner as usual. When I was ushered into our hosts' room I saw to my horror that I had miscalculated. I felt slightly reassured when I noticed that they were offering us a buffet with vodka. Alas, I was not then sufficiently conversant with the ways of the Russians to realize that this was just the *zakuski* – the overture to the banquet. Soup and four or five sumptuous courses followed. I felt like a comedian in a film as I valiantly tried to shovel the food down and show delight at the same time. Inwardly I wondered whether it was literally possible for a human being to burst. They must have thought us curious guests.

While we were living in this flat I had a car and a chauffeur put at my disposal. The driver's name was Pera. This very loveable young man came from a part of Yugoslavia which is called the Lika, where the inhabitants are renowned for their fighting qualities. But our Pera was short and would not have appeared to be a dangerous opponent in battle. He had many other merits, though. There was a patch of grass, an apology for a garden, at the steps of the block of flats where we lived and it was looked after by a Serb gardener, who, like many of his race, was rather lazy and was usually to be found snoring by the side of the mower. Pera used to come and sit in the car waiting to take me back to the Court; and I remember how on several occasions, after having read the football news in the paper, he would get out of the car, take the mower and do the gardener's work for him, breaking all trade-union rules. The gardener continued to snore and when he woke up he must have thought that some Robin Goodfellow had finished the job for him.

At first, my wife used to amuse herself by taking lessons from a riding master in the town by the name of von der Nonne. The name sounds German, but there are many Russians of Baltic descent who have German names. The whole of Yugoslavia was full of Russians and if you wanted something very cleverly done you could generally find a Russian to do it. Most of the doctors were Russian, and the best bootmaker in Belgrade was a retired Russian colonel who made my wife a superb pair of real Russian riding boots. There was also a splendid stationery shop kept by two Russian ladies, who sold attractive old Russian Christmas cards. But von der Nonne had an indifferent lot of horses to hire out to his pupils. The supercilious adjutants alleged that most of them came from Russian circuses and could be relied upon to perform all manner of tricks at the most unsuitable times. Once when I rode out with the King we met von der Nonne and my wife somewhere in the country and they lined up by the side of the track to give a salute as we rode past. At the very moment when this happened my wife's horse slowly lay down on the ground and rolled on its back with its legs in the air. With grace and skill she coolly disengaged herself from the stirrups. It looked so like a circus trick that it only confirmed the adjutants' warnings. The officers acompanying the King rocked with laughter. It was a long time before my wife could live the episode down.

Our flat was near a famous football ground, the Slavia stadium. I have found that in most Eastern European countries there are two rival teams, and every member of the public is a supporter of one or the other. I used frequently to go to football matches at the stadium and sometimes took Pera with me as he was a tremendous fan. An experience I would prefer not to remember was when Leicester City came out and were defeated by the Yugoslav team six nil. Later, Chelsea United appeared and were soundly thrashed on the same Slavia ground. On one of these occasions, I forget which, I was having a visit from one of my old schoolmasters – a former British international soccer player – and he, the chauffeur and I all went to the ground and watched the match. It was humiliating to see one of our leading football teams, regarded in Yugoslavia as a nine-day wonder, being walked over by players of a country which had not by that time attained much of a football reputation. Yugoslav excitability in football is notorious. Every year there was a day called the Day of Unity, which was instituted to commemorate the fact that the Serbs, Croats and Slovenes were one nation and made one state. On this day the Serbs and Croats played a match against each other and it generally ended with everybody, including the teams themselves, throwing stones at one another.

Our eldest son was born in Belgrade in 1937 in a private sanatorium. The birth was a very difficult one and the doctor, who was the Queen's, had a great tussle. My mother-in-law had come from Norway, and she and I helped, but I can remember one awful moment when the doctor came out looking as if he had given up hope. Hans Christopher arrived on 16th June at the height of the Belgrade hot summer. I had to go on to Bled immediately with the King, and as soon as my wife's health permitted she followed with her mother and the baby. Our son was christened by the British lay preacher, Mr. Sitters, in the garden of the villa where we lived on the shore of the lake. The Queen was away in England and Princess Olga came to the ceremony with the King and his younger brothers and cousins. It was an attractive one and the child was held by all the princes in turn. When my wife was later pushing him around in the perambulator a Yugoslav who had no particular reason to love me looked at him and remarked ironically: 'He'll *certainly* be well educated.'

With the baby's arrival, we began to find the flat too small and rather inconvenient. We were lucky enough to discover an almost new flat suiting our needs on a country road near the Banica, or military parade ground, which rejoiced in the name of 'Ledikoudriova'. Lady Cowdrie had been an English benefactress to Serbia. Here, we had the benefit of country air and a slightly pleasanter environment – as well as a bigger apology for a garden, which we shared with only two other tenants. There were two floors and we were on the top one. I cannot remember who had the ground-floor flat, but wedged in the middle was the Minister of Posts and Telegraphs and his wife. Theirs was a peculiar ménage. In the first place, their maid always used to throw all the slops and rubbish straight out of the window into the dustbin, a tour-de-force on her part, but a menace to anyone approaching the house. Madame Minister never got up before noon and then paraded about in a dressing gown and hair curlers for about an hour, after which she was not seen again until the evening when she reappeared all dolled up with sparkling jewellery. She then went out with her husband. It could also sometimes happen that there would be a tremendous shaking of the house accompanied by an awful caterwauling. Startled by this sound we asked our maid what was the matter. 'Nothing,' she replied. 'It's only Mr. Minister beating his wife.'

I am afraid that in those days Ministers did beat their wives and officers beat their men. I never actually saw any human being being beaten, but even the way the Serbs beat their wretched horses made my blood boil. Once when I was driving along, I saw a Serbian peasant violently belabouring his wretched under-nourished hack. I fell into a rage, stopped the car, got out and went up and shouted at him. I gave him a lecture in my bad Serbian and told him he ought to be ashamed of himself. The man stopped. He was completely bewildered and could not understand what I was at. As I drove off and simmered down, I looked back through the window and I saw him carrying on with the job. If you wanted to see horses well cared for, you had to cross the Yugoslav frontier and go into Hungary where they had a better understanding for them.

As for the treatment of the men by the officers I could only surmise what it was like. As I say, I never saw anyone seriously manhandled, but a stinging box on the ears was no rarity. One day when I was at Bled the senior adjutant on duty had a soldier up before him and was pitching into him for something or other. It was just at this moment that I brought the young King up. The adjutant could not see the King, because he had his back to him and he was in his room and we were at the doorway. But I could see the officer concerned and the bestial sounds that came out were so bloodcurdling and the expression on his face was so brutal that I took the King away as fast as I could. This man was in fact an English-speaking officer, and one might have imagined that he would have been the last to have acted as he did. Memories of the Janissaries were never far away!

I cannot remember what the matter was with our flat at Lady Cowdrie Street but we soon had another change. While King Alexander was reigning, Prince Paul had lived latterly in a little villa in Tolstojeva Ulica at Topčider, not very far from the palace but separate from it. In the same grounds there was a smaller villa which was used by his children, Prince Alexander and Prince Nicholas, and the governess, who was also English. When Prince Paul became Regent he moved up to the 'Beli Dvor' – the new building which had originally been designed for the Crown Prince – and the two villas in Tolstojeva Ulica became empty. It was decided to house the King's library in the larger of them, and I asked one day whether there was any possibility of our living in the smaller villa, which was certainly a far more congenial and secluded spot than Lady Cowdrie Street. The Prince Regent generously agreed and at about the same time he raised my salary, so we felt very happy.

My wife had previously been a trainee at the Princess Christian College of Nursing in Manchester for nearly a year. There she learned – apart from baby-craft – such important things as the fact that no lady drinks a glass of water down to the bottom, neither does she eat buttered bread with cold ham. More important for our future was her perfect mastery of English and her gift for assimilating foreign languages. Knowing all the Scandinavian languages, English and German, she quickly learnt to speak Serbo-Croat, Czech and Russian, while a two-year sojourn in Belgium helped her to add French, which she had never learnt at school. She had an intuitive understanding of foreigners and proved a wonderful companion and support to me on my Odyssey. Best of all, she had an excellent sense of humour and shared with me the capacity to laugh at any joke, however feeble, in almost any European language.

CHAPTER EIGHT ◇ THE FEVER AND THE FRET

◇ It was a problem to me that the young King was so much alone. It was bad for him to be with me all the time, and in any case he needed something to compensate for what he had lost by not being able to continue his schooling in England. But whom else could he be with? It had occurred to me that it would be a good thing to bring some children up to play games with him. This was initially – after the shock of the assassination – by no means an easy thing to arrange, but, as it chanced, King Michael of Romania, who was being educated in his own palace in a neighbouring country, took lessons in a school in his palace made up of specially picked school comrades. This made my idea acceptable to the Prince Regent and the Queen, and I started to try and put it into practice. But where was I to get the schoolboys from? I was anxious not to bring in the scions of Belgrade society, because I knew that there would be terrific jealousy among the Serbs about who had been picked and who not. There was a very select English-style public school called the King Alexander Gymnasium, but I presumed this was the school which 'society' patronized. Then I had a better idea. I knew of a patriotic sports organization called the Sokol, of which the King was patron. I had already got Mr. Kovač, an enthusiastic member of its organization to come and act as gamesmaster to the King. And so together we decided to pick out some boys of the King's age from the Sokol. It was a totally democratic organization and was patriotic at the same time, so that no one could really criticize our using it. Mr. Kovač collaborated superbly with me and soon we had a nice selection of boys who came up to play football, do sports or swim in the swimming pools in the summer. Once the King had got to know the boys on the sports field he began to show a special liking for this one or that and I gradually invited them up to do other things – to watch a film, have dinner with him or even go out on expeditions. We finally arranged an annual camp at Bled in Slovenia where the boys lived in tents, built bridges over the river Sava and played various games. When Prince Alexander, the son of the Prince Regent, was home for the holidays he took part in these too, and I believe he enjoyed it. The King became attached to many of the boys and they were genuinely fond of him. It seemed an excellent development, and it speaks well for them that I cannot remember any of them in my time being unsatisfactory or causing us difficulty.

Under this intensive system of sport, which included cross-country runs and other energetic exertions, the King's physique improved immensely and he began to lose his fear of hurting himself. He was no longer a forlorn-looking waif. No one could have said that he was a physical coward now. But I was more preoccupied with his mental and moral development and his preparation for the future, and I thought that it was essential that he should see more of the country than he saw in the normal round of holiday trips. I therefore planned a series of expeditions to various important districts, which would today be described as 'regional study tours'. The first was an exploration of Slovenia, which was easy to fix up because the King was at Bled at the time. We travelled by car all over Slovenia – particularly in the eastern part – and visited towns and regions which he would otherwise have never seen. We studied in advance the economic and cultural importance of the region and met leading people who were responsible for its administration like the 'Ban', or Governor, of the whole of Slovenia. Anyone who buys Yugoslav wines in London today will have heard of Ljutomer Riesling. At that period, it was not so well known, though I had heard of it, and when we went by train through the Ljutomer district someone boarded it by arrangement and brought with him some of the best bottles of this wine. It was a fitting application of Mr. Squeers' educational methods. 'Winder – go and clean it': 'Slovenian wine – go and drink it.' I should add that we were accompanied on the whole trip by an expert on the region, Mr. Bas, whom we christened 'the boss'. He was able to tell the King interesting things, which I could not have told him however much I might have mugged it up.

After this, we planned a trip to the Iron Gates – the region where the Danube crosses the Carpathians – which, before it was regulated, used to be dangerous for ships here. The northern bank of the river is Romanian and the southern Yugoslav, and on the northern bank there are important historic monuments, the principal among them being the Tablets of Trajan commemorating the Roman Emperor's first campaign against the Dacians in A.D. 103. They can be seen from a boat.

As far as I can remember, we travelled down the Danube on the Royal Yacht. We had not been warned of the terrible climatic conditions in this very easterly part of Yugoslavia. Icy winds blow through the Carpathians from the Russian Plain and, as one approaches the Iron Gates, they can attain hurricane force. I often wondered whether the ship would turn turtle in the storm we encountered. We managed to weather it, however, and we steamed safely back to Belgrade.

I had planned more of these study tours, but when I started suggesting a third, the Prince Regent told me that the Prime Minister was worried about the King's security, as any head of government might well be in the circumstances. He reminded me that the risk was appalling for any politician, let alone for himself as regent, and conveyed to me that it would be better if I desisted from them and from any more planning of this kind. I was sorry, but I accepted it as inevitable. He pointed out that it had been difficult enough getting the Government's permission for the King to visit Slovenia, because just at that moment there had been a considerable number of factory workers on strike, and demonstrations were feared. I began to realize that it was not such an easy task educating a king – or indeed being his guardian.

The trouble was that in this disturbed time after the assassination there was not much mutual trust in Yugoslavia. It was to my advantage since the Prince Regent, the Queen and possibly the Prime Minister found it safer to leave the King in my charge than let him go around with Yugoslavs who might be suspect because they were Croats or Slovenes or intellectuals or anything you like. However, I desperately continued trying to think up other ways of broadening his outlook, now that it was impossible for him to go abroad again for the forseeable future.

I had to confine my educational efforts to making the best use of his holidays and give up the idea of planning further tours around the country. Sadly, there were only two places where the King could stay. One was the villa of Suvobor at Bled and the other the Queen's newly built palace on the southern part of the Dalmatian coast at Miločer.

Some years earlier, the Queen and the children had been driving along the Dalmatian coast when they came to a beautiful expanse of sands just underneath the Montenegrin mountains. The Queen looked at the sea, the attractive little bays which were so well sheltered, and the small island of Sveti Stefan, which was nearby. 'This is where I should like to build a summer palace,' she said and, as in fairy tales, no sooner said than done.

There were problems, though, about this isolated spot. There was a road leading to it from the north, but it was not a good one and nothing like its modern counterpart today. Moreover, until fairly recently the Montenegrin hills had been infested with brigands. The Queen herself had told me that it was the habit of these brigands to stop people in their cars, strip them of their clothes, rob them and let them loose stark naked. She said, 'Sandro (King Alexander) and I felt that for us death would be preferable to this kind of treatment. We could never survive *that* humiliation.' But perhaps the worst risk was unforseen and of another kind: it was malaria. This part of the coast was not so far from Scutari and there were swamps in the area which were infested with malaria-carrying mosquitoes. In 1935, the Miločer Palace was just finished (although hardly so) and the Queen took the King and the other children to stay there in the summer. In planning the villa the Queen turned to me for help. She wanted to have special tiles in her bathroom which would have birds or fishes on them, and she knew an address in England where she could get them. She asked me to order them and said jestingly that she would like to have parrots in one of the bathrooms. I dutifully did what I was told and one of the bathrooms (the palace is now a hotel) still carries these emblems, I believe, to this day. It sounds compromising, but I never had a bath in that bathroom and indeed only had one brief glance at the parrots in it. Curiously enough, when I was in Moscow, I met the Italian Ambassador, who had been Governor-General of Montenegro during the war and had commandeered the palace for his accommodation. He knew all about the parrots and joked with me about them. Some of his other jokes about his experiences in Yugoslavia were understandably not relished by the Yugoslav Ambassadress, Mrs. Vidić (until recently Yugoslav Ambassadress in London). She was a Montenegrin and had been a partisan fighting against the Italians.

There was no doubt that in her anxiety to achieve her dream the Queen moved in much too soon, in fact before the villa had been properly prepared for royal habitation. Not only was it unfinished but there was next to no accommodation for the suite either in the villa or the neighbourhood. In the first place, it was a very backward and undeveloped area; and next insufficient thought had been given to the well-being of the suite. I found out later on that nothing had been arranged for my wife and myself, and as it was night time before I had finished settling the King in and seeing that he had everything he wanted, we had to take pot luck when it came to accommodation. They drove us to a point up in the Montenegrin hills where we were compelled to get out and walk because the cars could go no further, and we found ourselves at the small Orthodox monastery of Praskovic. It had the curious feature for a monastery that it contained both monks and nuns living together in happy harmony. It was indescribably primitive and I thought of what the Rector at Edinburgh Academy had said: 'If they want to have an Englishman, they must pay him an Englishman's salary.' At this moment I felt that it would be sufficient if they provided me with the sort of accommodation an Englishman would accept.

It was intolerably hot and stuffy in our little room in the monastery and at half past four in the morning all the bells started ringing and calling the brothers and sisters to prayer. The place was infested with bugs and my poor wife's back was furrowed like a ploughed field. For some reason, there were no marks on my skin at all, and I am glad to say that I have never actually seen a bug, because whenever I go to places they infest (and I have been to many) they always seem to shun me like the plague.

We could bear it no longer and we decided to get up. I was the first to rise and was dressed only in a shirt without my pants when suddenly the door opened and the Mother Superior barged in. She showed no surprise at my state of undress and placed a tray with *šlivovica* (plum brandy) on it before disappearing. If *šlivovica* is not exactly the kind of drink one desires to have in the early hours of a scorching summer morning after a tiring journey the day before, we were so crushed in spirit that we drank it with relief.

Some kind of permanent lodging had to be found for us. If I had been unmarried, I should have been accommodated in the villa and I believe that the Queen could have easily accommodated us both. At the suggestion of Prince Paul she had appointed my wife her *lectrice*, which would have justified such an arrangement, but a certain person was jealous and the appointment (which was anyhow unsalaried) never materialized. And so we were forced to take a frightfully primitive and insanitary room in a house in the fishing village of Budva, which was the nearest outpost of 'civilization' to the palace. Even so, it took some twenty minutes to get there by car.

Budva has excellent hotels today and is much developed, but it was then a completely one-horse place. My poor wife could hardly get anything to eat there, so primitive were the feeding possibilities in the village. I was eating at the palace and was of course well cared for, but there was nothing I could do about it.

Unfortunately soon after this, my young charge caught malaria and at a particularly bad time, just before the whole royal party were due to return to Belgrade for the King's birthday celebrations on 6th September. I too had been badly bitten by mosquitoes, but although I did not catch malaria I suffered from boils which followed from the bites, and in the end I had to go to a Russian doctor in Kotor to have them cut. It was a painful case and I had to hobble about with a bandaged foot.

When the inflammation was at its worst I suffered from terrible ague fits. My poor wife was terrified when the bed, the whole room, even the house began to shake. Sometimes she must have thought that the hovel in which we were accommodated would tumble down. Above my head was a thick cloud of flies, which we managed to reduce by means of fly papers. We had a royal visit during the time I was ill. One day we heard a call at the window and it was the Queen of Romania who was coming to see how we were getting on. *She* had certainly suspected something. We did not encourage her to come up, but I talked to her through the window. I felt like a leper.

The King was quite seriously ill. Luckily by that time I was cured, at least of my fever, so I could look after him, read to him and stay indoors at Miločer the whole day. At one time I was deeply worried about his condition and I was surprised how lightly the Court seemed to regard it. I am sure that it was wrong to have moved him when they did, but on the other hand the prospect of his staying there alone with me without his mother was rather frightening. His actual departure by car to the station was delayed as much as possible so that he would be fit enough to get out of bed. But he was far from well and during the whole car journey along roads lined with crowds he was continually sick. Even though I had provided for this, it was extremely difficult to try to get him to wave his hand on one side while on the other side I pulled down the curtains, brought him close to the sick basin, and helped him to vomit. I think this must have happened at least ten times during the journey. Officers who witnessed our arrival at the station gave a doleful account of it. First, the King, looking green and walking shakily, fell out of the car, and then I emerged hobbling along the platform as best I could. Lieutenant Stiglic with his usual humour described it otherwise. He said that as soon as the King's car stopped and the door opened, a slipper flew out and then we followed.

The drugs the King was given for malaria proved too strong and malaria was succeeded by jaundice. As a result he was on a very strict diet for a longish time. It did not do lasting damage to his health, but I was warned by the experience that in the future we must look after him better.

I sometimes wonder whether I did not in fact catch malaria too. Ever since then and up to fairly recently I have had bouts of ague fits, very reminiscent of malaric fever. It may have been due to something else but, whenever it has come, it has always reminded me of those harrowing days at Miločer. Twenty years later the King wrote that he was never completely cured himself and still suffered attacks.

The young King's attack of malaria and his subsequent jaundice made me feel that it would be inadvisable to take him to Miločer again in the summer. I felt he needed a more bracing climate. The Queen was against this, partly because she did not like Bled and loved Miločer, and partly because she felt that the representations I made to her about her son's health implied criticism of her. (One had of course to be very tactful and cautious when submitting reasonable and well-meant advice.) However, I got my way, and for some years we went to Bled for the summer holiday and to Miločer for the Easter holiday, although the Queen did not accompany us to Miločer. I spent a whole month there alone with the King and his cousin Prince Alexander, and it was a very healthy and enjoyable holiday for all of us. They were really delightful boys to be with. Later on, when the King got better and Miločer improved he went there again in the summer, and took with him some of his school friends. With the help of rafts and various swimming equipment and assisted by our sportsmaster, we had great fun jumping, diving, playing water polo and so on. Royal guests often joined in these games, especially Uncle Ali, the Infante of Spain, who was married to 'Aunt B.' and was very game. The Queen of Romania was there as well and I can remember seeing her going down to bathe when she was well over sixty. I suppose everybody has their childhood picture of what a queen is like, mostly based on illustrations in fairy books. The Queen of Romania preserved her beauty and her wonderful figure until her death, and I have never known anyone with more queenliness and grace. When you see people in bathing dresses and bathing wraps you don't think about their birth or position. But even in this attire, the Queen of Romania could never have been anything else but a queen. Sad to say she was already suffering from cancer, and it was only about six months later that I learned she was dead.

She had had a frustrated life. But she never showed it. I recollect a naval officer telling me that when her father, the Duke of Edinburgh, was in command at Malta, the garrison church was crammed every Sunday with young officers hoping to catch sight of the Duke's four beautiful daughters. The future Queen, who always ached for England, adored this life and remembered one of the officers attached to her as 'Captain dear'. Then she was torn away from it, married to a Hohenzollern Prince, Ferdinand of Romania, and condemned to live in the barrack-like conditions of the Romanian Court under the Prussian King, Carol I. One of her consolations was Carol's Queen, the romantic poet and art-lover Carmen Sylva. Queen Marie's husband, although a gentle and kindly man, had no guts. She told me how his valet once lost his temper with him and threw every scrap of his clothing at his head. She also openly admitted that 'it was sometimes necessary for her to give him a good pinch to make him stand up for himself'. However, in spite of such an unpropitious atmosphere the beautiful and gifted Queen certainly did not wither.

I missed her immensely because she always took a sympathetic interest in her grandson and appreciated the difficulties of his position. She once sent me two photographs of herself. It was on 6th February 1938 and on the back of them there was a letter in two parts after her usual custom. Characteristically, the photographs were taken in deliciously dramatic poses. In one, she was sitting on a wall in a fine draped gown looking reflectively at a rose. It was signed Marie and is reproduced in plate 15. She wrote on the back: 'I was so pleased to get your letter with such a satisfactory report about dear Peter. I think of him so much and deplore that (he) can have none of the liberty or advantages his brothers have. It must be hard for him to see them all leave, and he unable to be one of the party. My heart goes out to him. I only hope he does not realize as much as we do that (the letter continues on the back of the other photo) he is "un grand sacrifice". I am sure you make his life as pleasant as possible. He must always find in you a friend in whom he can trust and with whom he can talk things over. I am sad that we have not been able to be together for so long. I always loved Peter and saw his pathetic side. . . .'

CHAPTER NINE ✧ SCURVY POLITICIANS

✧ As the King grew older and his sixteenth birthday drew near, I pondered deeply whether he would be sufficiently mature and well enough prepared to take over the reins of his troubled country. He was by no means a strong character and in some ways still very much a child. Moreover, there were plenty of black sheep among his forbears on both sides. On the Karageorgević side he had a mad uncle, and both his paternal grandfather and great uncle had lived rather dissolute lives as young men, while on the Romanian side his grandfather had been a weak ruler and his uncles and aunts had been pretty unstable. Serb politicians were adept at exploiting situations where the personal weakness of the monarch was a key factor and had thrived on it during the nineteenth century. At the age of fifteen and a half he had the energy of his father but the utterly passive disposition of his mother and, like her, his opinions tended to be formed by the last person he had talked to – a fatal trait. How could he withstand pressures from those around him that would be motivated not by the interests of the country but by the personal aspirations of small cliques?

Inevitably the question had arisen as to whether the time was ripe for him to be slowly introduced into affairs of state. The Prince Regent and the government took the view that he should be left in peace until he had completed his education. Nonetheless, Prince Paul began to invite him to lunch when he had members of the government or foreign diplomats as his guests, and this was a good development. The King was little aware of what was actually happening in political circles in Yugoslavia or abroad. He read two Belgrade newspapers, but was interested most of all in the strip cartoons and items on sport or new inventions – especially mechanical things. Anything to do with politicians and politics left him cold. Even at the age of fifteen he had a somewhat childish mind. He was not encouraged by his government to take an interest in political affairs and submissively accepted the role which had been laid down for him. The Prince Regent was undoubtedly right in believing that he was not yet mature enough intellectually to begin to form judgements on these matters. But what I continually asked myself was this: if he never starts, will he ever achieve that maturity?

The situation was a delicate one within the country and it was not helped by the international tension, which was increasing. Internally, Prince Paul was trying to bring about a détente and establish a common platform on which Serbs, Croats and Slovenes could co-operate in governing the country. But he had soon found himself faced with the same difficulties as had confronted King Alexander. The more he tried to conciliate the Croats, the more he forfeited the trust of the Serbs.

The Prince was always friendly to me and from time to time we talked politics. I remember one day asking him why he did not occasionally see the leaders of the opposition parties and listen to their point of view. He stared at me in frank amazement. 'Mr. Parrott,' he said, 'do you realize that if I so much as looked at any of them, the Prime Minister would hand in his resignation the next day? You really have no idea of what the situation is like here.' My own inward reaction was that if I were in his place, I should let the Prime Minister go to hell and form another government with a Prime Minister possessing a more tolerant attitude to other parties. However, the Prince Regent was right. The system of government and political parties was very different in Yugoslavia from anything I had been used to in England or western Europe. British political methods would have proved as irrelevant in Yugoslavia as they have in Ireland.

After the King's murder, Milan Stojadinović, a Serb, had believed it was possible to bring Croats, Serbs and Slovenes together in one government and maintained he knew that this was the programme King Alexander would have initiated had he not been assassinated. Prince Paul was persuaded by Nevile Henderson to invite him to form a government. Stojadinović was an able politician and not an unpleasant man in casual relationships. I remember once accompanying King Peter to a shoot which the Prince Regent had organized for King Carol of Romania. When I arrived at the assembly point the Prince Regent took King Peter and his guest off in his hunting carriage, and I was left standing by myself. Presently, up came a very smart hunting carriage with a portly gentleman in it wearing Tyrolean clothes and puffing a cigar, looking like a stage impersonation of a Hungarian count. Seeing me, he called out, 'Mr. Parrott, why don't you come along with me?' I knew that it was the Prime Minister, but had no idea that the Prime Minister knew me.

Of course, I was flattered. I drove a short way in the Prime Minister's carriage and we had an amusing and easy conversation *en route*.

Although he was both able and energetic, after he had been Premier for some time he started to exhibit signs of paranoia. It began to be bruited about that he was trying to make his own Fascist party and join the group of dictators. There would be Hitler, Mussolini *and* Stojadinović. When he arrived at railway stations his followers, whom he had organized into quasi-military formation, put their hands up in a Fascist salute and called him 'Leader'. Discreditable stories began to circulate. The word for leader in Serbo-Croat is *vodja*. The word for devil is *djavol*. If you say the Serb word for leader quickly and shift the emphasis you soon find that you are saying the Serb word for devil. This is what the crowds were said to be shouting at Stojadinović, although he understood it the other way round.

Stojadinović had created a big new party called the Yugoslav Radical Union or the J.R.Z. And another story was that he and some of his ministers – all members of his party – were once riding in a donkey cart when suddenly the donkey dug its heels in and came to a stop. One of the ministers got up and beat the donkey, but it was to no avail. Another offered it a carrot, but that did not help either. Finally, Stojadinović himself climbed out and whispered something in the donkey's ear. The Yugoslav leader had hardly got back into the carriage when to the general amazement, the donkey bolted at the speed of a racehorse. His colleagues asked Stojadinović what it was that he had whispered into the donkey's ear. 'I asked him whether he would like to become a member of the J.R.Z.,' he answered. The curious thing is that I heard this joke being told in Yugoslavia in 1966, but it referred then to the Communist party.

It was also said that when Count Ciano came to Yugoslavia Stojadinović, without the knowledge of the Prince Regent, arranged an 'orgy' for him in one of the royal hunting lodges.

Amusing as he was, Stojadinović was an opportunist and a self-seeking rascal, and it was not surprising that when he saw how things were developing in Europe he began to make himself agreeable to the Italians and Germans. He is said to have given a hunting party for diplomats and their wives. When the liquor had gone to his head, he sprang on to the table and pulled the wife of the German Minister up with him, dancing with her in the gay fashion of opulent Russian merchants who used to fill their top hats with champagne corks and drink champagne out of ballerinas' dancing shoes. Alas, Stojadinović was no ballerina. He was a man of considerable weight, physically as well as politically. The table crumbled beneath him and he and his diplomatic partner found themselves wallowing together in the remains of the buffet on the carpet.

Although Prince Paul was well aware of some of his misdemeanours, he nonetheless loyally defended him against criticism. Once he justified his choice of Stojadinović to me, speaking highly of him. However, another day an incident took place which made me realize that something was up. I followed the Prince Regent into his library and he said: 'I'm afraid it smells rather unpleasant here. It's that nasty cheap hair oil which the Prime Minister uses.' I rubbed my eyes. A day or two later he asked me to sit down in his salon and said hastily: 'No, don't sit in that one. It's broken. The other day the Prime Minister burst out laughing and rolled about, breaking my beautiful Louis XV chair.' Now I knew that something was up and I did not need to be a prophet to predict that the Prime Minister would be dismissed.

Stojadinović proved to be in fact a man of evil character and Prince Paul was undoubtedly deceived by him. But it must be conceded that few politicians in Yugoslavia at that time were honest and any politician with brains was likely to turn out corrupt. It is possible, though, that had he been retained, he would have been able to 'manage' the Germans to the material advantage of Yugoslavia, even if he would not have enhanced her reputation.

Before his death in the Argentine, he published his memoirs in which he said quite revolting things about the Prince and Princess, who had so often stuck up for him, and – to my surprise – about me too. It is an interesting experience to open a book of memoirs written by a politician to whom you have only spoken a word or two in a hunting carriage, and read two whole pages accusing you of the worst form of treachery.

According to Stojadinović, I deliberately conspired with the Prince Regent to spread the rumour that the young King was mentally deficient. He based this on a report I wrote for Prince Paul, which the Prince must have shown him. The report was drawn up in confidence. It showed how backward he was in many school subjects and how necessary it was to bring him on. It was written by someone who had for several years done his best to try and see that the boy had the best education possible, and had always presented him in the best possible light. This indicated just how unscrupulous Stojadinović was.

There were many people in Belgrade who whispered that the Prince Regent would like to prolong the regency on the pretext that the King was not mature enough to govern. I do not believe that such an idea ever entered his head. I am sure he would have considered it advisable to stay with the King, if possible, during the first years of his reign after his coming of age. But as an experienced and well-read man he realized that factions exist at courts and once young kings begin to rule on their own it is the factions who decide and not the ruler. It could easily happen that the young King would be suddenly surrounded by men who would influence him against his uncle. This is not very different from what did in fact happen in 1941 and after. The impression I formed from frequent talks with the Prince Regent was that he wanted nothing better than to complete his mission and withdraw. He seriously considered resigning twice – once in 1940, and again in 1941. His loyalty to his young ward was shown by his reluctance to introduce any constitutional changes before he came of age. Until then, the Prince Regent regarded himself as carrying out the job of a trustee.

Disillusioned by Stojadinović and the Serb opposition, Prince Paul felt an increasing distaste for Serb politicians, but with the Croat leader, Dr. Maček, he still hoped he had a chance of coming to an agreement. Maček seems to have trusted Prince Paul, and Prince Paul, who was sometimes over-trusting, returned this confidence. However, to dismiss a figure like Stojadinović who was a tricky customer and had gained considerable power and influence both at home and abroad, was a bold and risky step. Not only would it be hard to find anyone of comparable political stature to replace him, but the Prime Minister was capable of a lot of mischief in opposition. Not least, the Germans and Italians would be very upset because he was Hitler's and Mussolini's great hope.

Abroad the situation was becoming more and more intractable. Italy and Germany were a constant threat to Yugoslavia. Of these two powerful neighbours, Italy was the more dangerous because she had irredentist aims and had long planned Yugoslavia's destruction. Hitler did not want to destroy Yugoslavia; he simply wanted her to be his obedient tool. He was at that time too anxious for Yugoslav friendship to be likely to play Mussolini's game in his dealings with Yugoslavia. The Yugoslav government therefore sought to neutralize the threat from Italy by cultivating better relations with Germany. Yugoslavia had no country she could turn to in her hour of peril.

In the spring of 1939 the international atmosphere grew still worse. In March, Hitler invaded Czechoslovakia. Mussolini was soon to invade Albania. The five years I had set myself as my limit for remaining in Yugoslavia would elapse in the summer. What was I to do? On the one hand, I felt a solemn obligation to remain with the King and look after him. His father had said that he had placed him in my care. On the other hand, if I stayed longer I might easily find myself round his neck for most of my life, and it was a prospect I did not relish. I had no wish to end up as a royal pensioner. It was an important decision, and one which stirred deep emotions within me. Which side of the Rubicon should it be?

I eventually decided to resign and return to England. There was no possibility of my finding a job in England while I was stuck out in Yugoslavia. Moreover, war might easily break out and my position would then become very tricky. I should be only an embarrassment to the Prince Regent. I also had the feeling that King Peter needed a change of tutorial régime. Perhaps if I left and was not always managing his life he would acquire more self-assurance and independence. There are times when one feels that one may have outstayed one's usefulness. I was broken-hearted to have to make the decision, and it took a great deal of resolution to do so. One disturbing factor was that the Queen had left Yugoslavia for good and King Peter would be alone in his house, since Prince Paul's villa, though standing in the same grounds, was some distance away and he was naturally much occupied with state affairs. However, on deeper reflection I felt that my departure might have the effect of bringing the Prince into closer regular contact with his ward because as long as I was looking after him there was less need for it. I was happy to hear afterwards that this is what came about. As far as our personal future was concerned, we were right to return home, for six months' later war did break out.

CHAPTER TEN ✧ YUGOSLAV EPILOGUE

✧ In 1941, when I was in Sweden, I learnt that there had been a *coup d'état* in Yugoslavia: King Peter had been declared of age, and the Prince Regent had resigned and left the country. It was a sudden and unexpected echo of my recent past. I had had a few letters from the young King since I had left him, but as the war gathered momentum it had become more and more difficult to maintain contact, and he was not a good correspondent at the best of times. We had also received friendly letters from Prince Paul and Princess Olga. Meanwhile, I had been following with sympathy and foreboding the struggle to force Yugoslavia to come into the war on one side or the other. Would the Yugoslav government yield to British pressure and come in on the Anglo-Greek side, thus provoking a German invasion and the destruction and dismemberment of the country? Or would they give in to German demands and sign the Triple Pact, only to find themselves blacklisted by the Allies? When German pressure increased, they tried to procrastinate and spin out negotiations by making conditions they thought the Germans would never accept. But I never imagined in my wildest dreams that they would be overthrown by a British-inspired *coup*.

Part of the story has been told fairly authentically by one of the Prince's closest advisers, the then Minister of the Court, Milan Antić. 'The Prince's aim,' he declared, 'was to maintain the best possible relations with the German government so that with its help Mussolini's underhand hostility towards our country could be neutralized. We knew that the Italians were supporting the Croat Ustaši; they were also trying to draw Maček into their sphere of influence with the object of tearing Croatia away from Yugoslavia and taking it under their wing. We were aware, too, that Mussolini had intended settling scores with us at the end of 1939 and the beginning of 1940 but had been checked each time by the Germans, who did not consider it to be in their interest to have a conflagration in the Balkans. Finally, Mussolini attacked Greece, but without Germany's agreement, as Hitler himself told Prince Paul when they met at Berchtesgaden a few days before the signing of the Pact. . . .

'Already in November 1940, Ribbentrop had told us that he wanted us to join the Pact, because, he claimed, it was only in this way that our frontiers with Italy and the other neighbours could be secured. We refused, however, because the Prince wanted us to stay neutral, await further world developments and particularly see what would be the end of the German-Soviet pact of friendship.

'In the meantime we took soundings whether and to what extent the British could help us if we had to take up arms in defence of our independence. But there was no assistance to be had from this quarter, according to the report of our military delegate in Athens, who was having concrete discussions with British military representatives. Meanwhile the Germans were applying more and more pressure on us to tell them whether we would join the Pact or not. In view of our inadequate military equipment and our isolated position, any military resistance to the Germans would have meant the certain end of Yugoslavia as a state. And so the Prince decided to accept Hitler's invitation to go and see him in the hope of persuading him to leave Yugoslavia in her state of neutrality at least for the time being.'

On 25th February Prince Paul informed the German Ambassador of his intention to come to Berchtesgaden at the beginning of March. The visit took place on 4th March. Two days earlier German troops had marched into Bulgaria. Yugoslavia was surrounded and more isolated than ever. Prince Paul had taken this decision at the prompting of his Prime Minister and Foreign Minister. He had already refused Hitler's invitation twice before and his ministers were anxious not to offend the Führer, who, they imagined, might have some general peace settlement in mind and might want to suggest that Prince Paul should act as his intermediary with Britain. At the meeting Prince Paul told Hitler that the decision to sign the Pact would be particularly difficult for him, because his wife was Greek by birth and his own personal sympathies lay with Britain and against Italy. He also warned him that if he signed the Pact, in six months' time he would no longer be there, with which Ribbentrop countered that it would be truer to say that this would be the case if he did *not* sign it. When Hitler said that he could no longer protect Yugoslavia against Italy unless the government signed at once, Prince Paul had the impression that Italy was probably pressing for permission to attack Yugoslavia but that Hitler preferred not to let her be dismembered as long as the war lasted, since he needed at the moment all the resources he was getting from her.

What was the 'Triple Pact'? It had started as the 'Anti-Comintern Pact', concluded in 1936 between Germany and Japan, and was originally designed ostensibly to achieve co-operation in the struggle against Communism. It was joined by Italy in 1937, and by Hungary, Manchukuo and Spain in 1939. When the Germans began to pressurize the various small European states into joining it – Bulgaria, Finland, Romania, Denmark and Slovakia – all of them became members too. By the time it was Yugoslavia's turn to be approached, the treaty had been considerably changed and all reference to the Comintern had been omitted. Its main object had become the vague one of co-operating with Germany in the establishment and maintenance of 'a new order of things'. This was because the Germans hoped the Soviet Union would join. Indeed on 26th November 1940 the Soviet government had agreed to do so and turn it into a 'quadruple pact'. However this never came about because of the German attack on the Soviet Union. The Germans also tried to bring pressure on the Swedes to join, on the ground that Denmark had already done so and Norway probably would. But they never pressed the point so insistently as they did with Yugoslavia.

'At the meeting in Berchtesgaden,' Antić's account goes on, 'Hitler and Ribbentrop . . . made important concessions nonetheless: they promised the Prince that they would not demand transit for Axis troops through Yugoslav territory or military collaboration of any kind. In spite of this, the Prince left the question of signing open, explaining to the Germans that he would discuss the question with his government.'

What followed can only be pieced together from several sources. When the Prince returned to Belgrade he held several meetings of the Crown Council on whether Yugoslavia should join the Pact or not. All agreed not to accept the Pact but to start discussions with the Germans which would enable Yugoslavia to mobilize and procrastinate. But the news of the march of German troops into Bulgaria and the consequent isolation of Yugoslavia had had a depressing effect on General Pešić, the Yugoslav War Minister, and military commanders, who insisted that their inadequately equipped army was now completely surrounded by the enemy and in no position to offer resistance to the superior forces of Germany. When they heard this, the Croat and Slovenian members of the government, Maček and Kulovec, insisted that the Pact must be signed. Otherwise their peoples, who inhabited that part of Yugoslavia which was unprotected by mountains and most vulnerable to a German attack, would be the first to suffer, whereas the Serbs could always withdraw towards Bosnia and Greece.

In spite of this the Prince Regent and the Prime Minister tried till the last moment to make them change their minds. It was in vain. In consequence they were faced with the stark choice of signing the Pact or splitting the country. One element in the situation was decisive: the refusal of the representatives of the northern part of the country to contemplate war. Maček said, 'I have a conscience too and a sense of tremendous responsibility towards our people. I cannot lead them to slaughter and that is what we must expect if we precipitate a war with Germany.' Kulovec said that in the case of war Slovenia would be the first territory to be invaded. 'Qui habet tempus, habet vitam.' It was in these circumstances that the government reluctantly decided to sign.

The Prince Regent explained this to the U.S. Ambassador. 'While many Serb voices cry for war against the Axis,' he said, 'the deep silence of Croats and Slovenes marks their reluctance to take any step that would bring the armies of Germany and Italy into their land. Am I to hand over to King Peter a country which is intact, or one in ruins?'

Prince Paul had every intention of biding his time until Yugoslavia was in a position to come out openly on the side of the West. Hitler had already long suspected this and said to Ciano at Salzburg on 12th August 1939: 'Yugoslavia will only remain neutral as long as it is dangerous for her to go over openly to the side of the Western democracies. The very moment things go bad for Germany and Italy she will at once openly join the other side in the hope of giving the course of events a final twist to the disadvantage of the Axis.'

What Prince Paul had said to Hitler about his Anglophile sympathies, while frank enough in the German official report, was an understatement. He had been educated at Oxford and before becoming Prince Regent had spent much time in England, as we have seen, where he had many friends. His two sons were born in this country and he always spoke English at home with his wife and family. His children had English nurses and went to school in England. His wife's sister was the Duchess of Kent. Even the palace he had reconstructed for his official use was built in Adam style. Excellent French speaker and scholar though he was, he seemed most at home in our own language which he spoke and wrote faultlessly, and with a style and polish I envied.

When he learnt of the assassination of his cousin, King Alexander, in 1934, his first action had been to send a telegram to the British Minister, Sir Nevile Henderson, then on leave, urging him to return at once. If in the previous reign, the British Minister had been in a privileged position in the Diplomatic Corps and had received confidences from the monarch, the position of the British Legation as a whole gained from the change of ruler, because Prince Paul was on terms of personal friendship not only with Henderson and Sir Ronald Campbell, his successor, but also with other members of the staff nearer his age such as the First Secretaries 'Jock' (Sir John) Balfour and (Sir) Terence Shone. He even set up a direct personal telephone line with the Embassy. I should have been happy to serve in a mission which enjoyed such close and almost family relations with the head of state. When I compare what Prince Paul told me at the time, or has told me since, with what was reported in official documents by the British Legation to the Foreign Office, I can see that he must have kept few secrets from successive British Ministers. They knew what was in his mind, and understood and appreciated his attitude. He even refused to permit our Legation to be subjected to the police supervision which was imposed on other missions in Belgrade. This was incautious of him because partly, no doubt, thanks to this tolerance S.O.E. agents in Belgrade were able to complete their plans to overthrow him in 1941 and remove him from Yugoslavia without hindrance.

There were at least two outstanding occasions when Prince Paul rendered valuable services to the Allied governments. One day his Prime Minister Stojadinović brought him copies of two telegrams sent to Lord Halifax by Campbell. Prince Paul asked to have them, but Stojadinović begged to be excused, saying that he had promised to return them at once to Count Ciano from whom he had received them. Prince Paul just had time to memorize the initial paragraphs of the telegrams before returning them and then at once sent for Campbell to ask him whether he recalled having sent two telegrams on these lines. Campbell turned pale and confirmed that he did. He asked Prince Paul if by chance he had noted the numbers of the telegrams. Prince Paul repeated them to Campbell, who said that the copies were genuine. The Prince Regent then told him to say nothing to anybody, take a plane to London immediately and report to Lord Halifax that the Italian government had penetrated the British ciphers. Campbell did as he suggested, but when Prince Paul later came over to England and mentioned the matter to Chamberlain, the latter seemed totally unaware of the incident. Some fifteen

1. King Peter between the Princes Tomislav (left) and Andrej. One of the photographs which made me decide to go to Yugoslavia.

2. The Royal Guard marching through the streets of Hercegnovi in Dalmatia

3. The author at Hercegnovi in borrowed Yugoslav uniform

4. King Alexander Karageorgević

5. King Nikola of Montenegro

6. Villa Suvobor at Bled in Slovenia

7. A few moments before the double assassination at Marseilles–King Alexander and Louis Barthou

6068-CA6

8. The moment after King Alexander's assassination. A French cavalry colonel slashes at the murderer with his sabre. Bogoljub Jevtić, the Yugoslav Foreign Minister, is running up to help the King.

9. Leaving Sandroyd school in the early morning after the murder of King Alexander

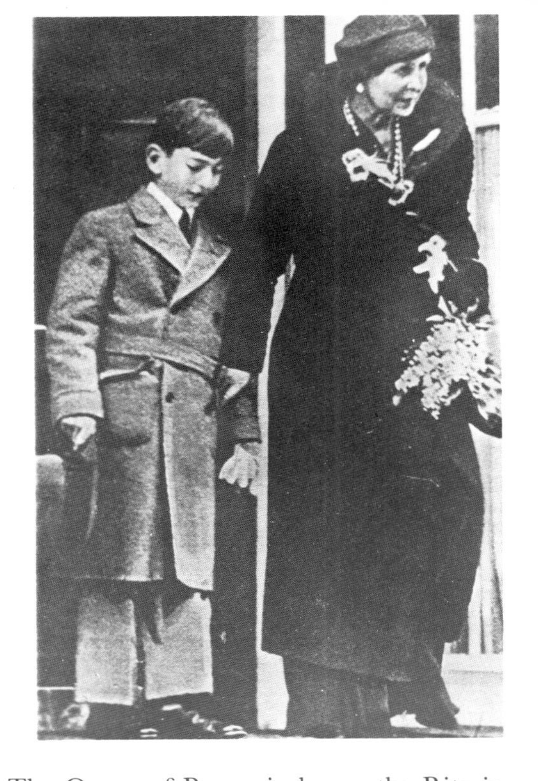

10. The Queen of Romania leaves the Ritz in London with her grandson on the day of King Alexander's murder

Београд. Дворац Њ. В. Краља на Дедињу
Belgrade. Dedigné. Le palais royal

11. The Palace of Dedinje at Belgrade soon after it had been built

12. Queen 'Mignon' of Yugoslavia with Princes Tomislav and Andrej

13. Prince Paul, Princess Olga and their children at Brdo, Slovenia

14. Smatzo with Tommy and Andy at the Mežakla in the Slovenian Alps

15. Queen Marie of Romania (see page 85)

16. The Queen's summer palace at Miločer in Dalmatia. Above and behind – the monastery where we stayed a night

17. King Peter with members of his suite so near and yet so far from the top of the Triglav

18. Norway. The *Altmark* in Jössingfjord (*A. S. Norsk Telegrambyrå*)

19. German troops march into Oslo, 9th April, 1943
(*A. S. Norsk Telegrambyrå*)

20. Nedre Möllergaten 19 – the notorious Oslo prison
(*A. S. Norsk Telegrambyrå*)

21. Stockholm in the peacefulness of war *(The Press Association Ltd.)*

22. German troops in transit through Sweden *(The Press Association Ltd.)*

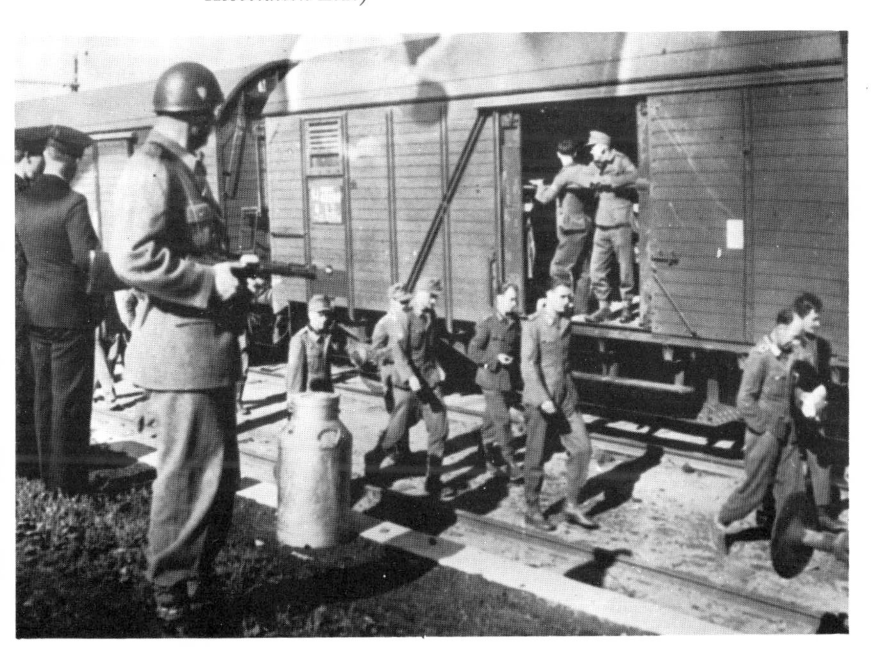

23. Shortage of fuel in Sweden due to Allied and German blockades. Typical Stockholm scene of streets stacked with logs *(The Press Association Ltd.)*

24. Madame Kollontay, the Soviet Minister in Sweden *(The Press Association Ltd.)*

months afterwards, Campbell informed the Prince Regent that the Foreign Office had at last caught the culprit. He had worked in the archives department and had had a Russian mistress. She had handed copies of the telegrams to the Soviet Embassy, and the Soviet Ambassador, Maisky, had handed them to the Italian Ambassador, Count Grandi, in order to cause the maximum mischief. A somewhat similar episode occurred with the Americans when Count Csaki, the Hungarian Minister of Foreign Affairs, warned Prince Paul that telegrams sent from Belgrade by the U.S. Minister were being read by the Germans, and Prince Paul in his turn passed the warning on to the State Department. One of the reasons why Hitler lost confidence in Prince Paul was that directly after his state visit to Berlin he went to England, talked to the British about it and discussed Yugoslavia's situation with the British Foreign Secretary. Later, when the Germans occupied France in 1940, they came across a batch of documents which showed that Prince Paul had authorized the holding of secret staff discussions with the French, and had sent a Yugoslav general on a secret mission to England with a view to coordinating defence plans with the West.

Much has been made of Prince Paul's anti-Soviet prejudices and his reputed Tsarist sympathies. I can confirm that he was anti-Communist and anti-Soviet. Indeed, very few Yugoslavs were enamoured of the Russians then, or are so today. But it was quite incorrect to suggest that he was pro-White Russian. On the contrary, Prince Paul viewed Russians of either colour with almost equal distrust – unlike Queen Elisabeth of Belgium who said 'she preferred them Red'. (King Alexander himself, who was reputed to be so well disposed towards Russia, had mainly kept to the society of Serbs while living in that country and in his heart of hearts was no Russophil.)

While I was at the Court it rarely happened that I was not aware of who were being invited as personal guests by Prince Paul and Princess Olga. Usually I had a chance of meeting them. Apart from his father-in-law and mother-in-law, who were of course frequently there, I can only remember two Russian emigrés staying with them for a few days during the five years I was there. One was the Grand Duke Dimitri Pavlovich, the co-murderer of Rasputin, whom I was particularly intrigued to meet. He was Princess Olga's first cousin and stayed only once for two nights. The other was Prince Vsevolod, who on his mother's side was a member of the Karageorgević family. Neither of them had any political status or influence. Nor was I aware of any political influence being exerted on Prince Paul by his Russian mother-in-law, the Grand Duchess Helen – and I am convinced there was none. In 1940, when Mussolini was concentrating troops on the Yugoslav frontier, Prince Paul decided to recognize the Soviet Union but kept the negotiations strictly secret because he feared an indiscretion. They were handled by Antić and the Yugoslav Ambassador in Turkey. In November of that year the Yugoslav government approached the Soviet government for war supplies. After initially promising help, the Soviet government later refused it, obviously to avoid disturbing relations with Germany.

It is often said, and now generally assumed, that Prince Paul turned away from the path of co-operation with the West scrupulously followed by King Alexander, and took Yugoslavia into the German camp. In fact, shortly before his death, King Alexander himself was already beginning to think of 'keeping the door open for Germany', because the situation in Europe was starting to change so radically. This is confirmed by Henderson's despatches. During the first half of the inter-war years Yugoslavia had not been exposed to the dangers of intervention on the part of the great powers. But on 28th December 1933, Henderson had reported: 'Instead of the Balkans continuing to be, as formerly, a constant danger to the peace of Europe, it is Europe today which is the sole danger to the peace of the Balkans.' In the same year he reported that 'An appreciation in this country of Germany's possible value as a counterpoise to Italian policy, intrigues and interference in the Balkans is beginning to gain ground. . . . It is therefore possible that the next few years . . . will see a marked advance towards a closer understanding between Yugoslavia and Germany. . . . The French alliance seems to be losing something of its enthusiasm. Its usefulness is less obvious than it used to be and in the northern districts of Yugoslavia it is actually unpopular. . . . The Yugoslav nation as a whole relies on England to maintain the peace of Europe. Piqued though they are by what they regard as British public indifference to their own country. . . .'

On the 16th April 1934, King Alexander told Henderson that there was no immediate danger at all of his going over to the German camp. He was bound by his alliances with France and the Little Entente, and he was not going to go back on his friends. But at the same time what would he do? Italy was still pursuing her policy of disrupting Yugoslavia. He did not and would never trust her. Mussolini's foreign policy was 'pure journalism'. It had no sense from an Italian or European point of view. So long as it continued on these lines he was bound to keep the door open for Germany, which was the country which was making all the advances. He would not do more, but no other course was open to him. . . . In his report of the conversation Henderson commented: 'Now in my humble opinion the attitude of the Yugoslav government and the King in this regard is reasonable and inevitable. It is Italy who holds the key of the solution. . . . It is this consideration which is largely responsible for the Yugoslav receptiveness towards Germany. This is only natural.' Later in his despatch he referred to the possibility of an Italo-German rapprochement after the Anschluss – a combination of Italy and all the revisionist powers against the Little Entente.

This was the very contingency Prince Paul was trying to prevent. His policy, in which he was closely following the ideas of King Alexander, as he himself told me, was not to allow Germany and Italy to come to terms at the expense of Yugoslavia. If they did so, they would at once be joined by Hungary, Austria and Bulgaria, who were all her enemies and had claims on parts of her territory. His first prime objective was to have peace at home and settle the Croat question. It took him years but finally he succeeded. In the field of foreign relations, Prince Paul actually improved Yugoslav relations with Hungary and Bulgaria. Even Italy became less aggressive when she saw that Germany – for selfish economic reasons – preferred to improve her relations with Yugoslavia too.

Chamberlain, and, by implication, the Conservative Party, has been attacked for the words he used about Czechoslovakia at the time of Munich: 'a faraway country of which we know little'. In fact he was no more to blame than earlier Prime Ministers of other parties. Lloyd George and Ramsay McDonald had in their time spoken in just the same way of Britain's attitude to the smaller countries in Central and South-East Europe. It was not part of British policy to defend countries like Yugoslavia, where British long-term interests were not engaged. The British government always made it clear to the Yugoslavs that they had not the means to help them militarily or equip them with arms and ammunition. Prince Paul was continually asking for military aid, and on 30th December 1936, the British Legation reported his 'second urgent request'. The answer he received was that Yugoslavia was one of the countries to which (if she were at war with Italy) Britain could in no circumstances give direct naval and military assistance.

British and French courtship of Mussolini, their betrayal of Czechoslovakia which led to her dismemberment and broke up the

Little Entente, and most important of all, the obvious French reluctance to move a finger to support her ally Yugoslavia left a deep impression on Prince Paul and the Yugoslav government, as I can well remember at the time. But one of the most serious consequences for Yugoslavia of the German occupation of Czechoslovakia was that, as the Škoda works were the main source of her supply of armaments, she became almost wholly dependent on Germany, who had taken them over. She could not immediately break off these vital commercial-military links, particularly as the West was unable to provide an alternative supply. The Germans played on Yugoslavia's defencelessness and held up arms supplies as they did with the Swedes.

The year 1940 saw Britain's unhappy interventions in Norway that led in the end to the German invasion – which Britain, to the surprise and disappointment of the free world, proved unable to prevent. The collapse of Belgium and Holland, which no foreign government had ever imagined the British could permit, followed by the disastrous capitulation of France cut Yugoslavia off from the possibility of help from the Western side, even though it had already been practically ruled out from the moment that the Western powers allowed Hitler to re-occupy the Rhineland. By 1941, it would have been a remarkable act of faith for a Yugoslav government to place unreserved trust in Britain's ability to save the country from Hitlerite aggression.

When Italy declared war on Greece in 1940, Yugoslavia was placed in a critical position. Italian and German policies in the Balkans differed. Whereas Italy had territorial claims on Yugoslavia and had long aimed at dismembering and destroying her, as we have seen, Germany had no such immediate policy. Hitler, it appeared, would have been content merely to have Yugoslavia's benevolent neutrality. He certainly had no wish to involve himself in a long drawn out war on his back doorstep in the Balkans, when he was secretly preparing his giant blow against Russia. However, the situation after the Belgrade *coup d'état* favoured a blitz war in the Balkans. On 6th April, the Germans invaded Yugoslavia and Greece and within three weeks they were both overrun and their Governments had capitulated. By provoking a German invasion the new Yugoslav régime had simplified and not complicated Germany's position, as Hitler himself stated to the Hungarian Prime Minister on the day after the *coup*.

To emphasize my point, Italy had been Yugoslavia's main

enemy ever since the end of the First World War. Discontented with her 'reward' for joining the victorious side in 1915 she had regarded herself as having been cheated by the Western allies when they failed to honour all the clauses of the secret Treaty of London, and the Italians worked for the next twenty years to encircle Yugoslavia. The situation became much worse under Mussolini and Fascism, when the régime no longer felt bound by any kind of moral scruple and began to act with unparallelled duplicity. After the murder of King Alexander at Marseilles in October 1934, for which the Italian government bore part of the guilt, relations between Italy and Yugoslavia deteriorated considerably. The British, however, seemed unable to understand why Prince Paul should be reluctant to deal with a government responsible for the assassination of his cousin. It was not merely a question of the personal feelings of Prince Paul: the whole country was strongly anti-Italian and it required much courage and self-control for the Prince Regent to try to overcome this and improve relations. He finally did so against an unpleasant undercurrent of secret talks which he knew were going on between the Italians and the Croat Ustaši.

The Yugoslav government were aware that, whatever German diplomats might say to the Italians, Hitler did not want to see Italian domination in the Balkans or the Adriatic, and consequently it was not unreasonable that the Yugoslavs, while trying to repair their fences with Italy, should seek to use the Germans to protect them from what appeared to be the more dangerous adversary. On 19th August 1935, Prince Paul had said to the British Chargé d'Affaires that he was 'merely a state machine and would be prepared to sink his own personal feelings if the interests of his country demanded it'.

A study of the history of Serbia reminds us that the policy of that country had always depended on playing one of the three great powers – Austria-Hungary, Russia or Turkey – against one or both of the others. When the Yugoslav government took its fateful decision in 1941 to sign the Pact, it was not doing anything inconsistent with traditional policies in the Balkans. Yugoslavia had no really friendly neighbours except Greece, and the powers whom she felt she could trust were far away and unable to protect her. An Italian or German domination of the Balkans was an evil equally to be resisted. Finland, which was certainly not Fascist, not only joined up with the Germans after Hitler's attack on the Soviet Union but sent her army to fight by their side against our ally. Sweden made many concessions to the Germans during the war: she refused transit for Allied troops through her territory to help Finland, while allowing the Germans later to send troops from Finland through Sweden to Norway – an act which not only violated her pledge of neutrality but was a breach of faith to her brother people, the Norwegians. She received for this Churchill's personal blessing. Turkey, in spite of British blandishments, refused to be drawn into war against Germany. During the war and afterwards the actions of Finland, Sweden and Turkey were accepted and forgiven. In *The Times* obituary notice on President Inönü on 27th December 1973, I noted the following sentence: 'His success in maintaining Turkish neutrality throughout the long-drawn struggle, in spite of the strongest pressures from both Allied and Axis powers, must be regarded as one of the most skilful operations of its kind.' The writer praised Inönü for having resisted Churchill's efforts to bring Turkey into the war. Only Prince Paul, whose government on two occasions refused German and Italian demands for transit rights and in practice did much less to help the Germans than the Finns and Swedes, and was only trying to preserve his country's unity and peace, continues to be written off as 'a friend of the Nazis'.

But if the British press and some British historians have been unjust to Prince Paul, the Foreign Office and the British Minister in Belgrade did not at the time necessarily share their views. On 5th November 1935, Sir Robert, later Lord, Vansittart minuted: 'Paul is still very clearly and warmly Anglophile. And I think it is clear that he has no intention of committing himself to Germany.' He suggested that the Prince Regent was trying to find a middle course. E. H. Carr who, when employed in the Foreign Office in 1936, recommended that Czechoslovakia and Austria should 'make peace' with Germany, minuted on Foreign Office papers regarding Yugoslavia as follows: 'There is no reason to suppose that this policy (i.e. a policy of cultivating good relations with Germany) is any way personal to Prince Paul. It is the policy of the Yugoslav government and more particularly of the Yugoslav Army, which probably has the last word.' Sir Orme Sargent wrote: 'The Yugoslav government are, as we know, still sitting on the fence waiting to see whether to throw in their lot with France (plus Italy) or with Germany. At present the chances of a German orientation are in the ascendant and so long as this is the case the Yugoslav government naturally do not wish to be identified with any scheme which has the appearance of thwarting German plans.'

We must also consider that the internal situation in Yugoslavia was very different from that of Finland, Sweden and Turkey. If the Serbs were ready to fight against the Germans (although they were more anxious to fight against the Italians), they knew that they could only do so with hope of success if they withdrew to a central position in Bosnia and Herzegovina and left the northern province undefended. This was something the Croats and Slovenes could never accept. Under conditions as unfavourable as these it was impossible for the Yugoslavs to contemplate a war with Germany.

Could the Yugoslav government have steered a middle path without signing the Pact? It has been suggested that Hitler's pressure on Yugoslavia did not actually take the form of an ultimatum and that the considerable concessions he made to Yugoslavia's objections showed how eager he was to preserve peaceful relations with her. If Prince Paul had opted for a policy of strict neutrality towards both Britain and Germany (or at least as strict as Swedish neutrality proved to be), would Hitler have been content? No one can be sure about this, just as no one can be sure that Hitler would have observed the undertaking he made in the notes appended to the Pact, which freed Yugoslavia from the obligation of affording him military aid. But it seems highly likely that Hitler would have regarded Yugoslavia's refusal to sign the Pact as a hostile act and that he would then have encouraged the subversion of Yugoslavia by the Italians and Bulgarians. In fact, like the British, he would have overthrown the régime from within, working through Croats as the British had worked through Serbs. If Prince Paul's policy had been carried out and war could have been avoided at that stage the lives of thousands of Yugoslavs would have been spared and the destruction of Belgrade avoided.

The *coup d'état* which took place on 27th March 1941 was a disaster for the country. Even Hugh Dalton admitted that the sequel was deplorable. It precipitated a German attack on Yugoslavia, when her main nationality problem had not yet been entirely solved and she was desperately unprepared for it. It sparked off a convulsion of maniacal rage in Hitler, who determined to punish Yugoslav 'faithlessness' by the most brutal means. The result was 'Operation Punishment' – the bombardment of Belgrade in which reportedly seventeen thousand people lost their lives in a single night. There followed in twelve days time the deepest humiliation a nation can suffer in its history, the utter defeat of its army and a degrading capitulation, while leaders of the *coup* fled the country and left the people to suffer the consequences.

It is sometimes argued that even the deaths of seventeen thousand people are justified if by this a nation 'finds its soul', to use the phrase which Churchill coined in praise of the *coup d'état*. In point of fact the *coup* achieved nothing, because hardly had the new régime been installed than its leaders found themselves in the demoralizing position of gradually having to try to worm their way back to the policy which Prince Paul and his government had followed, but without any hope now of it being accepted by the Germans and the Italians. The *coup d'état* was presented by its instigators as a protest against the Yugoslav government's capitulation to Germany. But in reality their motives had been entirely different. The signing of the Pact was only the pretext for it. The army had been misled into supporting it and the people into acclaiming it, because they genuinely believed that it would not only extricate the country from its predicament but bring them honour, victory and liberty. However, not very long afterwards the Yugoslav Foreign Minister, Ninčić, was desperately and vainly attempting to assure the Germans that the former policies would not be changed and that the new government would continue to adhere to the Pact. The conspirators were for the most part irresponsible Serb officers, who had little sympathy for the Croats and Slovenes, and whose object, apart from personal ambition, was to conduct a policy which was exclusively in the Serb interest. It was easy for them to misrepresent Prince Paul's important negotiations with Maček and his endeavours to bring about a Serbo-Croat understanding as a sell-out for the Serbs. But in spite of this the new régime set great store themselves in having the Croats and Slovenes as members of their government. After long hesitations, during which he had tried to persuade Prince Paul to stay in Zagreb and resist the *coup* with Croat troops, Maček agreed to join the new régime. But there was little confidence on either side.

◇ When I read about this in Stockholm I had scant knowledge of what had actually happened. Situated as we were in the midst of a war for our life and death as a nation, when fortune was going against us, it seemed on the surface to be good news that Yugoslavia had by popular consent flouted the Germans and thrown in her lot with the Western Allies. It was a consolation for me that it was my pupil who had allegedly given the lead. But when, on returning to

England, I stayed the night at my college at Cambridge, Peterhouse, and took advantage of my right to dine at the high table, discussion turned on the latest developments in Yugoslavia. The Fellows pressed me with questions. I explained what the situation had been when I was in Yugoslavia and pointed with some pride to the supposed achievement of my former pupil. One of the Fellows reduced me to silence. 'It was nothing to do with your pupil,' he said. 'It was entirely organized by us – S.O.E.' Now that the documents have been released, although not of course the S.O.E. documents, it is clear that he was absolutely right. There would certainly have been no *coup d'état* if the British had not planned it. When the British government found that they could get nowhere with Prince Paul's government, they decided to overthrow it, and him with it. Eden has stated this in his memoirs. 'You have my full authority for any measure you may think it right to take to further a change of government or régime, even by *coup d'état*,' he telegraphed to Campbell. 'We sent a wire to our friends to use all means to raise a revolution,' wrote Hugh Dalton, the Minister in charge of S.O.E. This was a unique case of the Foreign Office and the British Legation together with 'the Ministry of Ungentlemanly Warfare', as Dalton called it, engineering a *coup* against a government with which they enjoyed more than friendly relations and which was presided over by a British Knight of the Garter!

Sir Ronald Ian Campbell, the British Minister in Belgrade (who succeeded Sir Ronald Hugh Campbell), reported during the first half of March 1941 that Prince Paul's attitude showed the extreme difficulty in which he was placed. His own wish for a British victory appeared to be sincere. He felt, however, that he was not free to decide according to his personal inclinations. He had to judge the chances of military success; his advisors told him that his country could not hold out for more than a week, and that, even with British help, the Greeks could not resist much longer. He had also to consider public opinion, especially in Croatia. It was therefore impossible for him to come to a decision until he was sure that there was no way out between surrender to the Germans and fighting them. Looking back on the events of 1941 in full knowledge of all the documents and facts, there seems little to criticize in Campbell's final statement of the position before the signing of the Pact. When Anthony Eden was told by his Minister that if we needed the Yugoslav's help we must offer them military equipment and if possible make a demonstration in the Adriatic, his reply had been guarded. We could not promise to supply more than petrol and lubricants, he said, and later three-ton lorries.

The political and military disaster was rendered all the worse by the incompetence of many of those who took a leading part in the *coup*. General Simović was a bungler and had no idea what to do once he had seized power. The only good that can be said of him was that he succeeded in sparing the Prince Regent's life, when some of the younger mutineers were anxious to murder him in the Serbian tradition. When King Peter arrived in England soon after the débacle he had no words too bad for the incompetence of the general. Almost at once the Serbs in the régime were split into rival cliques and the Croat and Slovene representatives trusted neither. The quarrels of the members of the emigré government in England alienated British sympathies not only from them but finally from any traditional Yugoslav government. When I came over and talked with the Foreign Office soon after these events, officials dealing with Yugoslav affairs asked: 'What are we to do with *your* Jugs? They are impossible.'

In his book *Eastern Approaches* Brigadier Fitzroy Maclean writes that 'King Alexander's assassination did not lead to any change in the character of the régime he had established. If anything it became more oppressive under the rule of his cousin.' This is an astonishing statement. When I arrived in Yugoslavia before the assassination, the Croat and Slovene leaders were under lock and key. After Prince Paul took over, Dr. Korošec, the Slovene leader was released and made Minister of the Interior and the Prince set Dr. Maček free and repeatedly conferred with him about a settlement of the Croat question. Prince Paul had actually done his best to try to modify the dictatorial régime of King Alexander. He had achieved an understanding with the Croats. But he had received little help from the Western democracies and with his disappearance from the scene his country reverted to totalitarian rule.

Another criticism levelled at Prince Paul's government was that it had failed to take the country into its confidence. But Yugoslavia was not like Britain: it had no 'loyal' opposition. If the Yugoslav government in its extremity had disclosed every one of its diplomatic moves it would never have been able to carry out any policy at all. In times of crisis there have been many occasions when our own government has witheld vital information from Parliament and the electorate, as we all know.

✧ I was to hear later from two important witnesses what really happened on the day of the *coup*. King Peter gave me his account during the war and some years afterwards I was able to check it with the version given me personally by Prince Alexander, the eldest son of the Prince Regent. The latter told me that he had woken up one morning in his father's palace 'Beli Dvor' and noticed that the guards seemed to have been noticeably strengthened. His father had just left for Slovenia and he was alone in the palace with his mother, Princess Olga, his younger brother and baby sister. Aware that something was up, he telephoned the King and asked him if he had noticed that the guards had been strengthened. The King said that he had and that something strange was going on. Prince Alexander decided to go over and see the King in his palace of Dedinje which was about a quarter of a mile away.

While they were discussing the mystery, they decided to turn on the wireless and see if any news was coming through. Just at that moment they heard the voice of a boy, purporting to be that of the King, announcing that he had dismissed the Regency and assumed full powers as King. Prince Alexander and the King listened agape to this extraordinary pantomime. It was the work of the conspirators, who were compelled to resort to such deception of the public because the King would not have been prepared to come and speak himself. In actual fact they would not have succeeded in inducing the King to speak at that time, because it was only when Prince Paul resigned from the Regency on his return from Slovenia and Croatia that the King understood what the real situation was and agreed to play the part required of him. He spent the whole day with Princess Olga at Beli Dvor.

A third witness to the events of the *coup* is the Princess herself, who has kindly let me read and quote the entry in her diary for 27th March 1941. It runs as follows:

Thursday, 27th March 1941 A soft spring day. We were awoken by sounds of strange movements in the garden – saw troops in large numbers standing about with guns – was told it was to protect us in case of trouble, that General Simović, new head of the Air Force, made a *coup d'état*, seized power in his hands, proclaimed Peter as King, locked up the former govt. I was cut off from Peter all day, tried in vain to phone him – Alexander rushed up to see Peter at Dedinje – he (Peter) came over to me for lunch later and stayed all day – staggered to hear a young student had spoken on the radio, supposed to be himself – refused to make any move without Uncle Paul – was persuaded to drive round the various regiments with Simović to be seen. Paul returned only at 7.30 – went straight to the

War Ministry with the two other Regents to resign. We were told it was best all should leave for Greece tonight with our three children, English nurse and two maids – so little time to pack – poor little Peter tried to be brave and sensible, it was heart rending to leave him alone. As we parted, he cried and begged to go with us – the British radio broadcast several times we had fled for Germany.

But far away in Stockholm on the day of the *coup*, I had no idea what had happened and could only judge the position on the admittedly doubtful assumption that King Peter had put himself at the head of a *coup* and brought Yugoslavia over to the Allied cause. When Swedish papers approached me for an interview I gave what I think was a reasonably diplomatic account of the situation in Yugoslavia as I remembered it when I left. From these happenings there flowed various consequences for myself.

In the first place, like a governess who sees her charge as a child still, I wondered how King Peter could possibly manage to get on alone in his acutely difficult new situation. It occurred to me that I might have some useful role to play in Belgrade, and I discussed this with my Minister. He telegraphed to the Foreign Office the suggestion that I might be of some help to them and they might care to employ me there. (Sir) Philip Nichols, who was in charge of the Southern Department and was later to be my Ambassador in Prague, appeared to think the idea a good one. He discussed it first with the Yugoslav Queen Mother, who happened to be in England. Her reply was that one should perhaps wait a little, since it might be easier for the young King if he were not exposed to any outside influence for the moment. I think it was a wise decision and I am grateful to the Queen for giving this advice. If she had not, I might have been caught up in the mêlée in Belgrade when the Germans invaded. On past showing, I very much doubt whether in the *sauve-qui-peut* there would have been a place reserved for me in any Yugoslav plane, train or car. And had I stayed on with him when he was in London, I doubt whether I could have kept him out of the hands of the 'three Musketeers' – the young officers who took an active part in the *coup* and reaped their reward afterwards by becoming the boon companions of the King.

Meanwhile, the Germans were quick to pick up my interview. An article against me appeared in the Reich German papers and it was reproduced in the press of every occupied or German-influenced country from the *Deutsche Zeitung in Norwegen* to the *Ostasiatische Beobachter* in Shanghai. This article, based almost exclusively on what I had myself said in the interview, was such a remarkable specimen of Nazi journalism that I must reproduce it here, as it was published in the *Deutsche Zeitung in Norwegen* of 19th April 1941. It was headed 'Behind Peter Lurked Parrott' and sub-titled 'Career and History of the British "Educator" '.

Stockholm, 18th April 1941.

A touch of a spring breeze blows from Lake Mälaren over the square in front of the Royal Library in Stockholm. A shy sun shines from behind a veil of clouds and warms the just and unjust alike, Swedes and Englishmen. It warms as well a man who must be in his early thirties, whose round face reveals a pair of rather too large ears, and who has taken off his hat to enjoy this April sun, revealing thick dark hair, parted on the left. He goes hurriedly up to the nearest newspaper stand and buys *Dagens Nyheter*. With a frown he scans ill-humouredly the headlines on the first page, which tell the latest news from Yugoslavia. As he hands the newspaper vendor the 15 *öre* due to him there can be seen on his wrist the fine specimen of a heavy gold watch, decorated with the Royal crown.

This man is Mr. Cecil Parrott. He belongs temporarily to the British Legation in Stockholm on an undiscoverable mission. He has good grounds to be dissatisfied with what he finds in the newspapers, for the collapse now taking place in Yugoslavia is his finely contrived work too. He did not always walk disgruntledly through the streets of Stockholm, but was recently living in Belgrade. For five years he 'taught' the young King Peter, if one can use that expression.

Mr. Parrott studied in Cambridge. It was never known of him that he was a shining light of the pedagogic sciences, yet in the Secret Intelligence Service they were wont to smile benevolently and expressively at the mention of his name; he must of course have had his merits outside the spheres of learning.

At the age of 25, as a Cambridge student, he was ordered to the Serbian court, as King Alexander wanted to have his son educated in the British way. In accordance with his mission Mr. Parrott soon succeeded in convincing the King that a hard-dyed British education could only be fully attained on English soil, and so at the age of eleven King Peter went on a journey to London, near to which Sandroyd school lay waiting for him. Cecil Parrott was the sole witness when father and son took leave of each other on the then Austrian frontier without knowing that they would never see each other again. 'And take the boy with you for a trip through England each weekend', Alexander repeated once more at this leave-taking. 'I want him to get to know Britain well.' 'A monarch must know Britain and her methods well', Alexander continued in an undertone, more for himself, but Parrott had heard. Faithful to the King's intentions, he, Parrott, would see that the Crown Prince was accepted into the right school.

Seventeen days later King Alexander was shot in Marseilles at the side of the French Premier, Barthou. The Crown Prince had only made one weekend journey through England before the death of his father called him back to Yugoslavia, which he has not left since that day. He did not return alone; Mr. Parrott experienced the route London–Belgrade for the third time, and he had strict orders from his Government never to let the King take a single step alone during the next days. Britain knew what good services an obedient Serbia had rendered already once by the assassination at Sarajevo.

Parrott fulfilled his mission punctiliously. For five years he was like young Peter's shadow. He brought him up to be a blind worshipper of the British way of thinking. Not to be an Englishman, of course not. British pride would never allow a half-savage Balkan prince to become perhaps a second Prince of Wales. Cecil Parrott's efforts found fruitful soil in Peter. It was enough for him to point to the role which his father had played in rejecting the Austrian ultimatum in 1914, and the gain in Austrian, Hungarian, Bulgarian and Romanian territory which King Alexander in 1919 had been able to secure at the hands of the Entente for the 'victorious state', to awake in the immature boy childish hopes of a similar kind.

When Parrott at regular intervals sent the required reports of his activities to London, he never failed to point out the progress which Peter was making in 'democratic' thinking, the active connection which he maintained with the reactionary chauvinistic Sokol, whose President the young King finally became, and above all the popularity, which a clique, paid with British money, foisted on him to Britain's advantage by all well-seasoned methods. In deference to this popularity the young King, who would have greatly preferred to remain unguarded and unobserved in his weekend house among the royal vineyards of Oplenac, was obliged continually to appear as an enthusiastic sportsman and reap applause and a rain of flowers. As it will perhaps be recalled, at the relay race for the Olympic Games in Berlin he had to carry with his own royal hand the burning torch all the way from his father's grave over Mount Avala to the grave of the unknown soldier. Mr. Parrott is daily reminded of the sporting activity of his pupil, when he looks at the stop-hand on the gold wrist watch which Peter once gave him.

By means of Mr. Parrott, London played a clever game. It made the future ruler a complacent puppet on British leading strings, and, by forcibly making this England-thrall popular, unobtrusively won over through his person further sections of the Serbian population.

But the circumspect Britons were not content with that. King Peter was too young to act independently on his own initiative at the right moment. Some impetus was necessary to bring him over to the British way at that moment and, if necessary, by force. For this purpose General Simović was chosen, the same 'hero' who recently vowed that he would be in Vienna with his troops within two days.

Mr. Parrott arranged with skill the necessary purchase of the General, who, as a true Serb, was of course corrupt, if not cheap at the price. After that it was a question of making Simović acceptable in the eyes of the young King. To this end his predilection for all things technical was exploited. By corrupt side-channels the General was made Chief of the Serbian Air Force, and Mr. Parrott brought young Peter to the aerodrome at Zemun near Belgrade where Simović won the heart of the King by means of the performances of his airmen. Cecil Parrott, who had quickly established the necessary connection, did not subsequently neglect further opportunities of deepening the acquaintance of Peter and Simović.

When Britain knew that the future ruler of Yugoslavia had been sufficiently fettered to the bribed General, the stage manager of all this withdrew into the security of a neutral country. Cecil Parrott, once a simple student, suddenly became diplomat and was transferred to Stockholm. Soon afterwards Britain felt the time was ripe to tear Yugoslavia finally from the zone of peace, which the Triple Pact guaranteed for the country. The events are now known. By orders of London, General Simović staged his night *coup* and went in the early hours of the dawn to the sleeping child to tell him that he could now act the role of King. Naturally this immature boy very gladly did this as can be shown from the letter he had written shortly before to a friend of his in London: 'I am still only waiting for the day when Yugoslavia will decide against the Nazis, so that I can at least take over the command of my army.'

It all went off extremely well, and when Winston Churchill unleashed his premature congratulations in London two hours after the *coup*, he did not forget to tell his secretary to send a telegram of acknowledgement to Stockholm. Mr. Parrott smirked at the thought that he was remembered with gratitude. Today he smirks no more. He spent five years working on a King who could not rule properly for more than five days, before German Stuka bombers blew him out of his capital. Britain's efforts had been in vain and Mr. Parrott is now afraid that he will have to pay with his career for this fiasco.

Leading German papers took up the theme. The *Leipziger Neueste Nachrichten* triumphantly quoted a Reuter message that 'the principal companion of the young King was his English tutor, who not only taught him English but also generally controlled his behaviour and way of life'. The *Hamburger Fremdenblatt* made caustic remarks about the 'Gentleman – Ideal' in which I had brought up 'the marionette King'.

One of the amusing things about the article was that it appeared in many of the papers which we subscribed to in our Legation. All the versions included the sentence 'he (Mr. Parrott) belongs temporarily to the British Legation in Stockholm *on an undiscoverable mission*'. The *Grenzbote* of Slovakia actually sent the copy of the newspaper in which this article appeared to the gentleman with the 'undiscoverable mission' himself, addressed to the British Legation, Stockholm. I do not know whether this was due to Nazi inefficiency or Slovak sympathy.

The publication of these articles also had a sequel. As might have been expected there existed in Stockholm, as in all countries in Europe at the period, a small Fascist movement – what one might call a pro-German 'fifth column'. Naturally they studied very carefully everything that was written in the newspapers published by their masters and reproduced much of it in a little paper of their own called *Dagens Eko*, which had a minute circulation. Churchill was fond of quoting during the war the apparently biblical saying: 'though the mills of God grind slowly, yet they grind exceedingly small'. (The author of these lines was in fact a German, Friedrich von Logau, and Churchill was quoting Longfellows translation of them.) The verse goes on: 'Though with patience He stands waiting, with exactness grinds He all.' In this case I had to 'stand waiting' for about five months before the Swedish Quislings got on to it. I was therefore unprepared for the 'grind' when it came.

One day I passed a newsagent's shop with a placard. There to my amazement I saw my own name splashed up in huge capitals. It said: 'What is Mr. Parrott doing in Sweden? British specialist in revolutions here.' I went straight into the shop, which was presumably a Quisling shop, otherwise it would not have exhibited the placard, and bought a paper. The cutting which I made from it is one of my most precious acquisitions. In the article I am described as 'a well-known British globe-trotter who plans to "put away" King Gustav of Sweden just as he "put away" Prince Paul'. But it was the end of the article which pleased me most. It ended:

> There is, in other words, *danger afoot*. . . . We who are Swedish-minded must hold together, stand shoulder to shoulder, rank against rank and take up arms together against the agents of the enemy! Unity, comradeship, self-sacrifice – these are the demands that *Sweden* today makes on those who were already aware of the danger and are prepared to do their bit for people and country.

And now a few valedictory conclusions about the *coup*. Undoubtedly the British government were ruthless in their treatment of the Yugoslav government, and Prince Paul in particular. Churchill believed that there were no neutrals in the war – only non-belligerents – and that they must not be allowed to stand in the way of great powers fighting for their existence. For this reason, he ordered the British Minister in Belgrade to 'pester, nag and bite' Prince Paul.

But in judging his attitude we must also consider that small powers conduct a struggle for their existence too and have the right to seek their own ways of securing it. Churchill was not only very unsqueamish about the welfare of other countries during the war: he did not bother his head much about their future, as can be seen from his notorious remark to Fitzroy Maclean: 'Do you intend to make Yugoslavia your home after the war?' 'No? Neither do I.'

The results of Churchill's strategy did not justify the bloodshed and destruction it entailed. The great merit of the Yugoslav 'campaign' was always believed to be that it allegedly delayed the start of Hitler's invasion of Russia for two months and so involved the German army in disaster. But a closer look at the German military position at the time suggests that it did not delay it very much but rather that it came at exactly the right moment from the German point of view and had the effect of substantially speeding up the German operations.* In the treatment meted out to Prince Paul Anthony Eden was much to blame. He had been together with Prince Paul at Oxford and never liked him. The Prince Regent's and Princess Olga's internment in Kenya under humiliating conditions where he was treated as a traitor, until rescued and brought to South Africa by General Smuts, was unworthy of the British government, and the Foreign Secretary could certainly have saved them both from this ordeal if he had had more consideration for them. But Eden could be harsh and uncharitable in his judgements as his minutes on official papers show.

Here is a moving letter which Prince Paul wrote to his brother-in-law, the Duke of Kent, from his exile in Kenya on 18th August 1941 – nearly five months after the *coup*.

. . . To understand the situation one must know the inside motives of the so-called Belgrade revolution. Now this is only for your private ear.

One of the chief objects in view was the wish of a few ambitious (very few) military people to get hold of Peter and through him rule the country. In consequence I must at all costs be kept away from the child so that he shouldn't fall 'under my influence'. This is an absurd conception, I agree, but that small minority of people . . . do not understand how much I hated my job, (you knew it) and that the last thing I wish is to have anything to do with Yugoslav politics! I was longing for Peter's majority to release me from a dog's existence, and I was at the end of my physical strength when the

* See *Hitler's Strategy 1940–1941. The Balkan Clue*, by Martin van Creveld, Cambridge University Press, 1973.

March events took place. I did my best for my country, according to my lights during nearly seven years among the most eventful and difficult in the history of the world. During all that time I worked hard and walked hand in hand with your country till the last minute when I was unable to act differently owing to internal complications, when my efforts tended to prevent the splitting up of my country as Croats and Slovenes insisted on the pact being signed as well as the War Minister, and Chief of the General Staff. The short disastrous campaign that followed proved that the country was unable to resist, and that a large part of it did not desire to fight. . . .

It's childish to talk of our 'flirting' with Germany and of my visit to Hitler as if it had been a 'partie de plaisir' and a meeting with a pretty woman!

Hitler manifested for a long time the wish to see me and I avoided doing so for ages. I sent my Minister of Foreign Affairs first; then the Prime Minister and Minister of Foreign Affairs went together later.

Hitler again insisted on seeing me and for a few weeks again I turned a deaf ear. At last I was asked by my chief ministers including Dr. Maček to 'sacrifice myself' (that's the way they looked at it) and try and see if I could get round him.

As to what concerns Anthony* it's again linked with our attitude and fright of Germany. We were surrounded by Germans, Italians and Hungarians; Bulgaria and Rumania already had German troops, and it is nonsense to pretend that we were not frightened – we were – and I defy anyone not to be under the circumstances.

We carried on negotiations with Germany, and asked for terms which were very difficult for them to accept, and which we were sure they couldn't accept, but it gave us time to mobilise, which we did, as when I left we had 750,000 men *mobilised* and *concentrated*.

All the stories told since that I gave the orders to demobilise are pure fiction, probably to save the face of General Simović and explain in some way (at my expense) his failure.

Well, in a moment like that Eden comes to the East to try to organise a common front against Germany. Although I was longing to see him personally I had to give in to the arguments put forward by my Minister of Foreign Affairs that Germany would take it as a provocation. Had it been possible to keep such a meeting secret, but we were surrounded with spies. . . . We sent a General Staff officer to Athens secretly and without informing our legation there. This officer had meetings with the British and Greek staffs and the same day the German military attaché told our Minister in Greece (who knew nothing about it): 'Your officer is having a meeting with the Greek General Staff.'

In the old days I had a special way of communicating secret things to Halifax (often I opened their eyes that their secret documents at the F.O. were being stolen) but these last months there were

* Sir Anthony Eden.

no 'courriers' going. All the same I don't think that any foreign head of state has ever given you more information than I have. If you ask Campbell he can't not corroborate this, as I used to send him original documents – a thing which is never done. Besides I wouldn't have asked Anthony to take charge of Stojadinović, – the greatest Germanophile in the country (which he immediately and most kindly accepted) if I had been intending to give myself up to Germany. Stojadinović was removed by force through Greece a few days before we left, and this couldn't possibly have been to the taste of the Germans. . . .

Since September 1940 till my departure I only saw the German Minister three times and never once the Italian; the British I saw two or three times a week.

Dalton's comment on this event was: '[Prince Paul] had long deceived our diplomats. He now fled to Egypt and thence to Kenya, where we kept him in very comfortable quarters at his own expense, but under supervision as a political prisoner.' As anyone who has read the Dalton diaries will know, their author often deceived not only others but himself too.

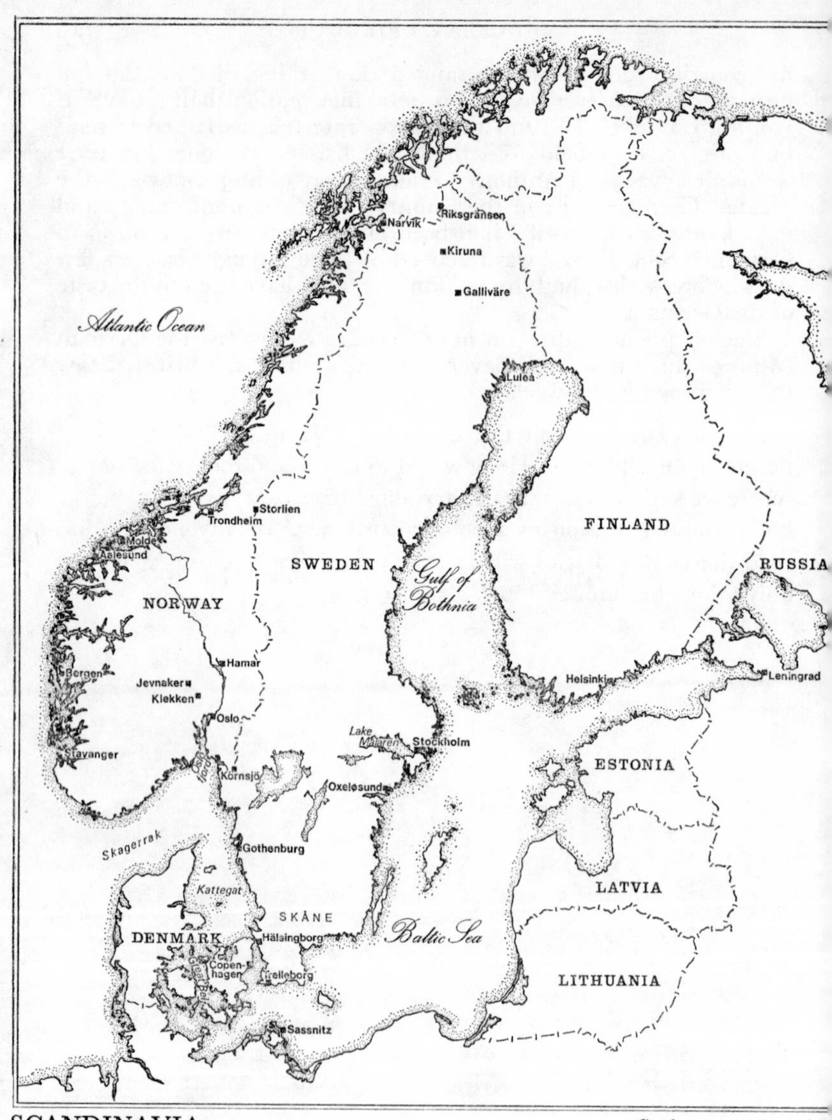

SCANDINAVIA *Scale* 1cm = 147km

CHAPTER ELEVEN ◇ WAR

◇ Before I left Yugoslavia in the spring of 1939 I had asked the Queen, whether she would help me find another job, and she wrote to Lord Astor on my behalf. When I arrived in England, he did not actually see me, but his secretary told me that he had a job in mind and would let me know about it as soon as he could.

As it was thought war was likely to break out in the near future, a hugh-hush shadow Ministry of Information was being set up. It was disguised as a Chatham House activity and had its base in a respectable building in Belgrave Square. I was asked if I would accept a job with it. The salary offered was a paltry three hundred and fifty pounds a year, which, taken all together, represented a considerable drop from what I had been getting in Yugoslavia, but I felt that I had no alternative but to accept.

It was an interesting set-up. The whole world was divided into sections for the purpose of organizing publicity work after the outbreak of war, and various dons and *soi-disant* experts came up from the country from time to time to work out blueprints for the future Ministry of Information. Among others there were from Oxford (Sir) Ronald Syme on the Balkans and Professor Wade-Gery on Greece, and from Cambridge (Sir) Peter Tennant on Sweden. The convenor was Michael Balfour and the 'Research Director' (Sir) Con O'Neil, who had only recently resigned from the Foreign Service – for the first time – in protest over British policy.

Since almost all the senior participants had other jobs and only came in periodically, a second eleven of younger people were needed to carry on the business full time. I was one of them and assisted my more learned colleagues on questions concerning publicity in the Balkans generally. We received our central directives from (Sir) Ivison McAdam, Director-General of Chatham House.

Although the company was agreeable, I found the work exceedingly trivial. I can remember having to work hard filling up questionnaires on how many picture postcards we would want to send to each Balkan country as a first step in our campaign to win neutral opinion to our side! In spite of the fact that Britain had had considerable experience of propaganda from the time of Northcliffe in the First World War, the efforts here appeared to me childish. I hated propaganda in any shape or form, but I supposed that if war broke out I could probably find a job in this organization.

The summer dragged on and we seemed to make no progress. My salary was so low that I could not afford to bring my wife and son over and establish them in England. I lived frugally and tried to save as much money as I could. I no longer bought newspapers but picked them up in trains. I also lived in extremely cheap and humble digs in a back street in London.

Eventually, the stagnancy of the whole operation, the uncertainty whether with the appeasers at work in Whitehall there would be a war at all or even whether Britain would stand up to anything any more, and my financial straits prompted me to see if I could find something better paid.

One day a member of the 'second eleven', who was a specialist on Latin America, told me that he had got a job with an organization called the Travel and Industrial Development Association. I had never heard of it. It was apparently an offshoot of the British Council and designed to deal with commercial publicity alongside the cultural publicity conducted by the parent body. Both institutions were under the direction of the late Lord Lloyd of Dolobran. When I asked my colleague whether there might be a job in it for me, he said that they were looking for somebody to be their representative in Sweden and advised me to go along and see them.

The headquarters of the organization was in Arlington Street and I was received in a very friendly way by a Mr. Meredith and a Mr. Brenan, who seemed delighted at the idea that I might be ready to take on the job. They needed someone who could speak Swedish and could open a branch of their Association in Stockholm to do propaganda for trade and tourism in Sweden.

When I said I could speak Swedish I had exaggerated. In fact I could only speak Norwegian. But the two languages are very close and I had read a lot of Swedish, so that it presented no problems for me. Also, I knew that English people found it hard to tell the difference between the various Scandinavian peoples and their tongues. The Queen of Romania had referred to my wife as 'the little Swede'. If I was the husband of 'a little Swede', then the language I spoke with her could well be described as Swedish. In time, I was invited to an interview with Lord Lloyd himself. He was the Empire-builder type, bluff and autocratic in manner, though capable of being benign to those who caught his fancy. He was not interested in whether I had any qualifications for the post but listened with absorption to what I had to say about my years in Yugoslavia. He knew Prince Paul and was intrigued by the whole situation there. I soon found my experiences with King Peter were going to be a trump card in interviews for any job whatsoever.

At last Lord Lloyd came to the point and offered me the job. 'You can have a contract if you like,' he said, 'but it won't make any difference. If I don't like you, I shall sack you.' Then in a lowered voice he added: 'If there's a war I shall use you politically.' It made me wonder. I remember once recounting this to a colleague of mine in our Legation in Stockholm, Roger Hinks, who commented: 'What an obscene remark!' The war did break out, but Lord Lloyd never used me politically, first because I would not in any case have allowed myself to be so used but also because by the time it had, he was no longer there to carry out his designs. Nor indeed for any practical purposes was the Travel and Industrial Development Association.

I was glad to have the job. It offered me the *princely* salary of seven hundred pounds a year plus a small entertainment allowance and the prospect of working in Stockholm, which appealed to me. On the strength of it I wrote to my wife to come over, and she and our son Hansi stayed with our splendid friends Mr. and Mrs. Martin Hopkinson at Longmeadow, Bovingdon, while I remained in London during the week. Martin Hopkinson was a publisher and the father of an old friend of mine, Jim Hopkinson, from Berkhamsted School. I was told by my new employer to go to Stockholm as soon as I could to try and decide how the Association's office should be decorated and furnished. They had taken premises in Birger Jarls Gatan, which was a fashionable and much frequented thoroughfare in Stockholm. My wife came with me to help us find somewhere to live.

When we arrived, we found the standard of living terribly high and the kind of flat we felt we ought to have far beyond our means. After some deliberation, we chose a beautiful duplex apartment in Stora Essingen with lovely wide windows, perched high up on the rocks looking out over Lake Mälaren. It was luck that in the end we never actually took it because it would have ruined us.

All of a sudden, it was brought home to me that I had obtained the job more or less under false pretences. A Balkan King's tutor, fluent in Slav languages and with a Norwegian wife, is not necessarily the ideal person to be the representative of an institution whose aim is to propagate British trade and tourism in Sweden. The thought first struck me when a leading member of the British business community rang me up, congratulated me on my appointment, said he was in the advertising business and asked me to give a talk in a month's time to the advertisers' club on my plans for publicizing Britain in Sweden. All the big advertising interests would be there. I realized I did not have a clue about publicity and would find myself hopelessly at sea among such super-professionals. I was just not up to the job.

But there was nothing to be done. I could not back out. However, at difficult moments of my life I have often been saved or helped by international developments. My anxieties were for the moment driven totally out of my mind by the unexpected press announcement that Germany had signed a pact with the Soviet Union. It was clear that this meant war, since Hitler would now have his flank secured and could continue his campaign of aggression in Europe. I wondered whether there would be any future for my Travel and Industrial Association Bureau. Who could tell indeed whether Sweden would be able to preserve her independence? I felt I must at once get in touch with the shadow Ministry of Information in case they required me at home. In answer to telegrams which I sent to Belgrave Square and Arlington Street, I was told to come back immediately for consultation. It turned out to be a more or less wasted journey, because the now no longer shadow Ministry was in chaos following the news, and there was nothing I could usefully do to ease its turmoil or contribute to its plans. I was glad to have a discussion with my new employers, though, and as they thought that I should go back to Sweden at once – in case anything should intervene to prevent me getting there at all – I set off again with a light heart. In the meantime, my wife and son had gone to Trondheim in Norway to stay once more with her parents.

I travelled by Swedish Lloyd to Gothenburg and was met there by one of the directors of this great shipping company. As it turned out, it was useful that he happened to be on the quayside. With the usual inexperience of a new set-up the Travel and Industrial Development Association had forgotten to provide me with a work permit, and it was a rule that no foreigner could enter Sweden without one. In the excited atmosphere of the time the authorities were taking no risks. On landing at the port I was arrested by the police and taken away under escort.

My first action at the police station was to try and contact the Consul-General. Eventually a member of the Consulate staff, possibly a Vice-Consul, came to see me and told me most helpfully that he could do absolutely nothing for me and I should have to go back to England by the next ship. This was monstrous *insouciance* on the part of a consular official towards someone who was coming out to Sweden as representative of a semi-official organization, but they had probably never heard of it and suspected the worst. As luck would have it, the director had great standing with the Swedish authorities and after softening up the Swedish police officer by addressing him by a title higher than he deserved, which generally flatters title-loving Swedes, he procured my release and permission for me to proceed to Stockholm, on condition that with the help of my own authorities I put my papers in order without delay. It was a dismal contrast to my arrival in Gothenburg only a week before when I had been photographed, interviewed by the press and honoured with prominent articles about my future activities in all the leading Stockholm papers.

In Stockholm, I found everyone tense with anticipation. The Molotov-Ribbentrop Pact had been concluded on 23rd August. Hitler launched his attack on Poland on 1st September. On 3rd September, Britain and France were at war with Germany. There was no time to do anything before the cataclysm.

I spent those anxious days in a little *pension* in Stockholm chatting with the correspondent of D.N.B. (the Deutsches Nachrichten-Büro). We listened together to Chamberlain's famous broadcast speech in which he announced a state of war between our two countries. 'Now we are enemies,' he declared. Although all the signs had long been pointing towards an international conflict it was still hard to believe that it was upon us.

Events then moved with astonishing rapidity. The Head of Chancery at our Legation, (Sir) William Montague-Pollock, rang me up and asked me to come and see him. He was fond of music and art and we had much in common. But this time he looked grave and said: 'There's no doubt that the Swedish authorities are very suspicious about your arrival here and your plans with the Bureau. I suppose they must think that there's something fishy about it. It's doubtful whether you will be able to go on with it, and I advise you to be most discreet about your activities. As it happens, we have just received an S.O.S. from our Minister in Oslo who is screaming for a Press Attaché there. Your wife is Norwegian and you know the language. Would you be ready to go there immediately and help out? He'll probably offer you the job.'

'But what about my present job here and my employers?' I asked. 'Well,' he replied, 'I don't think you should worry too much about that. War needs are paramount and someone is urgently needed in Oslo. Apart from that it might be embarrassing for us if you stayed much longer here in the present situation.'

I needed little further encouragement. First, I was getting cold feet about my suitability for the Stockholm job. Next, it was enticing to be offered a diplomatic post in Norway, particularly now when my wife and I might easily get separated from her parents. I knew that if I accepted the job it would be a great relief to her and she was in Norway at that moment. And finally, though Stockholm and Sweden attracted me I still needed to get to know more of Norway and was just as happy at the thought of working in Oslo, if not more so.

It was the weekend, and my passport was still with the Swedish authorities as a result of my efforts to get a labour permit. But Bill Pollock was insistent that I should go to Oslo as soon as possible. It is extraordinary what Legation and Consular officials can do if they are pressed. They made out a new passport for me, using as a photograph one of the snaps which had appeared in the Stockholm dailies on my earlier arrival. In a matter of hours I was in Norway.

The contrast in atmosphere between our two Legations was revealing. Every diplomatic mission has a character of its own and sometimes it retains it irrespective of the personality of the Head of the Mission or the officials serving under him. Our Legation in Oslo seemed to be run by three people – the Minister himself, Sir Cecil Dormer, who was elderly, courteous and gentle; the Second Secretary and Head of Chancery, Mr. Freese-Pennefather, who was a delightful easy-going Irishman with plenty of *laissez-faire*, *dolce far niente*, bureaucracy with a human Irish face and all the rest; and the archivist, Miss Nora Bing, who was the embodiment of devotion to duty and loyal observance of F.O. rules in all points which fell under her jurisdiction. As a complete neophyte, I was to learn a lot from her on what to do with my papers and what not, and our destinies were to be linked for a short time at a momentous period in Norway's and our own history. I was later to have additional proof of her sterling qualities.

The alarm which seemed to have struck our Legation in Stockholm was undetectable at its sister establishment in Oslo. It was the kind of post where the senior staff seemed only to work when a Bag arrived and departed. In between they would go ski-ing or sailing, or enjoy themselves in other ways. Moreover, the Bag was carried on to Stockholm or Copenhagen by members of the staff, who thereby got a free ride and enjoyable trip to the other capitals.

It was glorious weather, sometimes almost like mid-summer, and I can remember the golden look of Oslo and its gleaming fjord. Mr. Freese-Pennefather was a bachelor who lived with his sister, and unlike many other career members of the service did not look on me as an outsider, interloper, or greenhorn. He treated me exactly as if I were a new Second Secretary sent out from London to assist him. As might have been expected, we spent a lot of time playing tennis, in which the Minister joined.

But there were more serious things for me to do. I had to make sure that I was going to be definitely appointed at Oslo, and would not find myself obliged to return to Sweden later. Otherwise it would be better for my wife to stay where she was for the time being. The kindly Sir Cecil Dormer welcomed me with open arms and expressed delight at being able to count upon my services as his first Press Attaché. (There had never been one before in Oslo, because press affairs were handled by a Press Attaché in Stockholm who looked after Copenhagen and Helsinki as well.) My candidature was strongly supported by Sir George Ogilvy-Forbes, who had come to Oslo from our Embassy in Berlin – where, until relations were broken off, he had assisted Nevile Henderson (then Ambassador in Berlin) as Counsellor and Chargé d'Affaires. I immediately set about finding accommodation and furniture for an office, and engaged a secretary.

It was very cosy in the Chancery. The two 'perfect and gentle' knights, who made the little British Mission so top heavy with their brass, showed me all the letters and telegrams they were sending home about me, and from these I gathered that I was going to be offered the job of Press Attaché with diplomatic status, a salary of a thousand pounds a year plus rent, living and entertainment allowances, etc. This was so much better than what I had been going to get at Stockholm, and such a gift from heaven from the point of view of my wife and her parents, that I could do nothing but cross my fingers and hope my luck would hold.

Before I left Stockholm I had arranged with the Head of Chancery there that my employers should be told that, at the insistent urgence of the Legation, I had gone to Oslo to act as Press Attaché there. Everything had been turned topsy-turvy in London with the sudden outbreak of war, and something had gone wrong with communications, so that I had no idea whether in all the changes that had taken place in Whitehall, my Travel and Industrial Development Association still existed. The disadvantage in all this was that I had no source of income, because I had received no salary at all from my employers yet and the Legation in Oslo could not pay me until they had confirmation from London that my appointment was approved.

The days dragged on and I heard nothing from London. We were using up all the money we had and it was getting quite difficult. At first the Legation had taken rooms at the (for us) rather expensive hotel *K.N.A.*, and since the auguries looked good, my wife soon came down to join me there. But as time went on we had to look for cheaper accommodation. In the end we moved into a *pension*. It was not up to much, although it gloried in the name of *The Ritz*.

Before long we moved again to another *pension* rejoicing in the name of *C.C.15*. It sounds like a James Bond code-number, but the initials were those of the famous Norwegian poet, Camilla Collett – the address being Camilla Collett Street 15. This *pension* was as excellent as the other had been mediocre. The food was fantastic. On Sunday we had for lunch a delicious soup, a lavish portion of salmon, roast goose and a sweet which literally melted in our mouths. The company was interesting and select. We had what amounted to a little furnished service flat and lived in comparative luxury.

The reason we could improve our accommodation was that I was at last earning some money – or, to be more truthful, my wife was. But it was a sad story. As a result of the chaos in Whitehall, the Minister never received an answer to the telegram and letters he sent proposing my appointment. Instead, some months later, when we were completely 'broke', a curt telegram arrived saying that Mr. Rowland Kenney of the Foreign Office News Department had been appointed Press Attaché and would be arriving shortly.

Meanwhile, Ogilvy-Forbes, sincerely disappointed that I had not received the appointment he had proposed for me, showed us every sympathy and did his best to make up for it by nominating me for the post of Assistant Press Attaché. The job was nothing to write home about, nor was it very well paid. What was worse, it could not be sanctioned until the new boss came.

Rowland Kenney's arrival was a shock. He was quite an elderly man – in his late fifties, I think (and I was thirty). It turned out that he had been so disgruntled with the reorganization, or disorganization, of the Foreign Office after war broke out, and had become so fed up and irritable that they had decided to send him as far away as possible. He on his side was only too anxious to get as far away from them as he could. It was a combination of his asking for Oslo, their hoping to get rid of him and the Ambassador's telegram being mislaid which led to my not even being considered for the job.

He had strong qualifications for the post because he had held it in the First World War. (It was not the first time that the British government had considered that the methods and men used in the First World War would be suitable for the Second.) He proved to be most professional in press-work and very suitable for the Norwegian press-men, who were rather provincial-minded. They all knew him and he had a relationship with editors which varied between that of fellow clubman and that of master and slave. If it was necessary to tear a strip off the chief editor of *Norges Handels-och Sjöfartstidende*, Kenney was the man to do it, and the Norwegians took it like lambs since he was devoted to Norway and the Norwegians. And, like me, he had a Norwegian wife. But for all his good qualities he appeared rather rough in the disdainful eyes of a Cambridge graduate and at first it was riling to have to serve under him. All my drafts with their literary flavour (as I thought, at any rate) were ruthlessly crossed through and his ugly stylization was imposed on them. However, he taught me many wise things – like answering telegrams at once instead of waiting until you collected the necessary information. 'Send 'em a telegram back to tell 'em you got their message and are getting on with the job!' If only the F.O. and all Missions would act on that advice! The worst part of it was that I had to humiliate myself before him. Not only did I have to try to prove to him that I would be suitable as his Number Two, but I also had to beg him to employ my wife part-time in some secretarial capacity, as the meagre salary they had offered me, after the many months when I had received none, made it essential for me to find a way of paying my debts. He was immensely kind about this, accepted my appointment as Assistant Press Attaché and later engaged my wife as part-time archivist in the Press Department. Although she had been through a commercial school in Norway she was not a trained secretary. She was nonetheless a genius for putting things in order, and by the time Rowland Kenney had got settled in, the archives, which had been left unfiled since the outbreak of the war and were overflowing through the window, had all been put together in a masterly way. She certainly earned her keep.

When, in time, it became necessary to recruit another member of the Press Department staff, by a curious coincidence William Montague Pollock's brother turned up and asked whether his services could be used. He was Sir George Pollock, who was responsible for the advertising for Unilever in Norway. Kenney consulted me and we both agreed that it would be useful to have an advertising expert with us to deal with our publicity.

Looking back, I think we made a highly professional team. All three of us spoke Norwegian and had Norwegian wives. Two of us (Kenney and Pollock) had lived a considerable time in Norway. Our Press Attaché himself was one of the most experienced workers in the field. And so we soon divided the work up. In those days Press Departments had in the main to undertake two operations. They had to follow everything that was written in the press, spoken on the radio, published in books, or shown in films or the theatre, and provide the Legation with political information obtainable through the press. They also had to make sure that the British case was not misrepresented or left unrepresented, and initiate publicity themselves – that is to say, go round and try to persuade editors to publish favourable things about Britain or correct unfavourable comment, organize exhibitions or lectures, arrange for the loan of films, and so on. My job fell into the first category. I had to read the Norwegian press and report on it to the Ambassador and to London. George Pollock looked after the publicity side, as I have said, and Rowland Kenney strode above us both, visiting the editorial offices and indulging in a little arm-twisting of the editors or else asking them out for the evening and getting them tight on schnaps. The division of labour fitted in well with our abilities, our characters and our ambitions. We were a happy set-up. But it is characteristic of life that when set-ups are really happy they seldom last and something breaks them up. In our case it was the German invasion of Norway. Before dealing with this stupendous event, I shall say something about my work in Norway and my experiences of the Norwegian attitude during these first months of the war.

CHAPTER TWELVE ◇ INVASION

◇ In a Legation every member of the diplomatic staff is supposed to keep his eyes and ears open and report to the Minister. In Oslo, it was a matter of noting down conversations you might have had with prominent Norwegians and interesting comments vouchsafed you by other diplomats. Although the Minister and his Head of Chancery drafted the Legation's despatches and telegrams, they based them to a considerable extent on what we served up to them, and translations from the daily Norwegian press were their staple material. Among my other duties, I used to have to follow carefully what was going on in the Norwegian Parliament – the Storting. Whatever the Minister of Foreign Affairs said was for me a subject of special attention. Unfortunately, the Minister during this period was Mr. Halvdan Koht, a leading member of the Labour Party and also a fanatical supporter of 'New Norwegian', a new synthetic language gradually gaining ground in Norway. For a longish period there had been a movement to break away from the influence of Danish. The Norwegians had been under the Danes for four hundred and thirty-four years and their language had become very similar to Danish. When Norway was ceded by the Danes to Sweden in 1814 and then at last became independent in 1905, there was strong feeling in favour of making the language as national and Norwegian as possible. This new language, which was at first called 'Landsmål' (the country tongue) and later 'Ny Norsk' (New Norwegian) was an artificial language compounded of various dialects from Western Norway. Not only was Mr. Koht a great exponent of it, but he had his own particular variant of it. Unlike the other experts he felt that New Norwegian should be made up of dialects from *Eastern* Norway, and he created his own 'country tongue'. This could be most confusing at times, and on one important occasion when, as we shall hear later, the British destroyer *Cossack* penetrated into Norwegian territorial waters, the Norwegians were so outraged at what they held to be a violation of Norway's neutrality that Mr. Koht made a strong condemnatory speech in the Storting or Parliament, which it was my duty to translate. But alas, I could not make out what half the words he used meant. They were not the Norwegian my wife had been brought up to understand. In despair, I rang up some half-dozen editors, including the editor of the leading Oslo daily *Aftenposten*, and to my surprise and relief not one of them could give me a clear explanation.

In 1919, a cartoon had appeared in one of the Norwegian papers showing a Russian *muzhik* in the street of the Norwegian capital watching crowds of people behind barricades throwing furniture at each other. The Russian had approached one of the people at the barricade with an expression of keen interest, and was asking him: 'Well, and how is the Revolution going in Norway?' 'Oh,' answered the Norwegian, 'at present we are fighting about how to spell the word.' The witty Andre Bjerke, who made the Norwegian version of *My Fair Lady*, could not resist making fun of the language reformers. When he came to the passage, 'Why can't the English teach their children how to speak? Norwegians learn Norwegian; the Greeks are taught their Greek,' he translated it this way: '*Danes* learn Norwegian etc.,' adding the footnote: 'Professor Higgins has obviously not been informed that Norway is precisely that country where one does *not* learn one's mother tongue.' He also wrote: 'In Norway we have the paradoxical situation that Professor Higgins is being instructed by Eliza Doolittle on how to write and speak his mother tongue correctly. In this country Eliza Doolittle is not in the gutter selling wild blossoms; she is in the Language Commission handing out language bloomers.' And to make it more difficult for foreigners to understand the Norwegians' foreign policy, their Foreign Minister had to expound it in a special lingo of his own!

The Norwegians were supposed to be neutral. They were in reality very pro-British and anti-German, but they had no wish to be brought into the war. They had made themselves enormously wealthy by keeping neutral during the First World War and were hoping to repeat the performance. Moreover, they were a small people and realized that their survival as a nation could be at stake if they got involved. They watched their neutrality jealously when it was *not* in danger, but, as it happened, failed to guard it effectively when it *was*.

Any suspected infringement, especially when it was at the hands of their *friends*, the British, was regarded as the blackest crime imaginable, and when the episode occurred to which I have referred above and we defied Norwegian laws, sent a destroyer into territorial waters and boarded a German ship – even though it was for the humane purpose of rescuing British prisoners – there was a frightful hullabaloo up and down the country. So incensed were the Norwegians that we were advised it would be better for visiting English lecturers not to appear in certain Norwegian towns, and even my relatives began to look at me askance. Probably they would have taken the matter less tragically if they had realized that later the Germans would violate their neutrality on a much bigger scale and much more effectively.

In the meantime, it was becoming clear to me that being an Assistant Press Attaché in Oslo was not going to satisfy my ambitions. I felt that I had the capacity to undertake something more responsible and better paid, however agreeable it was to be in Norway where my wife's relations lived. It was a joyful occasion for me when I suddenly received a letter out of the blue from the British Council in London, signed by a very prominent academic. The gist was that they needed someone to take charge of all their undertakings in the Balkans and the person they were seeking had to have outstanding qualities. He would have to be very intelligent, endowed with great tact and diplomatic ability, possessed of considerable charm, a most cultured and outstanding representative of his country distinguished by high moral character and proven reliability. The letter went on to say that it might be thought it was impossible to find such qualities together in one person, but that someone had suggested they might be found in *me*! The British Council therefore asked me whether I would like to be considered for the post, and whether it would be possible for me to extract myself from my present occupation if it were offered to me.

I was thrilled with the idea. I at once conferred with the Legation authorities, who agreed with me that the job was just up my street. I then wrote a letter and sent it off to the Council in London hoping against hope that the post would materialize.

But our time in Norway was coming to an end although we did not know it. For those of us who were working in the less important parts of the Legation, British policy *vis-à-vis* Norway remained a sealed book. We were given little information about what was happening. We only saw from time to time that important visitors were mysteriously arriving and leaving, and we were sometimes aware of more intense and protracted periods of cyphering than usual. It came as a complete surprise to George Pollock and myself when the British decided to lay mines within the territorial waters of Norway. Those on the Legation who were in the know had been following the issue for quite a long time. My experience was to wake up on 8th April 1940 and read in the Norwegian press that at 5.30 a.m. that morning the British and French Ministers had informed the Norwegian government that mines had been laid by the Allies in Norwegian waters to prevent their misuse by German ships returning to Germany from their missions on the high seas. I did not know that the British and French Ministers had already on 5th April delivered notes to the Norwegian government warning them that this would happen. My instinctive reaction was: 'What will the German reply be?' And I realized that the Norwegians might be feeling extremely uncomfortable now that their carefully balanced neutrality had been given such a severe knock.

Very soon after the beginning of the war both the Allies and the Germans had begun to turn their attention to Norway. The British were the first to form definite plans. They believed the German war effort could be quickly brought to a halt if they could cut off the supply of iron ore from Scandinavia. The main sources of supply lay in Sweden in the ore-fields at Kiruna and Gallivāre. The ore was taken from there by rail either to the Norwegian port of Narvik or to the port of Luleå in Sweden and other smaller ports in the Gulf of Bothnia. The British thought to begin with that they might be able to persuade the Norwegians to prevent or limit the passage of ships carrying this ore to Germany, but it rapidly became clear that the Norwegian government were reluctant to do this for fear of reprisals from Germany. They were anxious to keep out of the war if they possibly could, and still believed that the observance of strict neutrality was their best safeguard. However, from the British point of view it was a fatal disadvantage that the German ships could make use of the vast stretches of Norwegian territorial waters to carry the iron ore or anything else into German ports unimpeded by the British navy.

The unpalatable truth was that the German ships were justified in making use of Norwegian territorial waters because the 'right of innocent passage' was acknowledged in international law. But on 19th September 1939 Churchill suggested to the War Cabinet that if pressure on the Norwegian government were of no avail, we might consider erecting a 'northern barrage' – in other words a minefield extending from the Orkneys to the Scandinavian coast – as we had done in the First World War. The War Cabinet agreed to the barrage but Churchill wanted to have it completed with a minefield across Norwegian territorial waters as well. Various objections were raised, since the Norwegians would obviously resist the operation, but closer examination convinced the Government that there was no other way to stop German ships getting back to their ports.

It was at this point that the French stepped in. They proposed a more drastic step, the invasion of Norway by an Anglo-French force with the object of occupying the Swedish orefields and thus securing them exclusively for the Allied war effort. The real motive behind the French plans to bring Scandinavia into the war was their desire to restore morale at home by putting an end to the 'phoney war' and keeping the active front further away from France.

The situation was further complicated by the Finnish 'winter war' with the Soviet Union, in which the Finns, in spite of their valiant resistance to Russian aggression and the severe defeats they had inflicted on the Russian armies, would soon have to surrender unless they received help from outside. However, as Russia was now in alliance with Germany and so far a non-belligerent, Britain was most anxious not to get involved in hostilities with her. In order to encourage the Finns and minimize the risk of armed conflict with the Soviet Union, the British government encouraged volunteers from Britain to go and fight on their side. One of these was Harold MacMillan and another was Hubert Howard, who was the son of a former distinguished British Ambassador, Lord Howard of Penrith, and later to be my colleague in Stockholm.

The real difficulty was securing the active co-operation of the Norwegian and Swedish governments. They were, as I have said, frightened to death of any action which might involve them in war. But both the British and the French governments thought that if they could somehow link their plans to cut off iron-ore supplies to Germany with aid to Finland, neither government could easily refuse their co-operation. And so the possibility was discussed of combining the limited plan – the exclusion of German ships from Norwegian territorial waters – with the wider plan, i.e. the occupation of part of Norway and Sweden as a preliminary to bringing armed help to the Finns.

As it turned out, the Allies spent such a long time discussing all the possibilities and were so careless about keeping them secret that the Germans got wind of them; and on 2nd January 1940 the German-inspired press in Norway were already putting it about that the Western powers were trying to extend the war against Germany into Scandinavia, and were using the pretence of helping Finland as a lever to bring Norway and Sweden into the war on their side. Once established in Sweden, they would cut off German ore supplies and build submarine bases on the Norwegian coast. However, Germany, it was stated, would not be caught unprepared.

Indeed, the Germans had in their turn been giving serious consideration to the question, too. In October 1939, Admiral Raeder had proposed to Hitler a German occupation of Norway and the creation of submarine bases on her coasts. Hitler had been doubtful about carrying out this plan in the face of British naval strength and had at first given it no encouragement.

On 6th January 1940, the British and French governments secretly notified the Norwegian and Swedish governments that they proposed to take steps to prevent the use of Norwegian territorial waters by German ships. But the reaction to their announcement, when it came, was far stronger than they had expected. The Norwegian government said that they did not consider that infringements of their neutrality by one belligerent authorized further infringements by another. (A Foreign Office memorandum prepared about two months later admitted that it was doubtful whether German violations of Norwegian territorial waters had been sufficiently numerous, recent and well-authenticated to justify retaliation on our part.) The Norwegian government, so the Norwegian Foreign Ministry said, could not believe that Great Britain would 'drive a small neutral country into a war'. The Swedes said that the consequences of the proposed British action would probably be a German occupation of Denmark and possibly the end of the independent existence of all the Scandinavian states. The Head of the Swedish Foreign Office commented: 'I should have thought that the British government had the fate of a sufficient number of smaller states on their conscience as it is.'

Then an episode occurred which stiffened the resolution of both sides to take action. A German auxiliary naval vessel called the *Altmark*, which was serving as a supply ship to the German cruiser *Graf Spee*, had taken on board about three hundred British seamen from merchant ships sunk by that cruiser. After the British had destroyed *Graf Spee*, the *Altmark* attempted to reach Germany with the prisoners, using the safe passage of Norwegian waters. It provided a good excuse for the British to intervene. It was not crystal clear whether carrying interned seamen could be regarded as 'innocent passage', but humane considerations were involved and on 16th February the British destroyer *H.M.S. Cossack* went into Norwegian waters, sent a party to board the *Altmark* and took off the prisoners. It led to a dispute between the Norwegian and British governments as to the legality of the operation. The Norwegians were outraged by our action because they feared that it would instantly provoke countermeasures from the German side. They were right since it was in fact only after the *Altmark* episode that Hitler finally gave his agreement to the plan for occupying Norway and thus forestalling a British invasion.

Later, both the Norwegian and Swedish governments made it plain that they would not agree to the passage of foreign troops across their territory to help Finland, and the Swedish Foreign Minister even insinuated that we were more interested in using Scandinavia as a battle ground for 'our war' with Germany than in saving Finland.

The British had hoped that Finland would make a public appeal to Britain to send her military assistance, which would put the Scandinavian governments in an embarrassing position, but in the last event she failed to do so because she had been given clearly to understand that we should not be able to produce the strength in men and planes she thought essential. The Finns saw no alternative but to ask the Russians for a cease-fire, and on the morning of 3rd March the British Minister in Helsinki was officially informed that an armistice between Finland and the Soviet Union had been signed.

Despite the ending of the 'Winter War', the British Cabinet decided on the 1st April that plans for intervention in Scandinavia should go ahead. The Allied governments would first warn the Swedes and Norwegians in general terms that they intended to stop the ore traffic to Germany, and then occupy Narvik and advance along the railway to the Swedish frontier. They did not believe that the Germans would retaliate by invading Norway, but should they do so, they expected to be able to land troops in Norway with the consent of the Norwegian government. As a result of this misjudgement, preparations for the landings were made at once. One British brigade of three battalions and a French force with one light anti-aircraft battery were regarded as sufficient for the occupation of Narvik. Five British battalions were assigned to the occupation of southern Norway to prevent German retaliation. No artillery was considered necessary and there was no mention of air support. An expedition to Stavanger (in the south) would be ready to start on 5th April; the other forces would sail as soon as possible after that date.

Meanwhile, on the German side the order to complete preparations for invasion had been given as long ago as 1st March. The

Germans had been planning to begin their invasion on 20th March, but owing to the severe winter were prevented from doing so by ice in the Baltic and Great Belt. The date finally fixed for the opening of the German attack was the fatal 9th April. It was not until 2nd April that Hitler actually settled on this date.

The Allied Ministers at Oslo and Stockholm delivered their notes to the respective governments on 5th April as planned. The Norwegian Foreign Minister protested against their tone and wording. The Swedish Foreign Minister's reaction was: 'This brings our countries very close to war.' He said he would never have expected to receive such a note from two governments which he had always regarded as Sweden's friends. At 5.30 a.m. on 8th April the Ministers delivered another note to the two governments informing them that the mines had been laid.

When I came back to *C.C.15* that afternoon, the evening papers were reporting rumours of a German invasion. A German troopship had allegedly foundered off the Norwegian coast and horses were being washed up. As I went up in the lift, a normally peaceable and friendly fellow-guest nearly tore my eyes out. 'Look what you British have done!' she exclaimed. 'Now you've dragged us into the war.' It was not a pleasant experience and I felt, as one generally does when one is in a situation where one has not been let into the secret, that we had acted wrongly and that Norwegian anger was fully justified.

I cannot remember much about that evening, but as we were going to bed there was suddenly a black-out in our immediate neighbourhood. We sat in darkness and saw from our windows that most of the town was in darkness, too. There were also air-raid sirens and we realized that we might be in for an enemy air raid. Later, the lights came on again. No aeroplanes came over, and we retired to sleep with slightly – but only slightly – easier minds.

At about four o'clock we were woken by a sharp ringing of the telephone. I took the receiver and heard the tense voice of my chief, Rowland Kenney. 'They're closing in on all sides,' he said. 'You'd better come at once to the Legation and help burn the papers.' We did as we were bidden. When we arrived there was a huge bonfire, which had been lit at 2 a.m. and everything was being thrown into it, files, cyphers and all the rest. We had been doing this for some hours and the day had begun to dawn when a Norwegian came along and watched us. 'What on earth do you think you are doing?' he said. 'Are you lighting the way for the Germans to invade our country?' He turned out to be the editor of *Aftenposten*, Norway's leading daily. One can judge from this the sort of mood many of the Norwegians were in after our energetic *démarche* of the early morning. It was not the mood of an ally.

But were they closing in – and who were *they*? We were told that German troops had landed at numerous points and were marching towards Oslo. It was a matter of hours before they would be here. We did not know it then, but at 2.15 a.m. the Norwegian Foreign Minister had telephoned Dormer with the news that four German ships were on their way up the Oslo fjord, five were at Bergen, and one at Stavanger. 'So now we are in the war,' Mr. Koht, the Norwegian Foreign Minister, had commented.

When we had done our job and everything had been incinerated, we hung about wondering what to do next. One of the Secretaries came out and said: 'The King and the government have gone to hammer!' 'To hammer what?' I asked myself. I realized that it was the English pronunciation of the official concerned. They had gone to the Norwegian town of Hamar.

It now became known amongst us that the Minister and his immediate staff were about to set off to follow the King and the government. Those of us who were not of the elect and select continued to stand around waiting for guidance. I can still see the tall figure of Dormer getting into his car with his staff, waving and feebly calling out to us: 'Why haven't you all gone away?' His caravanserai of cars left at 6.50 a.m.

Yes, why hadn't we gone away? But how could we get away, and where were we to get away to? This was the unhappy sequel to a conversation George Pollock and I had had with the Head of Chancery, (Sir) D. Lascelles, a week or two before the invasion. We had both been worried about what would happen to our children if the Germans invaded, and had asked him whether there were any plans for the evacuation of the families of the staff. Lascelles replied that nothing had been worked out, but that it was only reasonable that something should be done and that he would look into it. Before he had had time to do so, the Germans were there. The Legation cars had all been commandeered by our top brass and we had none of our own. At length my wife, with the resourcefulness she displays in times of crisis, managed to lay hands on a taxi. This was practically impossible by that point, as German troops were marching on the town and no taxi driver wanted to venture away from it if he could help it. Standing beside us were Miss Bing, the archivist, and Miss Church, one of the Chancery typists. They asked us if they could share our taxi and we were glad to help them. They confessed that they had aged mothers in the town and asked if they could collect them as well. I groaned as I thought of the jackboots coming nearer and nearer, but we could not refuse. We sped to the flat of each of them in turn and waited what seemed an age as these poor harassed elderly ladies, who had been taken completely by surprise by the turn of events, were persuaded to get up immediately, pack and leave with us. We learnt afterwards that Rowland Kenney, with his typical public spirit and resourcefulness, had secured two cars and taken care of about half a dozen other members of the junior staff.

My wife and I were on tenterhooks, because some weeks earlier our little boy had been rather ill and we had decided to send him into the country with a Norwegian nurse. They were staying at a farm near Jevnaker some two and a half hours away from Oslo. Wherever anyone else might want to go, we had no alternative but to go there and pick him up and we were desperately afraid the Germans might block our route. The ladies had to come with us. So we set out and just managed to get clear of the town before the Germans came in. On the way, we found the Norwegian armed forces were making road blocks by felling trees. Although it was with difficulty that our driver managed to negotiate some of these obstacles, we succeeded nonetheless in getting to the farm, which was our destination. Since it was a *pension* as well, it was no bad choice. The ladies could rest there peacefully, and it looked as if we might be well outside the firing line. What would happen to us afterwards we had no idea, but we were all of us convinced it would not be long before the British came and drove the Germans out again.

The kind proprietress of the *pension* was at some risk in harbouring us and my wife, who could of course pass for a Norwegian subject, set out on foot clad in her ski-ing trousers and boots to find the Fylkesmann (the representative of local government in the region) to report our presence and in this way legalize our position and that of the proprietress. After a long, tiring, dangerous walk, she succeeded in finding him. But she could not get much satisfaction out of him. She returned without having accomplished anything except the formal reporting of our presence. I was extremely glad to have her back again and felt cowardly at not having accompanied her. All the same, no one could have taken her for anything but a

Norwegian and she was a woman, while any man might easily have been taken by the Germans.

During the night we could not sleep a wink. We seemed to have been caught in the crossfire and could hear Norwegian rifle shots to the right of us and German guns to the left. We were fully dressed and ready to rush away at any moment. At one stage the rattle of machine-guns came painfully close and seemed to be encircling us but it was a false alarm. It turned out that the noise came from a neighbouring room. It was one of the elderly guests snoring.

From the elevated position where our farm was situated, we could now see Norwegian troops coming up the very road we had driven along when leaving Oslo. They were retreating, and were being pursued by the advancing Germans. We learnt afterwards that there had been a pitched battle at Klekken, which was not far away, and that the Norwegians had been defeated. Presently we saw the field grey of German uniforms. They were coming up the road not more than two or three hundred yards from our farm. They threw grenades into various farms lying just off the road as they advanced, which immediately went up in flames. It was a terrible moment. We waited for them to come up to us and do the same. But they passed us by. They encamped in the little village at the bottom, making a fire and sleeping in their tanks.

Soon the fighting was over, the Germans seemed to have cleaned up the whole area and we were in the power of an army of occupation. It was not easy for us in the farm. We were the only English people; everyone else was Norwegian. Most of the others had children with them, because the place had been ear-marked as an evacuation place in case of danger. And so quite a lot of the guests consisted of people from the city who had fled in panic at the news of the invasion. Now that the tumult and shouting had died down, they were anxious to get back to their jobs. It was they who had been the busiest colporteurs of horror stories of German atrocities. They had spread the rumour that the Germans were taking women and children and putting them at the head of their advancing columns. One can imagine the effect this had had on the majority of the guests who were themselves women and children. But when the danger seemed to have passed they were the first to become anxious to leave and to assure everybody that everything was all right and that the Germans presented no danger. Actually, they had no need to fear for themselves. It was not quite the same for us or for the lady who kept the *pension*. By this time Quisling and his Nasjonalsamling party were in power and we heard him say over the radio: 'Skutt vil blir enhver som . . .' '– anyone who does the following things will be shot.' One of them was harbouring British subjects.

We felt we should not put our good lady at further risk by staying in her house longer than was absolutely necessary. But what would we do? It was impossible to get any form of transport and in April the snow lies deep in Norway. The roads are almost impassable, let alone the fields. And our farm was right in the middle of the country.

When the danger seemed to be at its greatest, we planned to set off with the two younger ladies and leave Mrs. Bing, Mrs. Church and our little boy behind in the *pension*, since no great harm was likely to befall them, and disappear one evening without trace. We were told that at the top of the hill below which our *pension* was situated, there was a hut and it was suggested that we might take shelter there. It happened that some Norwegians who had skis were planning to go and reconnoitre this hut, and we asked them if they would let us know later when they came back, if it was suitable for us to stay in. On their return, they told us that our plan was out of the question: the hut was a concealed ammunition dump and we should be in even worse danger if the Germans caught us there than at the farm.

Several of the evacuees finally succeeded in organizing transport to take them back to their homes in Oslo. I asked one of them to leave a message with the American Consulate to tell them that we were here and needed help in getting out of the country. With the evacuation of the British and the completion of the German occupation of Norway, the Americans were looking after British interests.

In the meantime, the Germans had moved with their tanks from the village square where they had been encamped and, as none of them appeared to be in the immediate vicinity, we went out and examined the lie of the land. I was amazed when I went into the village shop. Although I had heard a lot about German atrocities and barbarity, I had never imagined that Germans could behave as they did here. The whole shop had been completely looted and plundered, and the troops had urinated in all the corners and often over the goods. It was particularly strange because the Germans had always claimed to be fond of the Norwegians and to regard them as their far-off Nordic cousins. Their attitude to them was entirely different from their attitude to the Slavs, whom they regarded as sub-human. In fact, the German army tried as a rule to leave a good impression on the Norwegians, and there were many German local commanders who won the respect of the people they were occupying. To people who set such a high store on cleanliness and decency as the Norwegians do, it was a disgraceful sight indeed. However, I was to learn afterwards that the looting of shops was not the prerogative of German troops alone. When the British military forces arrived at Aandalsnes, the local mayor had to protest to the O.C. against the looting of the evacuated houses and shops by the British forces billetted in them. In a small Norwegian town where stealing of any kind was almost unknown, the effect of that would have been deplorable, too.

We then got a message from the American Consulate that more transport was being organized and that we should go with it. We should persuade the driver to take us to the American Consulate and then the American authorities would negotiate our departure from the country. I need hardly say how relieved we felt, and when the next day a bus came and we all got into it, we thought that we had extricated ourselves from a dangerous predicament into which we had fallen through no fault of our own. However, we were speaking too soon.

In the first place, we had to pass through the German guards on the outskirts of the city, and we knew that there would be an inspection and that we would have no papers to show. It would be clear that we were foreigners and we should then be arrested and interned. To our great good fortune, when we actually came to the frontier post and German soldiers climbed into the bus, they only inspected the papers of a sample number of people at the front and we, who were all sitting in the back, were passed over. The driver of the bus took us to the front door of the American Consulate and the ladies, my wife and I got out and were taken in and given large glasses of Scotch by the hospitable Consul. It was interesting to see how the old ladies lapped up the whisky.

The American had organized the arrangements most efficiently – too efficiently perhaps. A German naval officer in charge of the evacuation of British subjects, who spoke perfect English, came along and the Consul handed us over to him on the understanding that we would be taken to a hotel and be escorted out of the country the following day.

The naval commander in question was a very strange man. He reminded me at once of a character in a spy film. He had a peculiar way of laughing a lot and suddenly dropping his left eyelid, after which a sort of iron curtain descended over his face. It was what I afterwards called the guillotine look. Just as when seeing a film one is suddenly struck by some unpleasant mannerism in a character, and so quickly suspects him of being the villain of the piece, so I formed at once a sinister impression of this naval officer.

But in many respects he seemed charming. He took us with him in a car to the Bristol Hotel – the finest hotel in Oslo. It had been commandeered by the German army and was full of officers of the High Command. We spent a peaceful night there, full of thanksgiving, and had an enjoyable breakfast next day in the dining-room, marred only by the presence of so many German officers sitting at tables around us. We then went upstairs to pack as we expected to be leaving immediately by train for Sweden.

CHAPTER THIRTEEN ◇ PRISON

◇ While I was sitting on the bed relaxing and lazily discussing how we should pack our things, there was a sudden noise of heavy footfalls and a sharp knock on the door. I said, 'Come in,' and in marched two bayonetted German soldiers commanded by another German naval officer – not the one who had accompanied us to the hotel but a more junior one. He did not look any younger and turned out to be an officer from the German Merchant Navy who had been transferred to the Naval Reserve. Asking me who I was, he curtly ordered me to pack my things and come with him. 'But where am I supposed to be going to?' I asked. 'I'm afraid I cannot tell you,' he answered. 'I can only say that I am going to take you to another place.' 'Another place!' my wife cried. 'But what does that mean?'

I hardly had time to kiss her goodbye before I was torn away, taken downstairs to the street and put into an armoured vehicle. A small crowd had collected outside. When I got into the car I said to one of the men escorting me (the naval officer was not accompanying us) that this was a breach of faith. We had come all the way from the country to the American Consulate and had been handed over to the Germans on the understanding that I should be allowed to go free, and now I was being taken off to prison. The soldier merely commented: 'Why didn't you try to escape while you were in the country?' I answered: 'How could I possibly escape when I had five ladies with me, two of them very elderly?' The German escort dismissed my remark with a wave of his hand. 'You need not have worried about the women. The German army never hurts women.' Meanwhile upstairs in the hotel the lieutenant was trying to comfort my wife. 'Now, now, don't take on, madam,' he was saying in quite passable English. 'These concentration camps are not as bad as what people say. There aren't any shootings, you know.'

Presently the car drove into the courtyard of what I learnt later was the famous Nedre Möllergaten 19, Oslo's main prison. After a perfunctory interview with some prison official in the outer office, I was pushed into a cell in the dark and dank interior and left by myself. I was locked in and given some wishy-washy food through a little hatch in the door. It was extremely cold and the bed was so abominably hard that I had to put the meagre bedding provided underneath me, and use my overcoat as a coverlet. But it was not enough to keep me warm. I hardly slept a wink, not least because my cell 'looked out' over the courtyard – if one can say that a cell 'looks out' over anything – and all night I heard the roaring of cars coming in and going out. It seemed that thousands and thousands of people were being arrested. To add to my discomfort, our own planes began to bomb Oslo and through the high barred window I could see all the colours of the rainbow. My spirits had sunk to their lowest ebb. I was convinced that the R.A.F. would drop a bomb on the prison and I would never get out of it alive.

The next day and for the remaining days I spent in the prison, I was free to walk up and down the corridor until 9 p.m. at night. That was a relief, but from the moment the cell door was locked I was overcome with terrible claustrophobia. It was as much as I could do to prevent myself pounding on the door with my fists and yelling. In the daytime, I met one or two people from other cells who were British personnel and had been picked up by the German army, too. Among them was a retired naval officer and a member of the Consulate staff in the north of Norway. He was called a shipping observer and his business had undoubtedly been to keep watch and report on German naval movements. Another of them was a young and military-looking gentleman who was rather cagey about his movements. There was also a young Jewish businessman travelling in textiles. He had had the misfortune to arrive in Trondheim the evening before the invasion and wake up next morning to find that the Germans had occupied the town. After passing the night in a cell like the Black Hole of Calcutta he was grateful for the improved conditions here with us.

Some of my fellow-prisoners came to chat with me alone in my cell. The military-looking man, who knew that I was on the Legation staff, confided to me that he was really a serving officer of H.M. forces and that if the Germans got to know this he could be shot, as he was not wearing uniform. He had only been married a fortnight when he was called up, and since then he had not seen his wife. The Jew told me with red eyes that it was just his luck to be a Jew. He would have no chance. They would at once send him to Germany and liquidate him. The retired naval officer, who was a good deal older than the others, looked tired and said little. They were pleasant companions but our companionship was flawed. They had small hope at best of escaping internment. I, on the other hand, as a member of the staff of the Legation, was entitled to be set at liberty and sent to a neutral country. But I did not realize then that the German authorities were in a frightful state of panic. The invasion had not gone as smoothly as expected, and was by no means consolidated yet. The *Bismarck*, carrying the German occupation top brass, had been blown up in Oslo Fjord. In such conditions, anything could happen and I could not be at all sure that I would be treated in the way international practice demanded.

We did not have too bad a time in that prison. The gaolers were Norwegian and the night gaoler was a great tonic to us whenever he appeared. He was violently anti-German and used to tell us the most extravagant stories about Allied victories, which turned out to be totally untrue. However, he really believed them. Whenever a German turned up we always knew that we were in for some unpleasantness, but we were left to ourselves most of the time and our Norwegian guards actually offered to let us get food from restaurants outside if we paid for it.

We talked, we read, we played cards, and we did not even have to work, because real prisoners, i.e. professional Norwegian prisoners, cleaned our cells for us! We were also allowed to take exercise outside for a short period each day, which meant walking about in a yard that was only slightly less oppressive than the main prison.

My wife, who was distraught, went at once to the American Consul and complained bitterly at what had happened. We had put ourselves under his protection and he had handed us over to the Germans. The Consul was a kindly and conscientious man and he did his best. She was allowed to come and visit me in prison and she brought our little boy with her. One day the naval officer with the 'guillotine look' telephoned to her in words of almost parental warning. 'When you come to see your husband next time I wouldn't advise you to take your boy with you. It isn't exactly good for him, is it?'

Our confined existence began to make us rather lazy. It was not that we got up late, but we took a long time to get dressed. We hung about in our dressing gowns talking, arguing always about the same thing: my prison mates maintained that the Germans had no right to detain us, and we were entitled to be set free. But would that happen? One day, when we had been discussing this as usual, there was a heavy tramping noise in the corridors. A disagreeable German under-officer appeared and, observing us contemptuously in our deshabillé, snapped out, 'You three, get dressed now, pack your things and come with me at once to the airport. You, Herr Parrott, will remain here for the time being.' We deluged the man with questions. But he was having no nonsense and merely resorted to a series of barks and growls, hustling the unfortunate men he was about to march off. The army officer in mufti tried to argue with him: 'You have no right to take us off to Germany. We were taken prisoner in Norway and not in Germany. Norway was a neutral country. You cannot send us to Germany.' The Jew looked as if his last hour had come. We all helped the old retired naval officer, whose hands were shaking, to cram into his case the clothes he was hastily trying to pack, for the under-officer would brook no delay. He was pushing and stamping around. I had the advantage over the others in being able to speak German and I asked him to show some indulgence to my colleagues. They had had no notice that they had to go off to Germany and had not been given time to prepare themselves. His reply was: 'Look how slowly he's doing it!' The poor old naval officer fumbling with his bag was a pathetic sight. I helped him shut it. I felt in some way ashamed that I was being separated from them and was staying behind. We waved goodbye and they went off almost at the double, the bully shouting at them. The last glimpse I had was of the naval officer's bag with his underclothes bursting out. There is no one so detestable as a boorish German under-officer.

I was left alone in solitary confinement. Life became much duller and I became impatient for my release, since I now had some hopes that this would come about. I had time to think back over the recent events and count my blessings.

Once before the invasion some students had come to me and asked whether I would give their Union a talk on British music. I was not then an experienced lecturer and was doubtful of my ability, but I was fond of music – not especially of British music, it is true – and, thinking that in wartime I should do my bit, I accepted. Soon I began to have second thoughts. Would I really be able to talk about the subject? Did I know anything about it? And however much I read it up, would I not get the composers muddled up, talking about Bax when I meant Delius, or Walton when I meant Vaughan-Williams? I collected various scripts on the subject from the British Council and even succeeded in obtaining a whole talk with records. Armed with this material, I felt sure that I could emerge from the ordeal with success, particularly as it was only a talk to students.

The more I brooded on it the more I feared it would be an appalling fiasco just *because* it was to be given to students. Norwegian students are lively and jolly people, and when I got up to talk ponderously about British music, they might titter and I would be put off my stride and become utterly inarticulate, and the evening would be a ghastly failure. It preyed on my mind each evening as I tried to impress on myself such things as the difference between the various periods of Vaughan-Williams' music. Now, as I sat alone in prison, I had at least one comfort: I should not now have to give the talk.

One day, the naval officer with the 'guillotine look' came and announced that I was free. It was a great joy to be re-united with my wife and little boy. She told me that in our absence the Germans had ransacked our rooms and taken every single thing away. I informed the German naval officer responsible for repatriation and he said he would try and help us find our possessions. We were taken to a building in which there was a huge hall where the belongings of what seemed to be all the Englishmen in Norway, and many Finnish volunteers too, were lying scattered around rather like the preparations for an Oxfam sale. I picked up my dinner jacket but could not find the trousers for it. At length I scrounged another pair which were obviously German – I do not think they could have been Mr. MacMillan's. Afterwards, when I wore this outfit as a diplomat in Stockholm, I used to say that the trousers were Hitler's.

I lost almost all my clothes and some precious souvenirs, including a few irreplaceable gifts given me by King Peter and the Yugoslav Royal Family. But somehow or other, and I cannot explain how, I have managed to retain the rest to this day. Of these a particularly precious memento was some cuff links given me by the Regent, Prince Paul, with his monogram on them. I kept these until 1964 when I took a holiday in Yugoslavia. It was stupid to take them with me, but no one in Yugoslavia today, or so I thought, would have recognized they they were given me by the Yugoslav Prince Regent. However, they disappeared in the course of my stay.

Presently the day came for us to be sent out of the country to Sweden. We had with us nine cases, as I remember it, including my little boy's tricycle and it seemed that a whole German platoon had been organized to carry them for us. Moreover, an escort accompanied us in the train for our protection. It was a curious situation. We were enemy subjects and I had recently been rescued from prison and possible internment. Now we were being treated just as though we were the royalty of a country allied to Germany! From that moment my son conceived an affection for the German military. He always remembered how nice they had been to him and how they had carried his tricycle. When my wife recounted the episode on her return to Sweden, she said: 'We came out with fifteen collies and the German soldiers carried them all for us.' In Norwegian a piece of luggage is a *koli*.

◇ It was good being in a neutral country and especially another Scandinavian one. The rest of our party had been evacuated the very day that I had been sent to prison. They had been horrified to hear of my fate and had imagined the worst. One of them had gone to our Legation in Stockholm and told a heart-rending tale of how I had been taken away. But the Legation showed little concern. When we reached Stockholm it was a relief to find a friend there – Bill Pollock, who was, I have said, the brother of George Pollock, my colleague at the Legation in Oslo. However, my first duty was to go and see the Military Attaché's Department and tell them about my unfortunate companion in prison. The Assistant Military Attaché looked very dubious. 'I doubt if he has much chance of survival,' he said. 'He was a member of the advance party for the planned secret British operation in Norway, which never got off the ground. The Germans will soon find out about this and all will be up with him.'

Later, we learnt that the Norwegian campaign had been a disaster. When it had become clear that British intervention had failed and the attempt to recapture the important port of Trondheim had finally been abandoned, the Norwegian government had been extremely critical of the British. The Prime Minister, Mr. Nygaardsvold, had advised his colleagues that Norway should make peace with Germany on the best terms she could obtain. Although in favour of continuing resistance, the Foreign Minister openly declared that the Allies had let them down. Others alleged that once the Allies had occupied Narvik, got control of the iron-ore situation and obtained possession of the whole Norwegian Merchant Fleet, they were no longer interested in what happened to Norway.

I never knew what happened to my friends from Nedre Møllergaten 19. Most of the British colony who were captured in Norway and transported to Germany for internment were not too badly treated, although they found it very boring. Among them was George Pollock and his wife who were taken off together with their children to a German castle somewhere – but that was a while after these events. They were excellent skiers, and possessing many friends in the country, had been hiding in a hut in the mountains. The Germans were apparently not aware of their existence until they decided to give themselves up. They could not go on living underground any longer. Had they not gone into hiding they would probably have been handled by the man with the 'guillotine look' and evacuated to Sweden. But having remained hidden for so long, they forfeited the treatment to which they were entitled.

It was easy to blame the Germans for putting me in prison and thereby breaching a diplomatic convention. The simple fact is that it was not they but the British authorities who were to blame. I discovered afterwards, and in fact was told by the Germans themselves, that my name was not on the list of the Legation staff. I did not have diplomatic status because at that time only a very few senior officials at our mission enjoyed it and as an Assistant Press Attaché and a 'non-career man' I was a mere dog's body. Had my name at least been reported to the Foreign Ministry, as is the normal practice in missions abroad, the Germans would have quickly identified me and sent me across to Sweden without delay. But by some oversight the Chancery had not reported me, and the Germans jumped to the conclusion that I was a secret agent. It explained their ransacking of our rooms at *C.C.15*. All I can say is that if that is what they believed, they treated me with considerable forbearance.

Dormer, who accompanied the King and the government on their headlong flight from the south to northern Norway where they were evacuated to Britain by the navy, had a difficult and dangerous journey. Accommodation was hard to find, and once having secured shelter he was forced to move on again as a result of the German advance. In the region of Molde the sole accommodation available was a lunatic asylum, but the director, though friendly enough, was nervous about having the British Minister to stay, fearing that he might compromise the Red Cross flag he was prominently flying. When the British government decided to pull their troops out of Norway, they kept their plans secret from the Norwegians and did not even tell the King what they were going to do. But their invitation to him and his government to leave Molde by British cruiser confirmed the suspicions the Norwegians had long been harbouring.

The state of the British troops and the ships which brought them can best be judged from reports sent to the Foreign Office byRowland Kenney. He had succeeded in reaching Aalesund, which the British forces had made into their temporary base, and established himself there. On 27th April, Major Lumley, the Officer Commanding British Troops Aalesund, wrote: 'The only two A.A. guns with which

I have been supplied would not only be an inadequate protection if mounted, but since they have been sent on an unsuitable type of mounting, and are unprovided with any height finder, any means of testing the sights, any trained personnel to man them or even any fuse keys to set the fuses, they are utterly useless and the ammunition a potential menace. There are, moreover, neither range tables, trajectory charts nor memos of examination, so that the M.V. cannot be ascertained.'

One of the ships hurriedly requisitioned a few days before sailing in convoy for Norway was the *Lochnagar*. When approaching the Norwegian coast the convoy had been attacked by enemy bombers for about two hours, and the ship had only just escaped being hit. Her condition may be gathered from the following particulars (from official reports). She had no chronometer, no barometer and no international code book so that she could not communicate with any other vessel. She was not armed – there was not so much as a rifle on board her – and she had no escort on her return voyage. There was no protection against possible splinters: there was not even one tin hat on board. Provisioned for about twenty-five men, she returned with about sixty, including nine wounded soldiers for whom there was no medical care of any kind. Through lack of spars, only two of her six lifeboats could be swung and held outboard, and even on these two there were no water-breakers, with the result that, if the passengers had had to take to the boats, there would have been no fresh water available. The only charts provided for the Master were for waters to the north of Trondheim. He had thus no chart for the Molde–Aalesund coast or for that part of the North Sea which he was to cross. The sole cargo shipped by the *Lochnagar*, which incidentally could have carried between three and four hundred men, was forty tons of petrol. And to carry this insignificant cargo she burnt, out and in, about three hundred and fifty tons of coal!

At least there appeared to have been one Howitzer – a naval gun. However, the young R.N.V.R. sub-lieutenant who had been sent out to operate it was a navigation officer in the Merchant Service and had been called up in the Navy. He had done a six-week course in gunnery, but there had been little time for him to learn much. His first real experience of a gun was when he was shown this particular Howitzer in Liverpool and informed that he was the gunnery officer in charge of it. Soon after, he found himself on his way to Norway. When he pointed out that he was not capable of taking charge he was given a manual on gunnery and told to mug it up. On arrival in Aalesund the Howitzer was taken over, to his great relief, by the military who were going to the front.

Norwegian officers were surprised and bitter about the British lack of artillery and effective equipment. According to the report of a British sergeant wounded in the engagement the British troops were not in any way armed to meet the heavily mechanized German forces. Even the anti-tank rifles they carried had a range of two hundred yards less than the German tank guns and were therefore totally ineffective. In this time of disillusionment, Norwegians were saying that the British troops went into the line with four footballs and fifty thousand cigarettes instead of the guns for which the unfortunate inhabitants of the occupied country had hoped and prayed.

However, there were serious faults on the Norwegian side too. The state of their defences was of course pitiful and security arrangements were neglected to such an extent that Quisling was able to install trained agents in several ports, ready to sabotage all resistance to German entry and oppose British troops. Many of the Norwegian civilian authorities lost their heads and in default of any other instructions either obeyed those sent out on the radio by Quisling or remained powerless and impassive. Some were understandably reluctant to be too closely identified with the British or French.

One of the worst features of the campaign was the succession of optimistic accounts which were being sent out by the B.B.C. At the very beginning of the German invasion, when I was still free and living from hour to hour on the news the B.B.C. dished out to us, I was able not only to feel its effect on myself but to note its effect upon others. The Norwegians immediately disseminated throughout the country everything the B.B.C. said and, as was their wont, tended to embroider the tale in telling it. It was easy to believe such Micawberish reports because none of us in Norway had ever doubted that the British navy would be able to defeat the German navy, and we believed firmly that as a result of their encounter the whole course of the war would be shortened.

It was mainly the French government and Churchill who pushed the British government into taking actions neither they nor the French were equipped to carry out. French feverishness to start a new front was puzzling, considering that they had held up the declaration of war on Germany for several days while making every effort to find a way out. As for Churchill, his brain was teeming with hare-brained ideas which did not take realities into account. The rest of the government were more prudent and sceptical about the possibilities. However, to do Churchill justice, the situation might have developed very differently had he been Prime Minister at the time and been able to override objections and put his plans into effect at once. The continual discussions about whether to take limited action and only mine Norwegian territorial waters, or take wider action and invade Norway and Sweden, cost the Allies precious time and prejudiced the success of either alternative since information about them leaked out and put the Germans on their guard. Above all, the government as a whole failed to take into account the obvious fact that Germany was exceedingly close to Denmark, Norway and Sweden, and was well placed to take forestalling action which Britain would have difficulty in countering, especially if conditions on the high seas were unfavourable.

CHAPTER FOURTEEN ◇ SWEDEN – ANOTHER INVASION?

◇ When we arrived in Sweden in the last week of April the Swedes had not yet recovered from the shock of the German invasion of Norway and Denmark. Indeed, while we were in the train on our way from the Norwegian frontier, the Swedish Foreign Minister, Günther, was telling the Norwegian Minister that he expected any moment to be receiving news that German troops had crossed the Swedish frontier.

On the day of the German action against the other Scandinavian countries, the Germans had sent a note to the Swedes calling upon them to observe strict neutrality and warning them not to take any military action which might be directed against the German occupation, including general mobilization. The Swedes gave the required assurances and Ribbentrop confirmed that Sweden would not be brought into the action, and that Germany wished to maintain the best relations with her.

But the Führer remained distrustful of Swedish intentions and Göring, whose first wife had been a Swede and who liked to pose as the German 'referent' for Sweden, was no doubt tipped off to turn the heat on the Swedes. He sent a message requesting that a group of 'trusted men' should be sent to Berlin at once to attend on him. Among those chosen to go were the Head of the Swedish Navy, Admiral Tamm, who was rather defeatist, and a Swedish friend of Göring's called Dahlerus, a business man who acted as his go-between with the Swedish Foreign Ministry. Fortunately the wiser and more robust Hägglöf, Head of the Commercial Department of the Foreign Ministry and later Swedish Ambassador in London, was also detailed to take part in this 'Hácha trip', as he described it.*

Göring assured the delegation that the Führer had no wish to drag Sweden into the war: the threat to Sweden came rather from the British side. But what would happen if the German troops at Narvik were forced to withdraw and the British pressed forward to

* Hácha, the President of Czechoslovakia after its dismemberment at Munich, was sent for by Hitler on the eve of the German invasion in March 1939 and forced to make a statement renouncing his country's independence.

invade Sweden and occupy the iron-ore fields? Could the Swedes effectively defend their frontier against British attack? If they would give him assurance that they could, he would personally guarantee that no steps would be taken by Germany against Sweden. Admiral Tamm gave the required assurance to Göring and repeated it subsequently to Hitler. Both seemed satisfied.

Göring also complained about the hostile tone of the Swedish press and indicated ominously that Germany might need to use the Swedish railways for transit purposes. Hägglöf explained to Göring that it would be 'unchivalrous' towards a brother people to permit the transit of troops, arms or ammunition to a power fighting against them. The argument seems to have had some effect on Göring, but it was hardly a safe one since once the Norwegians laid down their arms, it would no longer be valid. Any weakening of the principle of strict neutrality might lead them down the slippery slope.

However, these talks seemed reasonably reassuring to the Swedes, particularly when King Gustav received similar assurances from the Führer himself in reply to a personal letter he had addressed to him. Moreover, both the British and Soviet governments made it clear to Sweden that they would like to see her stay neutral.

◇ Arriving in Stockholm, we took rooms in a small *pension* and waited to see what would turn up. I was by now a professional job-loser. I had lost three jobs – the Travel and Industrial Development Association post, that of Press Attaché in Oslo (which never materialized), and now that of Assistant Press Attaché.

I was still hoping I might hear again from the British Council about the 'wonder job', but some time had elapsed since I had replied and there would be some delay before another letter could reach me. I could not wait on the slim chance that I would get it. I had to consider what else I could do. The Minister at Stockholm (Sir) Victor Mallet, sent a telegram to the Ministry of Information, who were my employers at the time, and asked them what they wanted done with me. They told him to send me back to the U.K. via Siberia and Japan! The next day I started making arrangements for the long journey. It was an incredible stroke of luck that on my way home I was going to have the opportunity of seeing Russia, not to speak of Japan. It would be a real enrichment of my mind. But the first thing was to try and get a Soviet visa. I went to the Soviet Consulate in Stockholm, only to be reminded that it was 1st May and that on this and the following day the Soviet authorities provided no services. It may be a tribute to my success in dealing with the Russians that I got the visas out of them by 2nd May.

We were all set to travel home when suddenly I was called in to see the British Press Attaché in Stockholm, (Sir) Peter Tennant. He told me he had an opening in his department and asked me whether I would mind putting off my journey and staying in Stockholm. I listened attentively to his eleventh hour request. He had a magnetic personality and was full of original ideas, and I felt sure that any plans he had would be worth considering carefully. He went on to say that in Sweden the provincial press was of substantial importance, since it consisted of a large number of dailies with large circulations. It was more important than the provincial press in other countries. He had received permission to create a special post of Assistant Press Attaché for the provinces. If I accepted it, my duties would be to go round the various provincial centres in Sweden, talk to the editors of the leading papers and try to win them over to the Allied point of view. My base would be in his department in Stockholm. I should have a car and spend most of my time travelling around.

This showed the priority the British government gave to influencing and possibly manoeuvring Swedish opinion. The idea appealed to me because I had originally come to Scandinavia in the expectation that I would be spending several years there, and my hopes had been dashed by the outbreak of the war. It was tempting too for my wife to remain in Sweden and be near her family in Norway. They were now living under German occupation and would certainly be suffering, and it should be possible for us at least to help them by sending them food parcels. On the other hand, the new job might not be a very active one when seen against the background of the war and the opportunities it offered. And then there was that entrancing prospect of travelling by the trans-Siberian railway across Russia to Japan.

Another factor I had to consider was the German threat to Sweden. What if the Swedes took courage and turned down the German requests for the transit of troops and arms to Norway? If we stayed and the Germans invaded Sweden we might find ourselves caught again, and we had no wish to repeat our alarming experiences in Norway.

It did not take me long to reach a decision. I find small decisions hard to make, but big ones never cause me headaches. All seemed quiet not only to us but to the Swedes as well. 'No jarring sound – A day of rest,' the Swedish Prime Minister wrote in his diary as he prepared his May Day speech. Reassured by this atmosphere I resolved to stay.

But the 'day of rest' was misleading. In no time, Göring had roused himself and summoned Dahlerus to Berlin. Another Swedish delegation was ordered to attend him. On 10th May Tamm, Hägglöf and Dahlerus were on their way to Germany once more. But they were for the moment unable to get further than Malmö. Germany had that day launched her great offensive to the West and communications were cut.

When Göring received them the next day, he addressed them from a position of still greater strength. Reaffirming Hitler's personal interest in the fate of the beleaguered German troops at Narvik, he formulated a definite demand for transit facilities. Sweden should permit the transport by her railways of artillery and ammunition in vans with Red Cross markings or should deliver three batteries of her own across the Norwegian frontier in return for three supplied from Germany. When Tamm conveyed his government's refusal, Göring simulated astonishment and threatened reprisals against Sweden's own arms supplies. Hägglöf argued that it was not compatible with Sweden's neutrality to permit an army, which had landed in Norway, to use her railways for the transit of war material. Göring turned purple, shouted at him and struck the table with his fist. Then after a moment's silence, he called an aide and left the room, leaning on his arm. A little later he returned looking much calmer, having had an injection of morphia in the intervening time, or so the Swedes thought. It was indeed a 'Hácha journey', except that it was the host who needed the injections, not the guests.

On the delegation's return to Stockholm Admiral Tamm gave the government a pessimistic account of the interview. Actually he went further, declaring he felt it his duty as the naval C.-in-C. to state his conclusion that Germany was bound to win the war. Hägglöf was called into the Cabinet afterwards and expressed a more robust view.

By this time, there were so many rumours of German war preparations, and the Swedish Legation in Berlin was calling so insistently for vigilance, that the government in Stockholm was expecting the arrival of German troops any moment. 'Rumour has it that today is fixed for the attack,' wrote the Prime Minister on 14th May.

On 16th May, Ribbentrop sent for the Swedish Minister at Bad Godesberg of all places (the Nazis had a pronounced sense of drama), and 'in all friendship' urged that the Swedish government should reconsider the German request. The German troops at Narvik were not fighting against Norwegian troops but against British and French. The transit of war material to Norway was therefore no unchivalrous action. The interests of Sweden would best be served if the Germans exorcized the threat of a British invasion. He made two specific requests – for war material for the troops at Narvik and for the safe return across Sweden of two thousand German sailors rescued from their wrecked ships. More precisely, 'three trains with thirty to forty sealed vans with war material and clothing'.

Arvid Richert, the Swedish Minister in Berlin, hastened to Stockholm and personally conveyed to his government Ribbentrop's demands. He recommended compliance. It would be an important gesture of good-will to Hitler, whereas a negative reply might mean 'extreme consequences'. In spite of Richert's choice of phrase – 'extreme consequences' sounded like 'extreme unction' – the government decided to accept the passage of the shipwrecked sailors but not to allow the transit of war material. Complying with the latter request might lead to Sweden being dragged into the war on the German side.

It was probably Sweden's greatest crisis of the war and it is a tribute to her democratic system that a question of such gravity was discussed in the Foreign Affairs Committee with all the risks of leaks which this exposed them to.

When the Committee met it supported the government's view. Günther's predecessor as Foreign Minister, Sandler, and his successor, Undén, were against the concession to the shipwrecked sailors, but the rest of the Committee advised acceptance of this at least. General Thörnell, the Commander-in-Chief of the Army, recommended accepting the German demands *in toto* on the ground that a German attack, if it materialized, would come at the very worst moment for Sweden's defences. It would be a long while before Sweden would be ready to defend herself in a war and she depended on Germany for her supplies. Germany was already holding her to ransom by cutting them off. But it was the government's view that, after having given a personal assurance in writing to the King of Sweden, Hitler would hardly be likely to take action without warning. There was still time to play with.

In conveying the Swedish decision to Ribbentrop, Richert stressed that Sweden's main reason for it was her obligation to a brother people. The requirements of neutrality took second place. He even went beyond his instructions in hinting that after the end of the fighting Sweden might permit the German Narvik troops to return home via Sweden. For this he was rightly rebuked by Günther. To volunteer this permission to breach Sweden's neutrality in advance was dangerous. Richert was the victim of his own misjudgement of the situation. His worst fears were never realized: Hitler was content for the time being to leave Sweden in peace. But later he would present the cheque which Richert had obligingly signed for him.

◇ Meanwhile, I was getting on with my job as Assistant Press Attaché for the Swedish provincial press. I started off by making a survey of the provincial papers and preparing to pay visits to their editors. I had cancelled all my arrangements for returning home. But only a few weeks after I had taken the job, something happened which radically altered its nature. An employee at the German Legation was arrested by the Swedes, tried and sentenced to five years imprisonment for espionage in the provinces. On examining the British Legation's request for permission from the Swedish government to establish my post, the Swedish authorities said that they well understood that I should not be indulging in illegal intelligence activities, but it would nonetheless place them in a difficult position *vis-à-vis* the Germans if so shortly after this episode they were asked to sanction the appointment of a British Press Attaché for the provinces. Tennant and the Legation had reluctantly to acquiesce in the Swedish request and drop the plan for the time being.

However, from our own point of view I had been appointed to the post. My salary had been fixed and was being paid, and it was necessary for me to do something to justify my keep. When I consulted Tennant, he suggested that I should carry on with the job 'internally', that is to say give up the idea of travelling around and do it in Stockholm. This was a great blow since the main interest and attraction of it had been the car and the prospect of travelling all over Sweden.

But it was wartime and there was nothing to do but buckle down and see if I could influence the provincial press by remote control, as it were: 'Maul halten und weiter dienen', as the Good Soldier Švejk would have said. The first thing I thought I would do was to send the editors a whole lot of material about Britain in the hope that a few of them would publish it. Unluckily, it was a bad time for such activities because, since the occupation of Norway and Denmark in April, contact between Great Britain and Sweden had been almost completely severed and extremely little publicity material in the shape of articles and so on was arriving. Somewhere dumped in the vaults of the Press Department I found a whole lot of outdated stuff which had been despatched long before these historic events took place and was unlikely to be of much use now. Even so, I fished out some articles that seemed to retain some sort of relevance, such as 'How the House of Commons faces up to War', and the like, and sent them off to about a hundred editors of Swedish provincial papers with the polite request that they might consider publishing them in their columns. I added that no payment would be necessary. I then sent copies of the articles to a press cutting agency and waited for results. My efforts were regarded by the other members of the Press Department with complete scepticism. I was clearly a lunatic. To the surprise of everyone, myself most of all, the press cuttings that came in showed that more papers had published the articles than had received them. It was because some papers in the provinces – those which appeared at irregular intervals – waited to see what others published and then shamelessly pirated material from them. Piracy is a good thing in war! I was thus encouraged to go on with my odd pastime. It appeared to be paying off.

Nonetheless, the gilt had been taken off the ginger-bread and however successful I might have been at the job I kept on telling myself that I could really do something better and that it was no fun being an Assistant Press Attaché for the provinces without any provinces or a car to get to them. My thoughts turned back to the British Council job dangled before my eyes in Oslo, and I asked the Head of Chancery if he would make enquiries and find out whether it had been filled. A reply came in time saying that it had not, and asking for a confidential report from the Minister on my capabilities. I was shown the Minister's telegram and felt unjustifiably proud when I read the opening words, 'Parrott is able'. It was very different from what I later learnt (from Foreign Office documents) to be the opinion of Sir Ronald Campbell, the former British Minister in Belgrade, when the possibility arose of sending me to Yugoslavia to advise King Peter (see page 108). 'What is wanted is a man of the world with wide outlook and plenty of authority. Parrott has neither of these qualifications.' I noted for the future how an Ambassador's judgement, albeit based on the flimsiest of knowledge, could make or mar a man. (We all had reason to fear Foreign Office personnel files to which we had no access.) For the moment, therefore, I was encouraged by the thought that I was still in the running for a job which I would have enjoyed a great deal more than my present one, and where my particular abilities would have been used to my greater satisfaction. My hopes were soon dashed again, because in October 1940 German troops marched into Romania and the situation in the Balkans began to look most uncertain. It was just as well that negotiations went no further, for the following six months saw the over-running of Yugoslavia by the Germans.

◇ Everything seemed to be quiet in Sweden once more. The calm was not to last for long. The Allies had evacuated Norway and the Norwegian forces had surrendered. Hitler now wanted to fortify the Norwegian coast and construct naval bases there. On 16th June Ribbentrop asked Richert to see him again. This time the *scenario* was a château in Belgium. He told the Swedish Minister that the situation had changed: war in Norway or against the Norwegians had ended and the grounds on which the Swedes had based their refusal to permit the transit of troops and war material were no longer valid. In these circumstances, the German government took it for granted that there would be no further difficulties over the transport through Sweden of food, war material and troops, especially those going home on leave. A refusal would be regarded by the Führer as an unfriendly act. Co-operation would wipe out the unfavourable effects of the earlier refusal and restore good relations. He held out to the Minister the promise of important economic advantages for both countries, if all went well. Richert was shaken and telegraphed to his government that a refusal would lead to the most far-reaching, perhaps even *catastrophic* consequences for Sweden, and would actually in his opinion be a *political impossibility*. He came to Stockholm and repeated his view at a meeting of the Cabinet. No one suggested a negative reply, but many thought it imperative that parliament should meet and discuss the question first.

At this juncture, a telegram arrived from Prytz, the Swedish Minister in London, reporting certain remarks by Halifax and Butler which he had construed as indicating Britain's readiness to seek a compromise peace, an interpretation later stated to be incorrect by the Foreign Office. But Günther's reference to the telegram – he read it out to the Foreign Affairs Committee – had its effect on those present, the effect indeed that he wanted to produce. Hostilities were over in Norway, he said. The British had left and the military situation had developed very much in Germany's favour. Sweden could not oppose German demands.

Again, Undén and Sandler opposed Günther, while the majority came out on his side. Günther informed the German Minister that Richert would the next day hand in a favourable reply in Berlin. In his diary entry for that date the Swedish Prime Minister wrote: 'And that was how our cherished and strictly observed policy of neutrality collapsed when confronted with the impossibility of accepting the risk of a war in the existing situation.' So much for small power neutrality in the face of great power pressure.

It was 18th June. German troops had entered Paris a few days earlier and Mussolini was already in the war on the German side. Even if Hitler did not intend to make war on Sweden, he would without question cripple her economically if she opposed him. What is more, new storm clouds were blowing up. Soviet troops were moving into the Baltic states. It could be a prelude to the break-up of the Molotov-Ribbentrop Pact and to war in the East. Sweden must at all costs avoid complications with any of the major belligerents.

The negotiations with the Germans were hard going. At first they wanted unrestricted use of the Swedish railways; but the Swedes succeeded in imposing limitations. The leave transports had to be shuttle services which did not increase the numbers of troops in Norway. However, the Germans kept on raising their bids until they succeeded in squeezing out of the Swedes one train daily between Kornsjö and Trelleborg with five hundred men instead of the original two a week. From Narvik to Trelleborg there would be one train a day in each direction, again to a presumed total of five hundred men. Other concessions were also made without anything being put in writing like the so-called 'horseshoe' transport between Storlien and Riksgränsen which carried troops on active service over Swedish territory from one part of Norway to another, not men returning to Germany on leave.

The British government reacted very unfavourably to the news of Sweden's latest concessions. The British Minister, Mallet, had orders from Halifax to 'check the Swedes in their downward career towards complete subservience to Germany'. But he judged the position more fairly than his masters in London. There was no question of 'complete subservience'. 'It is rather surprising that there has not been a more rapid and complete *volte-face* in favour of a pro-German policy,' he telegraphed back. To a similar complaint from the Norwegians, the Swedes replied that the concessions scarcely affected Norway's position in the war. On the general question of violation of their own rules of neutrality, they pointed out with reason that a neutral policy pursued by a neutral country must always be circumscribed by the possibilities open to it.

Since the Germans insisted that the troop transports must start while the negotiations were still going on, and the negotiations had to be kept secret, the Swedish public formed an exaggerated idea of the extent of the concessions and accused the government of misleading them. A hard-line lobby, backing the views of Sandler and Undén, grew up among journalists and intellectuals which was to cause the Swedish government some trouble.

CHAPTER FIFTEEN ✧ CLOAK AND DAGGER SPURNED

✧ In the meantime, a change connected with these developments in Europe occurred in my life. I have already mentioned that communications between Britain and the Continent had been badly impaired as a result of the German victories. A consequence was that the various departments in Whitehall, which were dependent upon the reading of the press and particularly of newspapers published in Germany and the German-occupied territories, were deprived of their source material. An urgent appeal came to the Legation from the Political Intelligence Department of the Foreign Office to buy all possible papers and journals published in countries overrun by Hitler and send them to London *via Vladivostok*! I saw the telegram and realized that it would take at least two months for any newspaper posted from Stockholm to reach England by this route. Even that did not take into account the inevitable time lag in obtaining newspapers from the countries where they were published. Then an obvious idea struck me. I minuted a telegram as follows and sent it back to the Head of Chancery: 'In wartime Departments in Whitehall will not be able to wait over two months for press information about the enemy and enemy-occupied countries. The best thing would be to set up a small branch office of the Political Intelligence Department in Stockholm, have some of the main papers read here and telegraph the more important extracts the same day as the papers are received and read. In this way our political intelligence will be more up to date.'

The staff of the Legation, although greatly swollen, was not large enough to cope with the voluminous material which passed through its hands. The Chancery often acted as a kind of Post Sorting Office and my minute got sent *tel quel* to the Foreign Office with the Minister's compliments or at any rate with the briefest of covering notes. I think I just knew that my suggestion had been put forward to London, but I gave it no further thought.

Very soon afterwards, I was told that (Sir) Charles Hambro was in Stockholm and wanted to see me. The name Hambro interested me as it was a Norwegian Jewish name. Karl Hambro had been President of the Norwegian Parliament; Hambro's Bank seemed to span Britain and Scandinavia. There were Norwegian Hambros and British Hambros, and one of the most influential of the British branch was Charles Hambro himself. After the outbreak of war, Dalton had appointed him head of the Scandinavian section of S.O.E. At the same time he was one of our principal trade negotiators with Sweden, since S.O.E. came under the Ministry of Economic Warfare. Bankers played a great part in Anglo-Swedish relations – Hambros on our side, and Wallenbergs on the other. Dalton said of Charles Hambro that he kept more 'balls in the air' than any man he knew, combining his S.O.E. assignment with his own banking business, the Court of the Bank of England and chairmanship of the Great Western Railway.

He proved to be an engaging character with a hail-fellow-well-met personality. There appeared to be nothing Norwegian about him and I do not think he even spoke the language. He made it plain to me that London had been extremely interested in my suggestion and would like to follow it up. He said that reports on these newspapers were urgently required by P.I.D. (the Political Intelligence Department of the Foreign Office) which I later learned was also used sometimes as a cover name for S.O.I. afterwards to be renamed P.W.E. (the Political War Executive), a department controlling propaganda against the enemy powers, and a Mr. Barman in particular – Thomas Barman, one day to be diplomatic correspondent of the B.B.C.

The real P.I.D. was staffed by a number of dons and other experts who did the straight work of issuing a bulletin of political intelligence for the Foreign Office. At one time, as it happened, they were housed at Woburn Abbey under the same roof as S.O.I., who were anything but 'straight' and from their hawkish position regarded them as fuddy-duddies. In fact, during the war P.I.D. started picking up the whispering campaigns which were being disseminated in Europe by S.O.I. next door, and reporting them in their bulletin.

S.O.2, afterwards to be called S.O.E., had been hastily put together under Hugh Dalton's direction and its staff was recruited on the 'old school tie' basis. Hambro had brought in one of his fellow directors, Harry Sporborg, and Sporborg in his turn had brought in most of the staff of his late firm of solicitors, Slaughter and May. The organization was flooded by representatives of big business and its ancillaries. I knew nothing of all this of course when I met Hambro.

Hambro said he would like on behalf of P.I.D. (sic) to authorize me to set up the kind of branch office I had suggested, and asked me to let him know how many staff I required and what the cost would be. I promised to work it out. But at this point he lowered his voice and hinted to me that there were some people in London who would be interested in such a bureau as a cover for other activities. It was very necessary to have a directing base for intelligence and other operations in Norway and Denmark. He invited me to consider whether I would like to take on this job, too, since I was well equipped in Scandinavian languages. The idea was that I would ostensibly be reporting on the newspapers and sending open telegrams about them to London but that beneath this cover there would be a secret and more important activity which I would be directing. He then went on to say that he would be returning home shortly and would like to have an answer from me before he left. If I would take on the assignment, he would put me in touch with a contact from Denmark whom I could recognize *because he had a missing third finger on his left hand.*

I admit that I was not prepared for this kind of development, although I should have foreseen such implications in my proposal and realized that things could develop quickly and unexpectedly. I felt fairly confident that I could implement the plan as I had outlined it. But I had grave doubts about the feasibility or desirability of my engaging in anything else besides or beneath, and I saw the undercover activity as a dangerous threat to it. The Swedes would swiftly discover that something was going on and close the office down, and then we should be without important sources of press information on which we were dependent. Moreover, I did not feel attracted to 'cloak and dagger'.

He probably saw that I was not enthusiastic, but I temporized and said I would let him have an answer when I had thought it over. The first thing I did was to consult Tennant, to whom I unbosomed myself in strictest secrecy. To my relief he agreed with me entirely and advised me to keep out of it. He promised to speak to Hambro himself and explain my feelings. Later I saw Hambro briefly, apologized to him for not being prepared to do what he was suggesting, and urged him not to let this prejudice the development of my original scheme which was a deserving one in its own right. From that time onwards I heard no more of such clandestine activities, although I was perfectly well aware that they were going on and who was carrying them out, but the main thing was that they were not to be done from my office.

I say 'my office' because from the day of Hambro's visit the situation changed rapidly. After I had sent to London the estimates for my Press Reading Bureau I soon received sanction to engage staff and start sending the press extracts by telegram in the way I had suggested. There was no room left in the badly cramped Legation. Even to accommodate me as Assistant Press Attaché for the provincial press they had had to knock the seat out of a small lavatory and make it into a workroom for me. Now I had to leave the premises and go elsewhere. The Minister gave up a room in his residence at Laboratoriegatan for my embryo outfit and we started there under pretty cramped conditions. At first I read the Swedish, Norwegian and Danish newspapers myself and telegraphed extracts to London, but in time I recruited special readers for this purpose, including a very competent and impressive British businessman from Copenhagen, Mr. Grew, who read the Danish press.

I was relieved not to have been forced to accept Hambro's offer and I blessed the name of Thomas Barman. For a moment I had feared that the powers that be in London had been interested in my plan solely for the cover it might offer them for their other activities. I had, as I thought, cogent reasons for not doing what Mr. Hambro asked. One was that I was quite sure that if I did I would soon be tailed by the Swedish police and be sent packing. And how right I was, for those who took the job on were successively 'blown' and had to leave the country in a hurry. Another reason was that it seemed absurd for me to have to restrict my activities as Assistant Press Attaché for the Swedish provincial press to Stockholm because the Swedes might accuse me of spying when I was innocent of doing so, and then take a job where I would be guilty of it – even if the activities would not be directed against them (or so I presumed).

However well- or ill-advised I was to think and act in this way – and I could not by my nature do anything else – it definitely paid off since I was able to arrange things as I wanted and in the end develop my organization to such an extent that it involved over sixty people. At no point would I agree that it should be used for any other purpose than the one which we declared to the Swedes that it was instituted for. It was abundantly clear that the Swedish police would have closed it down if at any time I had given them the slighest excuse for it. But they never did. In fact it was wound up in the normal course of events after the war was over and after I had left it.

The fate of the young man who took on the assignment our kindly authorities had prepared for me was less happy. He soon began to attract the attentions of the police and reports came streaming in to the Foreign Ministry about his activities. When in the end he allegedly started meeting his Swedish informants in the public lavatories under Norrmalmstorg – a square in the centre of Stockholm – and many of them were arrested, Erik Boheman, the Permanent Under-Secretary of the Foreign Ministry, summoned the British Minister and asked him to send his unruly attaché home. 'I told him,' he wrote afterwards in his memoirs, 'that if the British wanted to have more information about what we were doing about Germany, it would be much better if he confined himself to asking me. I had no intention of hiding anything from him and he would get much more reliable information by doing so. It was only natural that the British should want to know what the Germans were doing and in any case it was difficult if not impossible to prevent them finding out. But couldn't they engage rather cleverer agents so that a number of Swedes, who were mostly inspired by quite creditable motives, didn't get caught?' Mallet, understandably embarrassed, had to promise that his staff would mend their ways and that the offending attaché would be sent home. But the young man concerned remained undismayed. For a time he planned to defeat the Swedish demands by exchanging his identity with a young Czech, who was to fly over to England. The Swedish police would think that they had safely got rid of 'the spy' while he would still remain there as a 'Czech'!

Alas, Mallet had to blush vicariously and take the blame for many things he probably knew nothing about, because war was war and various departments in Whitehall, secret or open, were to cut across the otherwise strict dividing lines of command in the Legation and send their orders direct to their emissaries, whom they had perhaps smuggled in under some innocuous and totally irrelevant title. In May 1942, as we shall see, Boheman was forced to present Mallet with a list of 'sins' committed by the Legation.

◇ It was evident that an organization like my Press Reading Bureau was going to grow and could not be contained for long within one room of the Minister's Residence. The countries with which it was concerned were increasing in number all the time. As Hitler scored successive victories, more and more countries became enemy-occupied. It was a painful paradox that the more victories

Hitler scored, the greater success we had, too. That was why it was agreed by all concerned that I must find yet other premises.

It was not easy at that time to get hold of any accommodation at all since Stockholm had become an important observation point as the capital of a neutral country poised between the two sides, and every foreign mission was increasing its staff fourfold, if not more. There were also quite a lot of other new institutions like the Norwegian and Danish Refugee Offices, and the Swedish government had to increase the number of its own offices as well. Eventually I was offered a flat belonging to Mr. Wollebaek, the former Norwegian Minister, which would soon become empty because he had recently died. It was on the second floor of a building in Strandvägen, in a very fine part of Stockholm and only about two hundred yards from our Legation. Above us the Norwegians had retained one floor for their Press Office, which was combined with the Norwegian Telegram Bureau – the Norwegian Government's Press Agency – directed by Jens Schive, whom I had known from Oslo and with whom I had much to do. (He was afterwards to become Norwegian Ambassador in Stockholm.) An unknown private person lived on the ground floor. We had to have some alterations made, but the flat was a spacious one and provided enough room for us all in spite of our prodigious growth for the next four years.

There were advantages in being in close contact with the Norwegians, as they were obviously the best informed of our allies in all matters affecting Scandinavia. As it turned out, the main advantage of this contact lay on the Norwegian side because the Swedish government had to exercise strict control over the activities of the Norwegians to see that they did not use Swedish territory for anti-German activities. They were the free representatives of a brother country, which had been temporarily occupied by the Germans, and their activities were of course 100 per cent anti-German. But the Swedes for their part had to continue to maintain correct relations with Germany and try to keep Norwegian activities as far as possible within the bounds of the law. Schive sent telegrams to England at least once a day containing information which he called 'press information' but which often contained interpretations of the press that bordered on political intelligence. For some reason or other Swedish regulations forbade Schive to telegraph in English. He could only do so in Swedish or Norwegian. As the cheaper press rates applied solely to telegrams sent in the major languages, an arrangement was concluded between Schive and myself by which I signed all his press telegrams. And so technically they originated from the British Legation. This was within the law and saved the Norwegians a great deal of money. I had such confidence in Schive that I only looked through the telegrams very cursorily before they were despatched, and throughout the whole of the war I can remember only one occasion when I asked him to moderate something he had written in case it involved me in trouble with the Swedish authorities. But the Swedish authorities themselves looked with great tolerance on these telegrams and never took action against them.

By this time we had arranged to get a considerable number of newspapers and periodicals from Germany and the German-occupied countries, including France, Holland, Belgium, Luxembourg, Romania, Poland, the Protectorate of Bohemia and Moravia, Slovakia, Hungary, Serbia and Croatia. At first I had ordered the papers in my own name and had them addressed to the Minister's Residence, but when we moved to our new building I thought it would be safer to order them under an assumed name since otherwise the concentration of papers might arouse the suspicion of the Nazis. I had to decide in haste what Swedish name we should adopt and so at random I chose Stig Bergström – as good a Swedish name as one could think up. As the name change coincided with our change of address we watched anxiously after our move in case our newspapers failed to arrive. They were precious raw material without which we could not exist. To my horror it seemed that the papers were not coming, even allowing for the inevitable administrative delay. Had the Germans realized what we were doing and made arrangements to withold them? Knowing the inefficiency of the Nazis I doubted whether this was the case. There must have been some other reason. Perhaps the Swedish newsagents, through whom we placed the orders, had got cold feet? We checked up and found that there had been no change in the orders placed. And then one day we discovered a huge mass of papers outside the door of the tenant of a flat on the ground floor. It is scarcely believable, but this man was actually called Stig Bergström. It could have led to complications, but we were able to come to a friendly arrangement with Mr. Bergström and the postman, and after that our papers were all brought upstairs. I do not think Mr. Bergström suffered, and for us it was a most convenient coincidence.

Even so, I think the Swedish authorities did in fact begin to be suspicious of our activities, and from this time on I noticed that I received visits from several people of rather dubious type, some of whom, though by no means all, I connected with Swedish counter-intelligence. One of them was a devastatingly pretty young Norwegian girl in a very fetching fur cap and fur trimmed coat, who begged me to help prevent her being deported from Sweden. She sat and wept in my office and tried every possible blandishment on me. However, she was not aware of the fact that shortly before her arrival I had been tipped off by our own Legation and told that she was a dangerous German spy – which enabled me to 'handle' her with complete calm and detachment. The official who sent the warning added: 'In other times one might have had good fun with her, but war is war.' Another visitor was an enthusiastic Swedish sailor (a bit too enthusiastic, I thought) who tried to interest me in plans to blow up the Swedish iron-ore traffic to Germany. This was a pretty 'corny' plant, because it was well known that the Swedish iron-ore exports, which went by ship to Germany, were vital to the German war economy and the British were bound to do anything they legally (or illegally) could to try and interrupt them. There was in fact a sabotage case in Stockholm later, in which members of the British colony including leading British businessmen were sentenced to several years' imprisonment for plotting to blow up the harbour installations at Oxelösund. Unfortunately, when the police got on to their tracks, one of the agents involved had, according to the Swedish authorities, panicked, taken a taxi and dumped the explosives at the British Legation where the Chancery guard had in all innocence taken them in for a night. Their provenance was in any case highly questionable and the Legation were severely rapped by the Swedes. The case was one of the list of 'sins' presented to Victor Mallet. One of the members of the British colony implicated in the affair was the very same advertising expert who had asked me to give a talk in Stockholm and who had induced in me such a depressing realization of my inadequacy for the Travel Association post. I now saw why the Swedish authorities had been so suspicious of me when I arrived in Gothenburg! I wonder how many respectable business men are working for intelligence agencies! I was able to deal with all such diversions quite easily, but visits of this kind were disconcerting as however cautious you were, you could not deny the fact that someone had been to talk to you about an illegal matter. Out of the episode there might arise at best a host of misunderstandings.

I was also concerned to observe, when looking out of my window, that there was activity on the piece of rocky grass on the other side of the street opposite the Bureau. It seemed to me as if people were standing about with no special purpose reading newspapers, and watching our offices. After my experiences with detectives in Yugoslavia I had reason to suspect people with newspapers in their hands. Soon afterwards I engaged a young Swede to come and be our 'Swedish reader'. This meant that he read all the Swedish papers and extracted from them anything which conveyed information about Germany and the occupied countries. I noticed that from then on the rocky grass on the other side became uninhabited. Perhaps the Swedes had now got someone inside the Bureau and did not need outside watchers? No offence to our new recruit. He did his work admirably and was in an excellent position, if need be, to assure his countrymen of our innocence.

I must re-affirm that, in spite of all temptations to do otherwise, the Swedish police never interfered with our activities, as indeed they had no just cause to do since everything we did was open and above board. The situation was somewhat different at the main Legation, where of course activities which the Swedish authorities did not particularly like were bound to go on. I can remember how on one occasion the same kind of police surveillance was being carried out there and several plain clothes men were standing about behind the trees on the other side of the road. It caused a stir in the Legation and various members of the Press Department, including Tennant himself, went out and solemnly photographed these sleuths as they endeavoured without much success to make their presence less conspicuous. Like the Yugoslav general at the Court, they tried to make themselves more and more invisible behind the trees. As our Legation personnel became bolder and advanced to take close-up photographs of the intruders, a member of the police finally rushed out and kicked one person's camera from his hands. Some heated exchanges between the Legation and the Swedish Ministry of Foreign Affairs followed. If it appears to have been a foolish act on the part of the Swedish police it must be remembered that they were under considerable pressure from the authorities as a result of German threats and sometimes their nerves seemed to give way.

It was generally thought on our side that the Swedish police were more vigilant against Western activities then they were against the Nazis. They even gave the impression of favouring the use of Nazi methods themselves. Norwegian refugees suspected of carrying on intelligence or sabotage activities, whose guilt had not been proved, complained bitterly at their treatment by the police and the question was the subject of angry diplomatic interplay between the Norwegian and Swedish governments.

Countess Amelie Posse, the Swedish-born wife of a Czech artist, and herself a tireless campaigner against Nazi influences in Sweden, cited many cases of apparent Nazi sympathies on the part of the Swedish authorities. Her son, a young Czech refugee in Sweden, made it his business to do freelance investigations and ferret out Nazi organizations. He was clever enough to break into a Swedish Nazi centre and seize a hoard of Nazi material providing a complete list of all Swedes in official positions whom the Germans considered reliable as a 'fifth column'. Although his mother took this information straight to the top, the authorities were in no hurry to process the material or take steps to neutralize the activities of these alleged Nazi sympathizers. Her son ended by being 'punished' by those he was trailing. He himself was shadowed and then assaulted – probably by a German – so violently that most of his ribs were broken. Countess Posse maintained that the police were afraid of proceeding against Nazis in case they made an outcry. The Germans would then accuse the Swedes of victimizing those of their fellow-countrymen who were friendly to Germany and have a pretext for intervening.

Be that as it may, it was very difficult for the Swedish police to know where to draw the line. They received their instructions from the government, who no doubt tempered police activities to the exigencies of the political situation. And there were certain periods when the Swedes thought they had reason to fear that if the Germans were thwarted, Sweden's precarious neutrality would be at an end.

One day the British Naval Attaché found a strange piece of wire in his sitting-room. When he followed it to its origin, he stumbled upon a police agent sitting in the attic and listening in to his conversations on headphones. Also he observed that his visitors were being photographed from the house opposite.

But during the war every country did the same. Boheman relates that when he was in London he had an off-the-record conversation with the Permanent Secretary of the Ministry of Economic Warfare, Sir Frederic Leith Ross, and Charles Hambro in the Permanent Secretary's room, where a screen had been placed to conceal the wash basin. He observed a movement behind the screen and suddenly pulled it down, only to expose a shorthand typist with a stenographic pad.

While visiting Moscow with a Swedish trade delegation, Boheman lost his way on returning to the room in the Hotel National that had been placed at the disposal of his delegation. Opening the wrong door he came on several Russians sitting round a loud-speaker out of which could be heard coming some racy anecdotes in Swedish, punctured by loud guffaws. He immediately shepherded his delegation out on to the Moscow streets to overcome the problem.

Sweden was undoubtedly an interesting country to be living in. You could be sitting in a restaurant and find members of the German Legation sitting cheek by jowl with you at the next table, so close indeed that you could almost hear what they were saying. The Swedish government had normal diplomatic relations with both sides, as it was neutral, but whenever there were diplomatic functions they were divided in two – that is, into functions for the Western powers and functions for the Nazis and their satellites. Although Mallet had to try and bring pressure to bear on the Swedes to prevent them giving in to the Germans all along the line, relations between our two countries developed satisfactorily. A contributory cause was the tremendous veneration in which the Minister held the Swedish authorities. When he returned from a visit to the Swedish Foreign Office and reported on what the Head of the Foreign Ministry (called the 'U.D.') had told him, it was as though he had come back from Mount Olympus and was recording what the gods had passed on to him. Mallet was in some ways the 'Cup-bearer of the Gods'. The Swedes like such veneration from foreign diplomats and responded favourably. As for myself, living out on a limb in a separate building, I was not always in touch with the main diplomatic problems troubling our governments. However, I would soon feel it if relations became unfriendly.

CHAPTER SIXTEEN ✧ HITLER ATTACKS RUSSIA

✧ I must briefly explain how our Press Reading Bureau was organized. Every occupied country, as well as Germany itself, was assigned one reader for the political reporting and one for the economic. These readers, who were often nationals of the country they were studying, except in the case of Germany of course, prepared telegrams containing lengthy direct quotes from leading articles, statements by leading Quisling politicians and local Nazis, etc. Direct quotes were necessary because the B.B.C. or our 'black propaganda' (i.e. so called 'underground radio stations', clandestine newspapers and so on) took them up immediately and quoted them back to the countries concerned with an appropriate commentary on what was being said. Every country had its own pet Quisling, and each of them was given special treatment. Seldom has so much idiotic and treasonable nonsense been sent by wire. If we turned up any specially revealing facts of a political, economic or military nature, we generally sent them by the diplomatic bag or cypher telegram as we did not want to make the German censorship aware that these heavily censored papers could at times publish things which could be of interest to us.

Some of the press items we detected were of outstanding value. We received congratulations in two cases at least. One was a reference to General Field-Marshal Witzleben, one of the high-ranking officers involved in the plot against Hitler's life. The other was a revealing interview by Henlein published in the Sudeten-German paper *Die Zeit* in which he admitted having duped everyone by pretending not to be a Nazi, while all the time preparing for the German annexation of the Sudetenland. Sir Robert Bruce-Lockhart, who was at one time British representative to the Czechoslovak National Council in London, told me that our report strengthened his hand in his efforts to secure recognition for a Czechoslovak government in exile.

The team I gradually collected were devoted to their jobs and, most of them being emigrés, were extremely grateful to have any job at all. A considerable number were Jews and I got to learn a great deal about the Jewish character from my dealings with them.

They were wonderful people and I could not have got on without them. They were the pillars of our establishment. There were two particular things which I always noticed. First, they regularly carried on their private business by telephone and it was rare to find the department's telephones not being monopolized throughout the day by one or other of them. One could not complain if they spent too much time on this because they worked all the harder afterwards if the business they had been negotiating had been successfully concluded. The other thing was that they were a very excitable people. It did not affect my personal relations with them, although occasionally we had a few flare-ups, but they were apt to listen to rumours and assume that the Germans were going to invade Sweden the next day. On such occasions they often came to me to seek comfort and I always felt keenly for them and appreciated the anguish they must have felt. Not all our staff were Jews by any means, however. They were drawn from all creeds and walks of life. There were retired or exiled diplomats, businessmen of standing, an aristocratic Dutch countess, a Polish journalist, a Dutch pastor, an Austrian doctor, the son of a British Ambassador, the son of the last British Embassy Chaplain at St. Petersburg, exiled German and Austrian Social Democrats, a former Commander-in-Chief of the Hungarian Red Army under Bela Kun, and many others.

One day I needed a Norwegian political reader and was told that I would do well to consider a young man named Willi Brandt. I had imagined that he was a Norwegian, but when I was told that he had assumed this name and nationality and was originally a German by the name of Willi Bauer, I had some misgivings. We took in almost anyone *except* Germans. I was reassured, though, when I was told that he was a Social Democrat and the Norwegian Home Front had complete trust in him. I interviewed him and he seemed to me much like an ordinary young Norwegian. I should have been glad to have taken him on but he told me that he had some political work to do as well and asked me as a special favour whether it would be possible for him to do his work for me at home rather than keep regular office hours. His request was unfortunately one which many of the readers made of me. It was far more convenient for them to sit at home and do their work (or sometimes their commercial business!) but that was very difficult for us since there were always points in the translations we had to discuss with them. Moreover, there might at any time be a query from London on which we needed an immediate answer. I had granted such a request to our Czech political reader, who was in fact an anti-Nazi Czechoslovak German from Moravia, because she had begged not to have to appear personally in the office in case it brought down trouble on her relatives in the Protectorate. Since she was able and reliable, and the motive seemed genuine, I agreed to it, but this could not be done for everybody and I was anxious to ensure that it did not become a habit. I tactfully explained to Willi Brandt that he would have to keep office hours if he wanted to work with us. As a result he politely and regretfully declined the post. Another Chancellor-to-be was living not far from us, the future Austrian Chancellor, Bruno Kreisky. I did not meet him but learnt something of his views from a young and well-informed Austrian Socialist who was our 'Austrian political leader' and who was later to be his chef-de-cabinet in the Austrian Foreign Service – Mr. W. Reitbauer.

Sometimes we had difficulty with the nationalist feelings of our readers when they identified themselves with the national prejudices of the country they were studying. The principle on which we worked was that the Hungarian reader covered anything to do with Hungary in all newspapers, and so on. Almost all our readers knew English, the Scandinavian languages, German, French and other tongues, but if they came across a language they did not know an appropriate reader would translate it for them. We had special 'universal' linguists who marked the more generally used papers for all the readers concerned. There was particular controversy as to what was Romanian territory, what was Hungarian and what Czechoslovak. If I allowed the Hungarian reader to take more of Hungary than the Czechs and Romanians thought he should, then the Czechs and Romanians would begin to eye me askance. Similarly if I denied the Hungarian reader parts of Hungary to which he thought he was entitled, then he would become rebellious. In such cases I am afraid I was forced to become rather more pro-Hungarian than I would normally have wished to be, as the Hungarian reader, Willi Böhm, was a man with unrivalled knowledge of Central Europe and it was necessary to keep him sweet. He had been Minister of War in the Hungarian Bolshevik government under Bela Kun but was now a moderate and respectable Socialist. Even so he would still certainly have been shot if he had shown himself in Hungary. He was by no means a Hungarian chauvinist, but there are limits to the reasonableness of the most reasonable Hungarians all the same. (As the Good Soldier Švejk says: 'Some Hungarians cannot help being Hungarians.') I had to be careful not to overdo it, though. However well-disposed our Allies and their diplomatic representatives might be, they quickly became suspicious if I paid attention to anyone who came from a country at whose hands they had suffered, even if the man in question was an emigré and had suffered just as much personally at the hands of the régime there. Mr. Böhm's activities and my connections with him were watched closely not only by my Czech and Yugoslav friends but by the Russians too. It was good training in diplomacy, not merely the managing of this miniature 'United Nations' but also trying to deal with such minor diplomatic complications.

◇ The Swedes at this point were suffering from the concessions they had been forced to make to the Germans the previous year. The transit agreement was attacked in the Swedish press. Some sections of public opinion were getting more and more hostile to the behaviour of the Germans who passed through Sweden, although most Swedes either never saw the Germans or turned a blind eye on them. Countess Amelie Posse, than whom there was no bitterer opponent of surrender to the Germans, had no interest in turning a blind eye: she wanted to stir up as much trouble as possible and made it her business to visit Skåne, the southern part of Sweden, where – specially in the transit port of Trelleborg – she saw how German officials, civilian and military, had settled in and were throwing their weight about all round the harbour. Was it a Swedish town, she asked herself? Where the ferry to Sassnitz landed, and in its immediate neighbourhood, she saw masses of troops in field grey pouring out and speedily being stowed in the long train which was waiting for them. Once she succeeded in worming her way to a spot so close to the train that she could hear what the Germans were saying. A German lieutenant who was strolling up and down wanted to offer her a cigarette or a sweet. She replied with outraged dignity that no Swede would accept it at his hands. He looked astonished and asked why on earth not? 'Wir sind doch nordische Brüder und müssen zusammenhalten.'*

Countess Posse told him a few home truths. 'It's the Norwegians who are our brothers and every decent Swede is ashamed of this traffic, and abominates and despises those who have violated Norway's free land and maltreated her best citizens.' Non-plussed, the German took refuge in the usual propaganda arguments: the Germans had come to rescue the Norwegians from the perfidious

* We're after all Nordic brothers and must hold together.

British; most Norwegians acknowledged it and were grateful to be able to share in Greater Germany's grandiose future. The Swedish Countess could not be expected to swallow this and bawled out such offensive remarks that all the soldiers in the transit vans crowded to the windows to listen. At that moment a Swedish soldier with a fixed bayonet came up and said it was not permitted to *fraternize* with the German soldiers in transit and escorted her off. In Hälsingborg she was similarly enraged by the German officers who occupied the best hotel, behaved like 'cocks on dunghills', soaked themselves with drink, made a frightful hullabaloo in their rooms and the corridors, and even jeered at the English-born Swedish Crown Princess.

What troubled the Swedish government was that the Germans had started to cheat. Göring himself had suggested at the outset that arms could be put into Red Cross vans or Red Cross cases and this was sometimes done. And the thing that caused them most concern was that far more troops were being sent to Norway than were being taken out of it. In March 1941, the German 'overdraft' had risen to 4,200 men and Günther threatened that they might have to stop the traffic altogether. Then he had second thoughts and decided that it was better to try and regulate the question amicably than risk a deterioration of relations in a generally uncertain situation. With difficulty he won the government over to his point of view. It caused great excitement when one day the Germans demanded the transit of a back-log of '76,000 men', and Swedish relief was profound when they apologized next day and said there had been a cyphering error and the figure should have read '16,000'.

The situation was particularly delicate because the Swedes had information that Germany would soon be attacking Russia and that Finland would probably join with them. If they were unco-operative, Germany might seize part of Sweden to help in the build-up against Russia.

The German attack on the Soviet Union on 22nd June 1941, when it came, changed everything, and brought another crisis for Sweden. It eased her moral position: collaborating in any way with a Nazi Germany which was in close alliance with Russia, the age-old enemy of Sweden and centre of World Communism, was against all her traditions. But a Germany which had broken with the Soviet Union and was bent on destroying it was a different proposition altogether, especially as it meant that from now on the Finns would not be left to Soviet mercies but would have a powerful protector in

Hitler. Indeed, they had a good prospect of recovering the territories the Russians had seized from them.

It had naturally been the secret wish of most Swedes that the power of the Soviet Union would be smashed and that in the process Germany would be exhausted and forced to make peace with the West on reasonable terms. When in February Günther had been told of a German report that Hitler had decided to invade Russia at the end of May, he laughed incredulously and said: 'Some time luck will turn our way.'

But what if the campaign proved to be a walk-over for the Germans – which seemed quite possible at the time? Hitler would then emerge from it in such an unchallengeable position that he could turn with full force on Britain and subdue her and the whole of Western Europe before America had time to mobilize in their defence. It would have meant the end of Sweden's independence.

On the other hand, a German defeat held out the horrifying prospect of the whole of Eastern Europe including Finland being at Russia's mercy. In either case it would mean the end of the present Swedish government, which was regarded as not pro-German enough by the Germans and too anti-Russian by the Soviet Union. But the more immediate danger appeared to come from the Germans.

After the defeat of the Finns in the Winter War, the Swedish government had been active in trying to secure from the Russians the best possible terms for Finland. They had first explored ways of protecting Finland by associating her more closely with Sweden, but neither the Russians nor the Germans took kindly to this. Subsequently, as relations between the Germans and the Russians began to worsen, the Finns began to slide more and more into the German embrace. When rumours were rife that Germany would attack the Soviet Union the Swedes hoped that Finland would remain neutral, or at least on the defensive. Officially the Finns deceived the Swedes about their future attitude (although the Swedes had plenty of unofficial information about their real intentions). And so it was a disappointment, though no surprise, when Finland declared war on Russia and took part in the German invasion side by side with German troops.

The Swedes were still bound by their declaration of neutrality made at the outbreak of the Second World War. But during the Russo-Finnish Winter War, they had adopted an attitude of 'non-belligerency'. The Germans would expect them to do the same now, but the situation was a different one this time. The new war could not be so easily separated from the main war as the Winter War had been. The Soviet Union was soon to become an ally of Britain and later the United States as well. The Swedes therefore knew that they must steel themselves to resist new German demands. This time they would come jointly from Germans and Finns.

◇ On crossing the Russian border, the Germans served notice on the Swedes that for the time being they were not to attempt to shoot down any German planes which trespassed into their air space. Later in the morning of 22nd June the German Minister, accompanied by the top Nazi negotiator, Schnurre, handed to Günther and Boheman a list of Germany's demands in the new situation. The most important was the request for transit by the Swedish railways of a whole division – the so-called Engelbrecht Division – from the Oslo district to Finland. Further down on the list came transports for necessities for Finland; tonnage, including tankers, for joint Finnish and German needs; the use of the Swedish lines for telegraphic traffic; permission for occasional planes to overfly Swedish territory; information on airfields suitable for emergency landing; and agreement that crews making emergency landings should not be interned or their aircraft impounded. The Swedes were asked to mine certain waters and withhold from Soviet warships the use of the mine-free channels. German sea traffic over Swedish territorial waters should be maintained as far as possible under Swedish protection. German warships which sought the protection of Swedish territorial waters or harbours should not be interned, but Russians attempting the same should be denied any such facilities. Was this neutrality?

Sweden's attitude to Germany's action against the Soviet Union, the Germans said, would be decisive for her future relations with Germany and now was the time for her to make her political attitude clear. Permission from the Swedish government for Swedes to serve as volunteers on the Finnish front, or even official encouragement for them to do so, would make a favourable impression in Berlin.

Günther at once suggested that the troop transports might take place by sea, but Schnurre rejected this alternative as impossible, quite without reason, as it turned out. Günther then asked a curious question: how seriously would the Germans regard a Swedish refusal? (Did he really imagine that the Germans could answer 'Not too seriously'? It seemed that he was arming himself with the best means of persuading his government to accept the German demands.) Schnurre made the fullest use of the question by answering that it would be an understatement to characterize a Swedish refusal as an unfriendly action. But he stressed (untruthfully, as it happened) that the request for transit should be regarded as a one-time demand. He assured Günther that Sweden was not exposed to any threat of war herself and there was no question of German troops remaining on her territory or of German bases being set up there.

It seems clear that Günther, who had feared more far-reaching demands, had already decided that the German requests could not be refused. This was already obvious from the recommendations he and Boheman submitted to the Cabinet. But it was not fear of an immediate retaliation by Hitler which influenced them both to advise acceptance: it was the longer term fear that Sweden or at least the present Swedish government might be 'written off' by the Germans for the future. This could only be avoided if Hitler's war machine encountered such considerable reverses in the East that it was tied down there for a prolonged period and its striking power was seriously crippled; or if the Allies' successes elsewhere were substantial enough to bring about a turning-point in the war. Boheman could not at that time see either of these eventualities as likely. If Sweden refused the German requests, it could lead to Sweden and Finland ending up on opposite sides, which would be an absurd result in the opinion of the majority of the Swedes. On the other hand, Swedish consent would not, he believed, worsen relations with the West. He did not refer to future Swedish–Soviet relations.

In some ways these arguments were surprising coming from Boheman who was recognized as being probably the most pro-British element in Swedish diplomacy during the war. He was right to ignore possible Soviet reactions, for in fact the Russians were so glad that Sweden did not enter the war that they tended to overlook the concessions she made to the Germans. But the suggestion that 'relations with Britain would not be worsened' by a Swedish breach of neutrality in Germany's favour was a piece of self-deception and justified the 'strong arm tactics' of the British and Americans in dealing with Sweden in the latter part of the war. It must be remembered, though, that at that point it was not to be foreseen that Hitler would make such grave miscalculations in the Russian campaign and the German troops would remain so long bogged down there. Hitler's wars were still thought of as blitz wars.

Later in the day, Günther promised Schnurre that he should have an answer by 24th June, if this could possibly be arranged. Preliminary technical discussions could be started at once, partly on a 'naturally quite non-committal' provisional transit plan, and partly on mining and other naval matters. But how could the Swedes withdraw once they had started technical discussions? Once again, it seems to have been a manoeuvre to force the agreement through. Meanwhile, the Finnish Minister came to the Foreign Minister with a list of requests which was similar to that of Schnurre's. He argued that the German troops were too thin on the ground in Finland and the German division was needed to strengthen southern Finland's defences, where the Soviets had concentrated their forces.

Günther, in recommending to the Cabinet compliance with the German requests, stressed both the need to help Finland and the risks for the future. The Prime Minister emphasized the need for unity in the face of the new situation and, surprisingly, singled out the unique importance of the attitude of the Crown. The King, he told the Cabinet, had said that if they turned down the Germans' request he would 'accept the consequences'. There seems to be no doubt that the Prime Minister had interpreted these words as an abdication threat. There are, however, other possible interpretations. According to Boheman, the King was very upset at the strong opposition there had been in the Foreign Affairs Committee to the idea of yielding to the Germans, and, when the Prime Minister told him that he would face great difficulties from within his party group, Boheman heard the King say: 'If they don't support you, I shan't be here any longer.' Both Günther and Boheman interpreted this rather colloquial ambiguous remark as an expression of the King's fear that a war or a change of government might come out of it. But the German Minister, the Prince of Wied, who was a personal friend of the King, reports him as having said to him in confidence that he had had to go so far as to speak of his abdication. The King had expressly sent for the German Minister on the 25th June to tell him that the government had agreed to the transit of the Engelbrecht Division. Wied spoke of the 'joyful emotion' with which the King had communicated this decision to him and commented that it had proved to him once again how closely in his heart of hearts the King felt drawn towards Germany. The King confirmed to Boheman that he had mentioned abdication to Wied but only to make him understand how hard it had been to get the German request accepted by the Cabinet and that it would not be worth the

Germans' while to come back with further demands. A pro-German source who had an interview with the King twice towards the end of 1941, reported to the German Foreign Ministry that the King had told him he had had dramatic arguments with several Ministers and had threatened to abdicate if the German request was not accepted.

Be that as it may, the King's remark was grist to the mill of the Prime Minister, who could use it to good advantage in his struggle with some of his more refractory Social-Democrat Party comrades. 'It was a damned good thing that the old man said that. I shall use it in my party group.'

The 'abdication threat' soon became public knowledge and caused bitterness in British circles and among pro-Western Swedes. It seemed to confirm the impression the British already had that the King, whose mother and wife had both been German, and who had himself been demonstrably pro-German in the First World War, was 'at it again'. Günther had also by this time acquired the reputation of being pro-German too. How far was this justified?

As far as Günther was concerned, he had made it his policy to lavish as much attention on the Germans as he could in the hope of keeping them sweet. He believed that Sweden's independence during the war and her future status in Europe hung by a thread on the attitude of the Germans and he was prepared to make sacrifices to principles in order to appease them. No one could seriously maintain that it was in Sweden's interest to risk a German invasion or a complete German blockade for the sake of preserving the principle of strict neutrality.

Since he attached great importance to relations with Germany, Günther took personal responsibility for them himself. He was on a friendly footing with the Prince of Wied and frequently received Schnurre. His closest assistants, Söderblom and Kumlin, had close contacts with the German Counsellor, Dankwort. In Berlin, Richert was on excellent terms with the State Secretary in the Foreign Ministry, Weiszsäcker. This relationship may have appeared rather too 'cosy' all round, but Dankwort* and von Weiszsäcker were genuine friends of Sweden and could be relied upon to put a favourable construction on the Swedish representations. Günther left Western relations and relations with the Soviet Union largely to Boheman, who was himself very pro-Western and on terms of personal friendship with the British Minister and with the Soviet

* Dankwort was afterwards to become the German Federal Republic's Ambassador in Canada.

Ambassador, Madame Kollontay too, as far as this was possible. These were quite wise tactics on the part of Günther, because it inclined the Germans to turn a blind eye to the obviously pro-British sympathies of some of his staff, like Boheman and Hägglöf, and some of the members of the government. The Germans could thus always comfort themselves with the thought that their affairs were being dealt with at the highest level – by the Minister himself with the monarch in the background (and not always merely in the background). It is true that the Prince of Wied's despatches reporting his talks with Günther always give the impression that the Foreign Minister was very friendly towards Germany, but was not this what the situation required and was not Günther an accomplished diplomat?

It is interesting to compare the situation in Sweden with developments in Yugoslavia a few months earlier. Prince Paul under great pressure from Hitler and in agreement with the majority of the Yugoslav government had agreed that Yugoslavia should sign the Triple Pact on condition that Yugoslavia should not be obliged to allow the transit of German troops through her territory. Sweden for her part had accepted under German pressure the transit of what over the years amounted to a very considerable number of German troops. I cannot imagine Günther, still less King Gustav, telling Hitler how closely bound he felt to England, as Prince Paul had done. Indeed Günther seems to have left the Prince of Wied with the impression that he felt bound to Germany. How the King and Günther would have reacted in a personal meeting with Hitler, which would have been as great a test for a monarch as for a minister, no one will ever know, since Hitler never attempted to turn the full heat on Sweden as he did on Yugoslavia.

What would have happened if the King of Sweden had abdicated or had dismissed the government and installed a more pro-German one is hard to conceive. In the latter case, the British might have had to resort to the tactics of the Belgrade *coup*. There were plenty of 'rebellious' Swedes in touch with the British Legation and its secret agents. This was what the Swedish Fascist newspaper *Dagen Eko* had in mind when just about this time it published an article about me:

Shortly after Parrott came to Yugoslavia dissident circles began a lively propaganda against all 'policies of surrender' and the pro-German circles in the country, such as Stojadinović, were branded as 'traitors'.

Shortly after Parrott arrived in Sweden a lively propaganda against 'policies of surrender' began here too.

After Parrott had been in Yugoslavia a little longer, various circles began to play with the thought of a *coup*. The same thing has, as though by a special freak of fate, begun to happen here. There it was Cvetković and Cincar-Marković who were to be got rid of. Here it is Günther and Westman* who are to be removed. There it was the intention gradually to ease out Prince Paul. Here they are already discussing the possibility of the King 'quietly abdicating'.

Who knows? Maybe *Dagens Eko* was not so far from the truth. If I had accepted the S.O.E. job and met the man with the missing finger, I might have ended up by removing Günther and King Gustav, in spite of the fact that I certainly did not remove Prince Paul – no, not even by remote control from Sweden.

It is worth recording that the Germans made an attempt to get Sweden into the Triple Pact as they had done with Yugoslavia, although it was a rather half-hearted one. Schnurre raised the subject with Günther on 4th July. He offered a guarantee of the integrity of Sweden's territory and of her independence in return for accession to the Pact. Günther argued that the Pact was not appropriate for Sweden. Schnurre half agreed, but warned of Hitler's possible displeasure and suggested that as Sweden might be pressed to sign some sort of a pact with Germany, a special Nordic pact might be the best substitute. It could manifest the Nordic states' solidarity with the European block without affecting Sweden's desire to remain outside the war or her position as Scandinavia's leading and central power.

Fainter echoes of these proposals were heard by Richert from Ribbentrop and Weizsäcker, and after Schnurre's visits and Richert's reports, Günther was not at all sure that Sweden could go on holding out. He 'wondered whether they ought not to consider whether they could reach some other agreements with Germany which would meet her need to have everything ordered in her so-called "New Europe" '.

Richert predicted a German diplomatic offensive to try and get Sweden into a pact system with Germany and recommended preventive measures against it – the greatest measure of apparent will to co-operate and avoidance of all provocative utterances. But Schnurre, it seems, had gone further than his instructions envisaged. Ribbentrop showed little interest in negotiations for a pact and

* Swedish Minister of Justice.

instructed Schnurre to wait for his personal directives before proceeding further. The Swedes heard no more of Schnurre's initiative, probably thanks to the straight talking the head of the Scandinavian department in the German Foreign Office, Von Grundherr, got from Richert at the beginning of July. Richert told him roundly that the Swedish government were not inclined towards any pact-making at all and advised him that he had better see that the whole proposal was shelved. When Von Grundherr objected that Sweden would sooner or later come into a position of such dependance on Germany that a pact of some kind would be unavoidable, and that Sweden had some sort of moral obligation to adopt a policy 'which conformed to Swedish traditions and declared her full support for Germany's war against the Soviet Union', Richert replied: 'One day you enjoin on us extreme caution and vigilance towards the Soviet Union, warn us to keep our fingers off Finland, and display an icy frigidness towards Sweden, and the next you expect us to join you noisily in sudden war-whoops for Finland and Germany against Russia.' Sweden could not be expected to make such a political *salto mortale* as Germany had done towards the Soviet Union, Richert assured him. No one could say that Richert did not speak out if he thought the circumstances warranted it!

At the end of July, Schnurre came to see Günther again – this time to convey a request from Hitler for the transit of a further division to Finland. Günther rejected it out of hand. It would arouse such resistance in Sweden, he said, that there was no chance of its being accepted. Schnurre said that he had been instructed, to present the Führer's request to the King himself, if necessary. After consulting with the government Günther was able to convey a final 'no' to Schnurre and to tell him that a visit to the King would be hopeless, as the latter shared the views of the government and had asked Günther to tell him so. It was a double defeat for the high-level Nazi negotiator, who had been accustomed to having his requests complied with.

It is however an ironic comment on events in Sweden and Yugoslavia that, after Sweden had, in the words of the British aide-memoire presented to Sweden on 3rd October 1942, been 'assisting the enemies (of Britain) in ways which . . . constitute infractions of the obligations of neutrality' which H.M.G. 'cannot fail to view with the utmost gravity', and while she was still being 'a nuisance' over the Norwegian ships (about which more anon), Boheman was received by Churchill in London with great warmth and was told by him: 'I like the open way in which you defend your country's interests. I regard you as a friend.' No pressure would be put on Sweden from the Allied side to make her enter the war, Churchill assured Boheman. The British government wanted Sweden to remain neutral, even if more strictly so than up to now. It would be a great misfortune if Sweden were occupied or defeated.

If that was so, then it is clear that Swedish policy had been wise and successful. How fortunate it would have been for Prince Paul if he had received such gladdening assurances.

CHAPTER SEVENTEEN ◇ RUSSIAN CONTACTS

◇ After the German invasion of Russia we 'took over' the Russian press and at the time our press reader was the *Times* correspondent for Russia, R. O. G. Urch, who had until then worked from Riga. When things had consolidated, however, and we had become allies of the Russians, we gave this assignment up except as far as concerned those parts of Russia which were held by the Germans. Our own embassy in the Soviet Union would have normally been in a better position to cover Russia proper, but it had been evacuated from Moscow to Kuibyshev – the former town of Samara, far away on the Volga, where the famous Stenko Razin had his hunting ground.

The Russian colony in Stockholm came out of the purdah imposed on them by the Molotov–Ribbentrop Pact and I developed cordial relations with the Soviet Legation. I made an arrangement with the intelligent and forceful Soviet Press Attaché, Madame Yartseva, to exchange telegrams about the Scandinavian press. For about ten days a Russian despatch rider arrived each day and brought me a copy of the Soviet press telegram, and I gave him in exchange a copy of our own. The arrangement then lapsed without explanation. I did not pursue the matter, because I was sure from the beginning that it would not last. Indeed I was extremely surprised that it had ever been agreed on. And in any case the Russian telegrams were of no use to us. They only consisted of uninteresting reports on what the Swedish press were saying and we were in a better position to cover this ourselves. Possibly the Russians found that our telegrams were of little use to them, either, although I doubt it, or possibly they found other more convenient ways of learning their contents. But knowing Soviet conditions, I would imagine that the suspicions of some higher authority had been aroused.

A spur to my activities in this field was my anxiety to keep up my knowledge of Russian, which I had been cultivating in Yugoslavia with the help of White Russian emigrés and the cousin of the last Tsar of Russia. I had been baulked of my trip over the Trans-Siberian railway and felt I had to make up for it in some way. In the Yugoslav Embassy there was a Consul General called Mr.

Šajković whom I met from time to time who was a great Slavophil and spoke perfect Russian, his wife actually being Russian. Later, the Yugoslav Chargé d'Affaires, Brale Marković, who had just come from the Yugoslav Legation in Moscow and whom I got to know very well, proved to be another excellent Russian speaker. He had spent his youth in Russia. He was, in addition, one of the ablest and wittiest diplomats I had met. But since we were now allies with the Soviet Union I also had ample opportunity to try out my Russian on the Russians themselves, and I reserved for my Yugoslav friends the doubtful pleasures of my Serbo-Croat.

I cannot remember a time when our relations with the Russians have been so close. Exchanging telegrams by despatch rider is an exceptional enough state of affairs, but there were other things which happened which were on a par with it. I was a frequent guest at Soviet film shows intended for the Russian colony or for their closer friends. Time and time again we were asked to go out with them and they would also go out with us. We went to pass the evening with one of the Soviet counsellors, Mr. Vetrov and his wife, and were soon singing Russian songs round the piano. I went to dances and danced with the wives of the Russian diplomats, and one day I made a quite innocent assignment in a public library with the attractive Ukrainian wife of the Soviet First Counsellor, Mr. Semenov, to choose English books for her to read and assist her in the study of the language. From some members of the Soviet Legation I learnt that if any of the diplomatic staff wanted to entertain guests they simply rang up the Legation and food was brought along to their flats. Pictures or especially nice furniture could also be borrowed for the occasion.

At one stage, Mr. Semenov approached me about something his Legation could not do for him: he wanted me to help him find an English governess for his young daughter. When I questioned the word 'governess' and asked whether he meant an English teacher, he replied in a roundabout way that he wanted someone to teach his daughter not merely English but English manners as well. It was a strange request from a Soviet official but obviously had to be treated with the closest attention in view of Mr. Semenov's position. We could not allow the Soviet First Counsellor – afterwards to become a Soviet Deputy Foreign Minister – to have a second-rate English governess! They did not grow on trees in a neutral country in wartime. But we were lucky enough to have one ourselves who was giving our children lessons and as she was not fully occupied, I asked her whether she would like to take on the Semenov child, too. She said she would be glad to do so.

She was in fact an Irish girl and a Roman Catholic missionary, and the reason she was in Sweden was that she had been sent out to Finland to try and convert to the Catholic faith Orthodox Russian prisoners-of-war held in Finnish prison camps. I knew that the Russians did not worry very much about religion, but I had at the same time to take it into account that the war had changed some of their traditional Marxist thinking. Patriotism and the national religion – the Orthodox Church – meant something again in official Soviet eyes, and so I suggested to Mr. Semenov that he might like to share our governess but warned him about her background. I added that I was not a Catholic and would not like it if my children were taught a Catholic view of history but that I had no criticisms to make of her as a teacher, and I felt that he would have nothing to fear either. He brushed aside my remarks and asked if she could come and see him at the Soviet Embassy. I understood from her afterwards that she was engaged.

It was a curious episode because it was clear from the start that, however discreet she was, the girl might well tell us more about the Semenovs than she would tell the Semenovs about us. I interpreted their decision to take her on as an expression of their confidence in me. Many, many years later I learnt from reports of a Russian defector who had been in charge of security matters that the K.G.B. had fancied they were grooming me as a recruit for their organization. I must congratulate them on their approach. I was blissfully unaware of it. And if it really was only thanks to the K.G.B. that I had such pleasant relations with my Soviet colleagues during this period, then I am grateful to them nonetheless for providing me with the opportunities I so much enjoyed!

◇ There were times when it looked as if my relations with the Russians would become clouded. One day I determined to return their hospitality by organizing a performance of the Noel Coward film *In Which We Serve* in a small private cinema in the town. It could not accommodate more than thirty people and there were to be refreshments afterwards. The evening was to be a senior diplomatic one and I could only ask the three counsellors of the Soviet Embassy. From other friendly Embassies I asked only one counsellor because there was normally but one in each mission, if that. Judge my horror when at the appointed time there arrived not just three

Soviet counsellors but practically the entire Soviet Embassy, that is to say, some seventy or eighty people. The fear in the faces of some of my other guests, who had their own feelings about the Russian 'invasion' and had not expected to find themselves so outnumbered by them at my party, may be imagined. There was absolutely nothing to be done. The projection room could not physically take more than thirty people and there should have been no doubt that I had only asked the three counsellors. I had to take 'the bulls by the horns', and send them away! It was not an easy thing for any diplomat to do – especially to the Russians – and I was convinced that my whole future as a diplomat would be hopelessly compromised. I was to hear later that other would-be Russophils had had similar experiences. However, the Russians were good sports. I organized another performance for them and they all came again to a man and seemed to have forgotten my possible insult.

✧ I continued meanwhile to make the most of my contacts with them to improve my knowledge of the language. Russian and its glorious literature had become my greatest preoccupation and consolation. When Paris fell to Hitler and the whole British Legation went off on a bathing picnic, I stayed at home and read the works of Turgenev. It may sound very anti-social, but I just could not paddle about with other people at that terrible time. Turgenev helped me over our defeats.

I was never pro-Communist. On the contrary, as a student and as a young man I was non-politically conservative and the main attraction of my Russian studies had always been old Russia. Even when I went to the Soviet Union I was always searching beneath the layers of contemporary civilization for the remnants of what had gone before. In this I think I was perfectly right, for experience there taught me that whereas, superficially, there seemed to have been enormous changes in Russia, in actual fact Mother Russia or the old Russia of history and literature was still to be found buried not very deeply below. I came upon some lines of that great poet and Russophil, Rainer Maria Rilke, which explain what I felt. 'The deep, the real, the ever-surviving Russia has only fallen back into its secret root layer, as once formerly under the Tartar domination. Who may doubt that it is there?' And Russians, whether they are Red or White, have plenty in common, although they may not always like to be told so. It was therefore easy for me to be friendly with Russians who owed allegiance to a system I rejected. I also believed that we should try to have friendly relations with other countries irrespective of ideological differences. As a result, I came to be regarded as too rightist to be acceptable to Soviet Russians and Eastern European Communists and too leftist to re-assure conservative suspicions in England. No doubt both sides thought I was an agent working for either the one or the other.

My passion for Russian was so great that, as my wife has recently reminded me, I used each morning to make the thirty-five minutes walk from the station to my office and back carrying in my pocket little pieces of paper with Russian words and phrases written on them. These I used to repeat to myself as I went, with the consequence that I never noticed anyone I passed in the street. Complaints soon began to be heard that I kept my nose in the air or was deliberately cutting people. It was not in the air. It was in dictionaries. Even today I often spend my time translating imaginary sentences into foreign languages and continue to cut people in the street. A Russian dictionary is a wonderful companion while waiting for a train or a dentist, provided it is not too bulky.

I was simultaneously having to keep abreast of developments in Germany and the occupied countries to ensure that our work was being carried out properly. I was talking Norwegian with Norwegian refugees who came over the frontier, Swedish with Swedish officials, and Serbo-Croat with my Yugoslav friends – in a desperate attempt not to forget a language which I had managed to acquire fluency in – and I was already blossoming out into Czech, which I discovered was a fairly simple language for me to pick up after having learned both Serbo-Croat and Russian. And suddenly in the midst of all this I perversely started learning Hungarian! How this came about was rather singular.

I was something of an amateur footballer. To keep in training I used to go for long runs around my house. And once I played in a team for the British Legation against the American Legation. During the first few minutes of the match there was a break-through and I nearly scored a goal. Then when I got my breath back, I saw everything dissolve into rings and stars. Deciding that something was radically wrong and that I had better leave the field, I went to my wife, who managed to get me home. I was very ill and feverish. I was worried because I saw this as the end of any attempt on my part to play football or take active exercise. I was only thirty-two and I feared I might have developed a weak heart.

It was an enormous relief when the doctor came to see me (he was our Austrian 'medical press reader' from the Press Reading Bureau) and diagnosed it as jaundice – infectious hepatitis, which had been brought back to Europe by German troops.

Jaundice is a most boring illness. I had never had it before and soon found that I had to do something to occupy myself during the intolerably monotonous period in which I was compelled to lie in bed. I concentrated on three things. The first was Mrs. Beeton's cookery book, where I feasted my eyes on the coloured plates of all the most savoury dishes, which I was not allowed to have of course. The second was a street plan of old St. Petersburg on which I followed the movements of the main hero of Dostoyevsky's novel *Crime and Punishment*. And the third was a Hungarian primer. My preoccupation with the topography of St. Petersburg came from my good fortune in having found a 1914 Baedeker of Russia in a second-hand bookshop with a marvellously detailed plan of the city. *Crime and Punishment* was particularly fascinating when I could follow exactly where Raskolnikov went. As for Hungarian, it is a very difficult language, but it has the characteristic that once you have broken its back, it becomes much easier. By the time I had finished my diet and was ready to get up, I had both broken its back and cured my liver. In counter measure, I had absorbed a great deal of Dostoyevsky and no longer thirsted for Mrs. Beeton.

While I was deep in *Crime and Punishment* for the second time and was in a jaundiced Russian mood, news was suddenly brought to me from the office that one of our Polish readers, Mr. Fuchs, had hanged himself over his door in his bedroom. It was a sad reminder of the terrible fate of many of the people who worked in our Bureau. He was a Polish Jew. It was not clear why he had taken his life: probably at that stage in the war he would have felt there was little hope for the future.

He had been a great bibliophil and he loved collecting books on languages and topography. We had had friendly competitions to see which of us could outdo the other in purchasing unusual books on unusual languages and countries. After his death, his collection of books was put up for sale in the Press Reading Bureau and I bought a number of them. If it was a tragic end to our rivalry, his legacy was to prove most valuable to me.

◇ My principal occupation was to deal with what the press wrote, but although I still resisted attempts to involve me in secret intelligence work, opportunities did arise to supplement the information we were getting from the newspapers by talking to neutrals who had been on visits to the enemy countries. If through friends I heard that some Swedish businessman or Swedish journalist had visited Germany or one of those countries and it seemed possible to meet him either at someone else's house or have him to lunch, I did so. With my knowledge of languages and a good day-to-day grasp of what was happening in the various countries, I was in a good position to cross-question such neutrals on things that really mattered. I did not enquire about military or detailed economic matters since that would only have frightened them, and anyhow I was quite inexpert on such topics and could hardly have evaluated what they told me. I was interested in general political developments: how the people felt about the war, how they regarded Hitler and his Quislings in the various countries, and what hard news there was about the Nazis themselves. I cannot say that any of the information I gained was of great importance, but we used to send it home by diplomatic bag from time to time just as a diplomatic officer would.

Most of the staff of the Press Reading Bureau probably viewed their assignment with us like a 'Colditz': they longed to escape from it but could not. They bore my somewhat tyrannical direction with good humour. Our Belgian reader, Mr. Bellens, told us that as soon as he was 'out' he would write a book called *Under the Heel of the British.* I believe he went into the Belgian Foreign Service and I often wondered whether he found the Belgian heel any more bearable. Such was the 'Parrott House', as it was nicknamed.

The news we obtained was supplemented by further information supplied by the press readers in the Bureau, some of whom had good connections. I did not ask where it came from but sent it back to London, and sometimes it proved extremely useful. One important factor was that some countries were now regretting having joined the wrong side or having become involved with Hitler, and convinced of an Allied victory, were anxious to put themselves in the clear by the time the peace conference came. One of these countries was Hungary. My Hungarian press reader, Willi Böhm, who, as I have said, was an ex-politician, was always a mine of information. Indeed, many emigrés collected information to prosecute the interest of their own countries and very often this information was slanted in specific directions. As far at the Hungarians were concerned, the ruling régime were anxious to whitewash themselves as far as possible in British and American eyes – and if possible to find an alibi. There was however a world of difference between the world of Willi Böhm, which was Social Democrat and international and the world of the Hungarian Minister in Stockholm, Mr. Ullein-Reviczky, which was traditionally nationalist and conservative. Willi Böhm would have been shot on the spot if he had returned to Hungary, and at one time Mr. Ullein-Reviczky and his nationalist friends would probably have been the first to see that this was done. But now all Hungarians felt themselves to be in the same boat. Much as they hated each other and disagreed in their political views, they were united in one thing – they had to do everything they could to prevent Hungary being further mutilated after the Second World War, through which they would all suffer. Hungary should at least try to emerge from it better than she had after the First World War.

I started becoming the recipient of approaches and information from various groups of Hungarians. Mr. Böhm began to provide me with copies of fascinating diplomatic despatches from officials like the Hungarian Military Attaché in Berlin, the Consul-General in Belgrade, the Minister in Bratislava, etc. No doubt the Hungarians were distributing these on a fairly wide scale. Were the documents I was shown forged? I had no means of finding out. The Foreign Office who liked to read them allowed me to maintain discreet relations with the Hungarian Legation in Stockholm and I was the object of much hospitality from some of its younger members. I was careful about the Minister himself, who was obviously a much more exposed personality. One of our difficulties was that any sign that we were being friendly with the Hungarians was at once seized on by the Czechs and Yugoslavs and thrown in our faces. Worse than that, we could never be sure that the Soviet Embassy in London would not start making démarches on the subject in London – as they in fact did.

One very good example of Soviet nagging and British compliance was the case of the citizens of the Baltic states. We covered the Baltic newspapers in the Press Reading Bureau and had on our staff people from the Baltic countries as well as Britons who had spent most of their lives there, were more Baltic than British and had Baltic wives. There was in Stockholm a Baltic emigré community, too, of some distinction which got on well with the Swedes. The Finns and Estonians are of common stock and their languages are not so dissimilar. Because the Swedes had a special tenderness towards the Finns, they extended this to some extent to the Estonians and to a lesser degree to the Lithuanians and Latvians as well. They accorded such emigrés good treatment during their forced period of exile in

Sweden as a result of the Soviet and German occupations. However, as the fortunes of war turned and Russia not only started to demand the permanent annexation of the Baltic States but seemed likely to overrun them anyway, the British government thought that it was not worth while spoiling Anglo-Soviet relations for the sake of – a ha'porth of Balts. Under Russian pressure, therefore, they began to take a tough line with those of us in the Legation who had contacts with these worthy and much-suffering people.

One day the Foreign Office sent the Minister a letter drafted in the high-handed terms so characteristic of it at that period which instructed him to tell members of his staff that they were to break off relations with persons 'purporting to be Baltic nationals'. When this letter came to me my hackles rose. I was irritated by the arrogant tone of the letter, and scornful of its craven and inhuman implications. No account was taken of the fact that we were employing former Baltic nationals in our Legation or British subjects who were married to Baltic nationals and could not therefore avoid having contact with their wives' relatives or friends. I therefore wrote a minute to the Minister in perfectly reasonable terms explaining how difficult it was for us in our department to implement this instruction. Naturally, the letter was not meant for the eyes of the Foreign Office itself but for the indulgent attention of the Minister. But as so often happened in the dear old Chancery at Stockholm in those days, the minute was just 'bunged off' to the Foreign Office, no doubt with some brief covering letter or possibly with nothing more than a compliments slip, and in due course no doubt it found its way to the desk of the high official who had drafted the letter. As a result, we received another letter which was drafted in still more arrogant – even menacing – tones. 'Mr. Parrott would be well advised to carry out the instructions of Her Majesty's Government. Mr. Parrott should etc., etc. Mr. Parrott could etc., etc.' We now had no alternative but to break off all contacts with our Baltic acquaintances, all 'for the blue eyes of the Russians', as the Norwegians say. We could not dismiss our Baltic employees, of course, as it would have drawn Swedish attention to our surrender to Soviet demands. That was precisely what the British government were anxious to avoid. The Swedes were very anti-Russian and their attitude to the Western war effort might well be affected by signs that we were making too many concessions to the Russians. Nor could we dismiss those members of our staff who were married to Baltic nationals. They were British subjects, even though some of them could speak better Russian or

'Baltic' than they could English. However, it put paid to any contacts we might have had with the unfortunate Balts living in Stockholm, who were in fact quite good sources of information (as well as excellent Russian speakers). Some of their information may well have gone to the Russians instead, as the following incident will show.

Miss Church, who had accompanied us during our long saga in Norway, and who worked for a short time as my secretary before taking a more permanent post in the main part of the Embassy, became engaged to our Latvian reader, Mr. Danziger, from Riga. The wedding took place in the British church and was conducted by the British Embassy chaplain, a delightful man of old-fashioned views who would call on the members of the Legation staff and chide them for not going regularly to church, adding the veiled threat that he might not baptize their children nor, what was worse, even bury them. In his sermon he dwelt on the difficulties of marriage: to the congregation it seemed that he was reluctant to join the couple in wedlock because of the dismal prospects it held for them. When the service was almost over, the congregation had risen and the organist was hanging out of his seat to catch the signal for the Wedding March, his voice could be heard loud and clear: 'And where shall I send the bill, Mr. Danziger?'

Since Miss Church had no father and she was alone with her ageing mother in Stockholm she paid me the honour of asking me to give her away, which I gladly did. The best man was Prince Lieven, a scion of one of the great Russian noble families who came from the Baltic states. And a fine best man he made, too, being tall and large and very much the kind of Russian one used to read about. Today Russians all seem to be very short except Brezhnev and he is certainly no great height. Stalin and Khrushchev were midgets, in comparison with the Russians one met on the streets in earlier days.

Some weeks after the wedding, the best man was arrested by the Swedish police on the charge of espionage for the Soviet Union. He was subsequently found guilty and sentenced to a term of imprisonment. The probable explanation was that he had been helped out of Russia through the kindly offices of King Gustav of Sweden, who as a neutral king had influence with most European powers. But no doubt the Russians, while agreeing that he should go, had made it a secret condition that he should do some work for them. The unfortunate Count may have had to satisfy his former masters. There were many cases of the kind. However, this particular one showed that the citizens of the Baltic states were not necessarily always acting against the interests of the Soviet Union, and the Soviet government were perfectly happy to use them for *their* purposes when they wanted to.

◇ Stockholm continued to be an interesting sounding board for international politics and it became especially valuable when the Finns, who had been fighting against the Russians for the second time, began to put out peace feelers.

As the tide in Russia turned against Germany and the Soviet Army surged back towards Western Europe, the Finns had once again been put in a difficult position. Rumours were rife in Stockholm that the Finnish government had secretly sent a delegation to Sweden to take soundings of the Russians. Everybody was trying to find out what was really happening and I was extremely surprised one day to have a call from Mr. Semenov who asked me if I could come and see him. It was unusual for Russian diplomats to ask members of Western missions to visit them in their offices. It was even rare for them to make calls on us. However, anything connected with the Russians was interesting, so I went along and obliged him.

When I was ushered in, he greeted me in a very friendly way and talked about everything else but the matter he had wanted to broach. I still had no idea what it was. Then suddenly, looking very secretive, he advanced towards a big cupboard in his room. I was convinced that he was going to give me some secret information and that my career in the Foreign Service would be made. But to my amazement he took from the cupboard not a file of papers but a bottle of cognac. Pouring me a full tumbler he asked me to sit down. It was about half past three in the afternoon, and not a time I particularly favour for drinking cognac. I am usually just getting ready for a cup of tea. I was also too old a hand at the game not to realize what he was up to. I knew he wanted some information, but I was astonished when I learnt what it was. Turning to me confidentially, he said: 'I've been reading in the Swedish press that there are supposed to be some Finns here in Stockholm. Do you know what they are doing?' 'Well,' I replied cautiously, 'the Swedish press say that they have come to Stockholm to negotiate with you and I would have thought that you would know that.' He smiled enigmatically: 'Is that what they're saying?' he asked. And thus the conversation went on, while he tried to extract from me my views on the press report without giving anything away himself.

I was at a loss to know why he should have asked this question of me of all people. I was not a senior member of our Legation and it was not likely that I would have any information which would be of value to him. The explanation was probably that I was useful to him as a sounding board. He may have received instructions from Moscow to find out what the Western powers thought about these peace negotiations. He surely could not have imagined that I was the chief representative of the Secret Service in Stockholm? Once when I stayed rather long at a Soviet Legation reception and all the staff had had a drop too much, one of them came up to me and asked me if I knew Comrade So-and-So. When I said I did not, he leered at me and went on: 'Well, you certainly should, Mr. Parrott – that is to say, if I know your functions aright, *if I know your functions aright.*' (A big wink.) I concluded that Comrade So-and-So must be the chief representative of the M.V.D. (later the K.G.B.) in the Legation. As far as Semenov's approach was concerned the only other explanation I could think of was that the negotiations were being handled by the Soviet Minister herself, Madame Kollontay, and Semenov had been left in the cold and was trying to check up on her activities, either on special instructions from Moscow or on his own initiative.

According to Boheman, Madame Kollontay was much bothered by her Counsellors, particularly Semenov, whom she found too doctrinaire, too stiff and too full of prejudiced opinions. Moreover, as she told him, *they were too eager to look into everything she did.* 'But I have hit on an excellent way of getting rid of my esteemed collaborators, at least for a few hours a day. I have told them they can do nothing useful here in Sweden if they don't learn Swedish. I have found a few nice Swedish girls who can give them lessons. And these lessons are held during walks in Lilljanskogen. Then I can work in peace.'

As the story shows, Madame Kollontay was something of a law unto herself. She was a member of the Bolshevik Old Guard and was quite unlike any of the other Soviet diplomats of my day. She belonged to another age. I remember seeing her at the receptions the Soviet Legation gave on the occasion of the October Revolution. She sat enthroned like a queen with two ladies sitting one on each side of her, like ladies-in-waiting. At one time, she had been a very beautiful woman and a woman of temperament too. There were tales of how she had danced with the revolutionary sailors at Kronstadt. But, when I knew her she had become a little wizened, and her cheeks resembled dried-up but still rosy apples. I thought the way many of the Western ambassadors paid court to her was too servile. But she was a remarkable woman. Before becoming the first woman ambassador of the new Soviet state, she had sat in prison in various Scandinavian countries. No other diplomat could rival her in that kind of experience.

CHAPTER EIGHTEEN ◇ GUN-RUNNING

◇ Early in 1942 Anglo-Swedish relations were painfully disturbed by a sharp conflict of views on the Norwegian ships problem. It began this way. When the Germans occupied Norway, some thirty Norwegian ships were lying in Swedish ports. The Norwegian government immediately requisitioned them all and chartered them to the British government. Some of their captains and crews obeyed the Norwegian government; others submitted to the orders of their German-controlled owners and sailed back to Norway.

Right from the start, the Swedish government took the view that under Swedish law it had no power to prevent the ships from sailing freely out of Swedish ports, and that the ownership of the ships could only be decided by Swedish courts. It was obviously in the British interest that all ships still remaining in Swedish harbours should sail to Britain with as little delay as possible, not the least because some of them had valuable cargoes which were badly needed for the war effort. Our production of tanks was falling badly behind schedule and we were in a hurry to get the ball-bearings and the machine tools for manufacturing them which the ships had on board.

At the beginning of 1941, five of them slipped out unnoticed and reached British ports with full cargoes. It was a brilliantly executed *coup*, stage-managed by George Binney, an official in the Ministry of Economic Warfare, who was serving as 'Assistant Commercial Attaché' in our Legation. He was knighted at once for his exploit.

Binney was then just turned forty. Previously, he had by the age of twenty-seven led three research expeditions to the Arctic, among them the Oxford University Expedition which set up a record in 1924 by reaching latitude 80.15°.

The German warships that lay on watch outside the Swedish ports and were supposed to be in control of all outward and inward sailings were taken by surprise by this daring exploit and the German authorities were mortified. They vented their spleen on the Swedes and accused them of having been in league with the British. They threatened that if a similar break-out attempt were made with the remaining ships they would institute a general blockade of

Sweden and cut their life-line to the West. The Swedes became understandably agitated.

After some long drawn out and very complicated negotiations between the Swedish, German and British governments, the Swedes decided to refer the question of the ownership of the ships to their courts, and an interim embargo was laid on all of them pending the court's decision. The British government then appealed against the embargo on the grounds of immunity. The Swedish *Överexekutor** declared the embargo invalid, but was overruled by a higher court. However, as Swedish law then stood, the *Överexekutor's* decision could not be overruled in one specific case, so that the ships were still legally able to make a dash for Britain. To prevent this the Swedish government hastily introduced a bill to legalize the overruling by a higher court. Not unnaturally the British were incensed at such an action, which they regarded as anti-British, and trade negotiations which were being carried on with the Swedes in London at that moment, ran into heavy seas.

There was indeed something very phoney about this trumped-up piece of legislation. But the Swedish government were desperately afraid that if the Norwegian ships slipped out again the Germans would be true to their word and stop the Gothenburg traffic, which was indispensable for Sweden's economic survival. The Swedes were terribly short of oil. All cars were being run by producer gas instead of petrol, and huge piles of logs for the production of the gas were being piled up in the streets of the bigger towns. Oil could only be obtained through the blockade by agreement with the Allies and the Germans. They were dependent on Germany for their coal, too. They were therefore ready to change the law if it was not favourable to their immediate policies and might provoke a severe fuel crisis.

Finally, on appeal, the case was heard before the Supreme Court, where on 17th March 1942 the verdict was that the British could rightfully claim immunity and no restraint could therefore be laid on the ships. The British case was vindicated and there could be no longer any possibility of anyone preventing the ships' departure.

Now it was the turn of the Germans to vent *their* anger. They accused the Swedish government of having adopted an unneutral stance throughout the whole affair, of preventing the rightful owners from disposing of their ships and of unjustly favouring the British case. They ended by repeating their threat to stop the Gothenburg traffic.

* The equivalent of an Enforcement Officer.

At that point, the ten Norwegian ships which had been freed by the verdict of the court lay in the harbour at Gothenburg. The largest, *Skytteren*, was just over nine thousand tons, the smallest, *Lind*, about two hundred and forty-five, the average tonnage of the whole lot being rather over four thousand tons. All the ships were fully loaded with their valuable cargoes, and they were all set to leave. It was clear that as soon as an opportunity occurred, another attempt would be made to get them away.

And George Binney was still in Sweden and in charge. However, getting them out this time would be an extremely hazardous affair, because it was most unlikely that the Germans would allow themselves to be caught unawares a second time, and their warships were in a state of high alert. The prospects for a successful breakout were grim, and the casualty risk was very high. Not only were the Germans in a dominating position and on the watch, but they were using all the means they could in Sweden and within the harbour of Gothenburg itself to find out exactly when the ships were planning to slip away. It was almost impossible to conceal such information from them and the Norwegian ships were at their mercy. There was no hope of assistance from the British navy because since the occupation of Norway no British warship had penetrated into the Skagerrak or Kattegat and another consideration was that the crews were mainly Norwegian and there was therefore a danger that Norwegian lives might be sacrificed to no purpose.

The Swedish government were not slow to drum all this into Mallet, and to stress the dire consequences for Sweden if, as a result of a break-out, the Germans isolated her from the West. Similar appeals were sent to Washington.

From the Swedish point of view it would clearly be best if no attempt at a break-out were made at all; but if one had to be made it was vital that it should go off smoothly and that no naval engagements should take place within Swedish territorial waters. With the excitement and emotion which was mounting on both sides, anything might happen. The German warships could take the law into their hands and break into Swedish territorial waters; the British could send in their own warships in a last attempt to rescue the ships. The Swedes did all they could to minimize these disagreeable possibilities, and they ordered away a German ship which was lying very close to the Norwegian ships so that it should not be used as an observation point for spying on them.

Instructions were given that the Norwegian ships should go direct out of Gothenburg's harbour into the *outer* Swedish territorial waters. When they reached that area, they could put to sea from whatever point they wanted to. But they should not go and hide in some creek in the *inner* territorial waters where Swedish warships could not protect them from possible German violations of Swedish waters. If they could not get to sea, they should return to Gothenburg. The Swedes mobilized patrol boats and fighter planes so that they could protect the ships and control events during their passage out. They also arranged for the Norwegian ships, which were given Swedish pilots and control officers, to be stationed at various points in the mouth of the river Göta in order that they could get out of the harbour with a minimum of obstruction. They were not allowed to stop or anchor as they left for any purpose except to drop the pilots and the control personnel. German spies haunting the harbour were tailed, and special measures were taken to prevent unauthorized persons from visiting the harbour for intelligence purposes.

It was difficult keeping the Germans out. Two officials from the German Consulate and other German agents got into the harbour on the pretence of visiting the captain of a German ship lying there. Before it was removed, this ship had been moored in a position which afforded an unhampered view of the Norwegian ships. The officials telephoned the German Legation (the Swedish police listened in on their conversation) and kept them informed of what was happening. Police reports confirm that the German agents' reports were the immediate cause of the subsequent concentration of German warships and aircraft off the Swedish west coast. The officials were arrested by the Swedes for espionage and accused of being responsible for the untoward developments.

Before the break-out had been decided on, Churchill was shown the relevant papers and on 30th March he minuted on them, 'If there is no chance whatever of the ships escaping, is it worth while running all the other risks?' However, it was too late. It was said that Binney was afraid of being accused of cowardice if he called it off. At about eleven o'clock in the morning of the following day the chief of the Swedish naval district was informed that the ships would be leaving in the course of the evening, when it was expected that a layer of mist and snow would lie over the Skagerrak. Between 8.30 and 9.30 p.m. the ten ships left the harbour. It was clear moonlight. After midnight, visibility did deteriorate as a result of fog and snow, but not sufficiently to protect the ships. Between two and three o'clock in the morning some of them ran into German control ships on their way out to the north. They took various evasive manoeuvres and waited for a more suitable occasion to proceed further.

At seven o'clock in the morning, five Norwegian ships were observed by the Swedes to be steering back towards Swedish territorial waters. They were warned by the Swedish authorities that they must not shelter in Swedish inner territorial waters, whereupon they continued along and within the outer territorial waters in a southerly direction. As visibility became worse and more favourable for a breakaway, some of them were again seen veering in a westerly direction. In the meantime, they had been joined by two other ships, *Lionel* and *Dicto*, but these two returned to Gothenburg the same evening. No violations of neutrality took place in connection with the attempted break-out.

Only two of the ships, the 8,000 ton *Newton* and *Lind*, the smallest of them, reached British ports safe and sound. The remaining six came to grief. Three of them were sunk by German warships and three others scuttled themselves to avoid capture. According to the German accounts, two hundred and thirty-five men were picked up and captured.

The Swedish warnings had been justified. The Germans had been on their mettle and their control had been most effective. From the British point of view this second, almost desperate undertaking had been a failure. But the British authorities were not impressed by the measures taken by the Swedes to ensure the speedy and uninterrupted departure of the ships, and they complained that the Swedish actions had in fact had the reverse effect and had impeded the breakaway. It was from the Germans, however, that the Swedes were to receive the worst reproaches, and with good reason. Forty Norwegian sailors had reached London by train. Reuter interviewed them and published statements made by some of them, who boasted that they had 'shot off a Heinkel' with machine-gun fire. Now when the Norwegian ships had first arrived in the Swedish harbour they had carried no weapons. There was therefore every reason for the Swedes to enquire more deeply into the Reuter report. The Swedish Foreign Office had several times warned Mallet that the ships must not be armed during the time they were in Sweden and he had given them an assurance that nothing of that kind was intended. And so, when the Reuter report appeared in the Swedish press, Boheman called Mallet to see him and confronted him with it. Mallet's only answer was that he had no knowledge of any plan to arm the ships.

On 10th April the Swedish government received a long memorandum from the German Minister repeating all the complaints he had made before about an unneutral attitude on the part of the Swedes that favoured the British and the Norwegian governments. The Germans had quickly seized on the fact that the ships had been armed with guns and ammunition. One of the ships, they claimed, had fired with eight guns. The presence of so many guns and their emplacements on board, they complained, could not have passed unnoticed by the Swedish guards. They had proof that a British subject had been smuggled on board for the express purpose of mounting the guns. The Germans also protested that *Dicto* and *Lionel* had been allowed to return to a Swedish harbour, and insisted that they should be prevented from making any further break-out attempts.

Then in another note, the Prince of Wied claimed that they had evidence that all the ships had been supplied with arms towards the end of 1941 by Sir George Binney himself, who had used a car belonging to the British Consulate-General in Gothenburg for the purpose. The emplacements for the guns had been mounted on the decks of the ships while they were in the harbour, and with the help of the Consulate all the ships had been supplied with explosives for scuttling. The German government again protested at the fact that the Swedish government or the Swedish authorities had adopted a position favouring Britain throughout the affair.

Binney was himself on board *Dicto* when the ships set out and he returned with her to Gothenburg. As he was back in Stockholm, Boheman called both him and Mallet together to the Foreign Ministry to ask for an explanation. Mallet was extremely embarrassed. He apologized for having deceived Boheman, but said he had done so in good faith and requested Binney to tell Boheman frankly what had happened. Binney was not embarrassed at all but only disappointed that the venture had failed. He admitted without reservation that the ships had been armed, explaining that, as the person most responsible for bringing the ships to England, he had regarded it as his duty to do all that was in his power to protect the crews and the ships. On his own responsibility he had brought on board twenty light English machine-guns. The intention had been that British ships would meet the Norwegian ships at various points and transfer more powerful guns to them. This meeting had unfortunately never taken place.

In addition, Binney said he had provided the ships with tubing for the discharge of fireworks, and with a supply of fireworks too. He had done this, he said, to make the enemy think the ships were better armed than they actually were. Although Boheman expressed deep indignation during this conversation he confessed afterwards that, had he been in Binney's place, he would have done the same, if he had been really convinced that the machine-guns would increase the ships' safety, though, as it happened, he doubted very much whether this was so.

The British on their part complained that when the Swedish warships ran out with the Norwegian ships they only drew attention to the break-out and endangered their escape. When five of the ships, including *Lionel* and *Rigmor*, steered towards Swedish territorial waters, they were met by two Swedish destroyers and a mine-sweeper, who signalled to them: 'Put out to sea.' The mine-sweeper shouted through a megaphone: 'Get out of Swedish territorial waters.' One ship asked to be able to continue in territorial waters and possibly make for Gothenburg but was given short shift. 'If you go back to Gothenburg, you will never go out again,' she was told. Subsequently the Swedes admitted that the officers had behaved incorrectly. The British thought that the Swedish naval authorities had not only behaved incorrectly but disobligingly. Another complaint was that Gothenburg radio relayed a call for help from *Newton* and thus betrayed her position to the Germans.

Later the British Minister was also sent for by Günther who proposed that the remaining ships in Gothenburg should be laid up without prejudice to the Norwegian and British governments' right to their ownership. After what had happened, he declared, it was clear that Binney would have to leave Sweden. The Germans were told that machine-guns had in fact been smuggled on board but any complicity by Swedish authorities was denied. In a personal letter to the German Minister, Günther assured him that *Dicto* and *Lionel* would not be allowed to leave the harbour again.

When the matter was investigated by the Swedish authorities it was established to their satisfaction that the machine-guns had indeed been smuggled on board in small pieces by employees of the British Consulate. According to their evidence Reynolds, a clerical assistant in the Commercial Department of the Legation, used to carry with him on his visits to the ships bags or packets of various sizes. Sometimes he had on a long and wide overcoat under which he hid the things he brought. He stored them on board in the captain's bathroom. These employees had not had to undergo a personal search because of their Consular status. Only the captains on board had had knowledge of the smuggling. The machine-guns had not been brought out until the ships had left Swedish waters.

◇ Although these events gave rise to a series of exchanges of notes between the German and Swedish governments, no reprisals were taken against the Gothenburg traffic for the time being. The British laid off some of the crew of *Dicto* and *Lionel* and said that they would let the ships remain temporarily in Gothenburg with their cargoes on board.

It seemed that the problem of the Norwegian ships could rest. The Germans had done their job satisfactorily and the British had been the losers. But the 'peace' was not to last long. The Swedish Foreign Minister had been unwise to give the German Minister a specific assurance that the two remaining ships would not leave the harbour again. By doing so he brought his country into cross-fire from both the great powers, whose prestige was by now heavily engaged in the affair.

On 21st December 1942 two representatives of the Ministry of Economic Warfare, led by Mallet, called on Günther and left an *aide-memoire* in which it was flatly stated that unless the Swedish government gave permission for *Lionel* and *Dicto* to sail within two weeks, the British and U.S. governments would cut off all imports into Sweden from the West.

This was particularly awkward because Boheman had just returned from America, where he had negotiated a valuable trade agreement. The U.S. now informed Günther that the implementation of this agreement was dependent on satisfaction of the British demands for clearance for the Norwegian ships.

Günther was in a difficult position. He had always maintained that the Swedes could not legally prevent the ships from leaving and now he had tied his hands by the categorical assurance he had given to the German Minister. What was worse, he appeared not to have the whole-hearted support of the government, nor even of his own colleagues. Boheman argued strongly before the Cabinet for the release of the ships. One of the Ministers commented that the Foreign Minister and the Permanent Under-Secretary seemed to be following opposing policies.

The end was an anti-climax. The Swedish government saw that they were being held to ransom by the British and that they had no alternative but to give way, and they informed the Germans of their intention. Strange to say, the Germans took the announcement more calmly than the Swedes had expected. Hitler was already in trouble on the Eastern Front and did not want any further complications. However, what really exasperated the Swedes was that when the British were at last informed that the ships were free to leave, they did nothing about it! Apparently the Admiralty had decided that the risks of another break-out were too great.

Then the Germans suddenly announced that 'for operational reasons' permission could no longer be given for Swedish ships to pass in and out of Gothenburg to the West, and imposed their threatened blockade. But after painstaking diplomacy the Swedes succeeded in getting the traffic resumed at the beginning of May 1943.

◇ Relations with the British were not too good. Charles Hambro told the Swedish Counsellor in London that he could understand why the Swedes had felt compelled to pitch into us immediately after the arming of the ships had been discovered, but their continued nagging and carping had made a very bad impression in Britain.

When this was reported to him by the Legation in London Boheman was highly indignant and replied as follows:

This remark is completely incomprehensible, and I assume that you refuted it in the most forceful way not only to Hambro but also in the Foreign Office, who were behind it.

What are the facts of the case concerning the British Legation?

1. The personnel of the British Legation were implicated in the Rickman affair.* The British Military Attaché on his own admission stored the explosives.

2. There has been espionage activity by two British attachés, as is confirmed by numerous police reports and their own open boasts of it all over the country.

3. Admitted smuggling of arms by Binney and Reynolds.† Coleridge and Waring‡ gravely implicated. Reynolds was admitted to Sweden after the British Minister had given the most solemn assurance that former Finnish volunteers would not indulge in any activities contrary to our laws.

* A sabotage trial in Sweden, in which members of the British business community in Stockholm were tried and sentenced to imprisonment for attempting to blow up installations in a harbour where iron ore was being exported.

† Employee of the British Consulate-General in Gothenburg, formerly a Finnish volunteer, and before that allegedly a horse-trainer.

‡ Employees of the British Legation in Stockholm.

4. The transmission over the British cypher systems of a Czech espionage league's information including information about Swedish military affairs.

Our only reaction to all this has been:

1. A quiet request for the two attachés to be replaced. This was only made after many months.
2. A single mild rebuke in the press for the exceptionally mean way in which the arms were smuggled on board the ships. This rebuke was sensationally mild and not repeated.
3. A request that Binney, Coleridge and Waring should leave Sweden. Binney went almost at once. Coleridge and Waring are still being retained here against all international usage and we have been extremely considerate and have not pressed for their imminent departure. That this can be interpreted as 'a continual nagging and carping at the British Legation' seems to be the expression either of complete ignorance of what has been going on or of a mentality which I have difficulty in characterising. I cannot say more than that in our relations with the British Legation we have been as considerate as we could possibly have been.

I sincerely hope that the Legation will devote all imaginable energy to dissipating all misunderstandings on this question.

Well, it is a great relief for a diplomat to be able to 'blow his top' for once, because otherwise he had to suppress his feelings, and it can be like keeping the steam back in a boiler, as I well know. Boheman certainly had reasons for his indignation, and his resentment is further shown by his postscript to the letter where he mentions that a leading Danish member of the resistance had just travelled across Sweden with his family on a false passport issued by the British Legation. '*Very* considerate!' he adds with an audible snort. Britain was most generous with the issue of false passports in the war years.

Söderblom in a letter to Prytz, the Swedish Minister in London, gave further details of British 'sins':

Major Munthe's activities in Stockholm have long caused us irritation because we have clear proof that he has organized from Sweden an intelligence service on Norway by sending Norwegian and Swedish experts there. Some of these helpers are now being held in gaol or detained. . . .

After Mallet had given his word of honour that Munthe would not undertake anything which went beyond his obligations as a diplomat, there were additional indications that Munthe was nonetheless continuing with his former activities, and so the Foreign Minister took the matter up with Mallet again and was satisfied with further assurances from him.

Recently, however, a whole organization has been uncovered which is being led by an Englishman called Millar who uses the name of Mortensen when dealing with the Norwegians (he speaks Norwegian without an accent) and has been organizing and carrying out sabotage activities against the communication lines in Norway from Sweden. In connection with this certain Swedes and Norwegians have, among others, been sent to Norway to reconnoitre suitable objectives. From there they have gone by boat to the Shetlands and Scotland, and been trained in sabotage and supplied with explosives. After returning to Norway by the same means they have carried out their assignments and fled back to Sweden. Here some of them have been caught and have made full confessions. It is also now evident that Mortensen has been in close touch with Munthe. . . .

I do not need to tell you what dangerous consequences it may have for our country if activities of this kind on the part of the British Legation are tolerated. Perhaps I should add that some time ago the German Naval Attaché, Admiral Steffan, was sent home at our request after it had come to our knowledge that he had organized commercial espionage. I must stress that the charges laid against Steffan were much less incriminating than what can be laid against Munthe. The Germans immediately complied with our request and Steffan was replaced by a new Naval Attaché without any fuss.

But of course the British could not see that their arms smuggling and other peccadillos were so grave compared with the sins of the Swedes, who could be said to be smuggling considerable quantities of arms and men daily over Swedish railways to the German troops in Norway. What were one or two machine-guns in Gothenburg or some sabotage against the Germans compared with quantities of artillery and thousands of fighting personnel conveyed for years over Swedish railways and through Swedish territorial waters?

So the Swedes received little satisfaction from the British. Their protests were treated as of minor importance. 'I would point out that the conveying of this armament on board the ships in question appears to constitute at most a minor offence against the relevant Swedish laws. The captains concerned have already been fined and in the circumstances my government desire to express their regret that this incident should have occurred.' That was the sum total of Eden's reply to Prytz.

Mallet subsequently came to tell Boheman of secret plans for sending a number of specially built civilian motorboats into a Swedish harbour to take off the cargoes on board the Norwegian ships. The Swedish government saw no reason to object, provided Swedish laws were complied with. Nor did they oppose a British request that *Lionel* and *Dicto* should be moved to a more secure harbourage. Eventually, in this way, all the valuable cargo was safely 'ferried' to Britain.

CHAPTER NINETEEN ✧ BACK TO SLAV ENCHANTMENT

✧ Although I was resolved not to get drawn into any underground activity, I was not left in peace for long. Hambro's original invitation to me to go into this kind of work had been disposed of comparatively easily. But later on, and particularly when I began to meet neutrals who had been visiting Germany and other occupied countries and sent reports home of what they said, other secret intelligence organizations of ours became interested, as might have been predicted.

I remember a brigadier who came out on a secret errand. He had a game leg, presumably from a war wound, and I saw him continually stumping up from Stockholm towards Strandvägen, where the Legation and my office were, and back to his hotel. (There were times when the weather conditions were such that our planes could not safely fly over enemy territory from Stockholm to London and visitors were marooned in Stockholm for a much longer period than they would have liked.) This brigadier came to see me and tried to persuade me to hand over all my 'sources' to his organization. It was absurd because I had no 'sources'. The people I received information from were never regular contacts. They were *ad hoc* acquaintances. I do not think I ever met anybody before they went to Germany and said to them, 'Oh, when you go there please find out exactly this and that and come back and report to me.' I simply got in touch with people who had come back from Germany and were willing to talk about it – mainly journalists, businessmen and diplomats – and I did it in a very open way. Thus I resisted take-overs from two secret organizations which from one side or the other attempted to get hold of me and all my 'bags of tricks'. If I succeeded in keeping the flag of the Press Reading Bureau flying, I cannot say that my attitude endeared me to these organizations, and no doubt some people would say that I failed in my patriotic duty. But at least I maintained successfully and uninterruptedly what I had originally undertaken to do – namely, to set up and operate an 'open' organization of restricted scope. My objectives were limited ones but no less useful and patriotic for that.

· · ·

◇ And now a word or two about my own private life in Stockholm during these years. I was still suffering from financial and material difficulties because I had had no real job for so long. I had stayed in Sweden in order to take the post of Assistant Press Attaché, but that job had come to nothing. After that I had been told to set up a Press Reading Bureau. But whenever something new is set up, especially in wartime when communications are bad and even departments in Whitehall seem unable to communicate with each other across the road, it takes a long time to get one's salary fixed. Although I did eventually get a salary, I was not given any allowances since I was considered to be a 'local employee'. More and more people were sent out from London to form the staff of the Legation and they were all regarded as 'home-based' and given tax-free rent and foreign service allowances, which made their salaries considerably higher than mine. We had also lost a lot of our clothes and other possessions in Oslo so that we were both of us in a bad way sartorially. It remained hard to find furnished accommodation, and as rents were high (furnished accommodation was the only possibility for us then), we moved from one furnished flat to another I don't know how many times.

The first flat we took had had no bathroom, though it had a very delightful old Swedish piano, a so-called *Taffelklaver*, but we were soon forced to take another one, which belonged this time to a Finn. It was a newly furnished modern flat and after we had been there some six months we heard that the landlord was ready to sell us all its contents for an incredibly small sum. However, we had no money at all and it was not possible at that time to borrow any, with the result that we lost the chance of acquiring possessions cheaply and had to move on. Finally, we took a small villa in the country district outside Stockholm. Even there we had trouble, for the landlord failed to put in all the things he had promised – including a bath. It looked once again as if we were going to stay dirty, but this time I resolved to have no nonsense, bought a bath and forced the landlord to pay for it.

On the whole, the Swedes were very chary about letting flats to diplomats because of the so-called 'diplomatic clause', which permitted the lessee an escape from the contract, and also because some diplomats are reckless and careless tenants. But when they learnt that my wife was Norwegian, they generally changed their attitude. They had considerable sympathy for their Norwegian brothers and sisters, as was proved to us on many occasions.

During this time we acquired two more children, both sons, Michael and Jasper, and my wife had her work cut out trying to look after the children on a shoe-string without any help. Looking back, I have no doubt that our government treated us very badly and very unfairly compared with other members of the Legation. My work was difficult and demanding. I used to have to go into the office on Sundays since we had to work every day: there was certainly no five-day week for us during the war. This meant that I was not able to give much help to my wife and I returned home exhausted to find her more worn out than I was.

But if we both of us were subjected to serious strain during these four years, we could also count ourselves lucky, because we could look up at the sky in Sweden without fearing that a doodle-bug would fall down on top of us, or a rocket land in our street. It was a precious thing for our children to be able to grow up in a relaxed atmosphere. Of course, there were repeated scares that the Germans might invade Sweden, but as the war continued both sides seemed to derive advantages from Sweden's neutrality and it became more and more unlikely that either would disturb it.

It was perhaps because my war job in Sweden followed so closely on the very dedicated job I had in Yugoslavia that I grew accustomed to regarding my work as something which should take precedence over everything else. After the war I found myself unable to get back into the tempo of peace because I had scarcely known what it was. My life in Yugoslavia had been a race against time. Could I develop the King in the short time at my disposal so that he would be capable of taking over the reins of government? Then came the war years, and again everything had to be done at blitz-like speed. I can remember being woken up in Stockholm in the small hours of Christmas Day by a telephone call from the Legation. I was told that an urgent telegram had come in and I must come and see it at once. It had the kind of prefix which meant that it must be dealt with instantly and personally. I dressed and set out – I think that at this time I was living on the outskirts and it was quite tricky getting in at night. Imagine my feelings when on reaching the Legation and reading the telegram, it turned out to be a request for me to purchase a book at a booksellers and post it to London! It seemed inconceivable that anyone could think that the purchase of a book could justify someone being dragged out of bed early on Christmas morn. This was the *senseless* war tempo.

. . .

◇ It gradually became clear that Germany would soon be defeated, which meant that I should be without a job. I could not believe that the Travel and Industrial Development Association existed any more and it was therefore very necessary for me to secure my future. I was approaching thirty-six, and had a wife and three children. I had enjoyed my role as a political observer and the most obvious thing for me to do was to apply to be taken into the Foreign Service. I made my application, and as the process would take a long time I tried to find a temporary job first.

◇ We all of us had great hopes for the period after the war. It would be a new world and a better one. As far as I was concerned, it would mean starting a new life. I had never really had a career. Now was the time for me to settle down into one. When I had been a boy at school – I suppose I must have been about thirteen or fourteen – my classics master asked me what I intended to do when I left, and I remember answering: 'Join the Consular Service.' He stopped and looking at me in surprise, said: 'Then why are you doing classics? Why aren't you doing modern languages?' I was so dashed by his remark that I abandoned the idea of being a Consul.

What was it that attracted me about being a 'Consul'? Of course I knew nothing about the Consular Service, as it then was, or I should certainly have said an 'Ambassador', which was what I eventually became. It was just that I had a vague idea of the fun of being somebody who represented his country abroad and lived in foreign parts.

The idea that a classical education was the wrong preparation for the Foreign Service was sheer nonsense. In point of fact my best subject at school was French and I had no doubt that I would get on well at other modern languages. However, in those days the teaching at schools was best on the classics side and the élite of the schools tended to read classics. Languages and the 'modern' side were equated with a commercial career which was considered intellectually inferior. It is not surprising that our thinking has changed since then, but even today a modern languages degree is not highly rated. At the same time, there are many people today who would still think that a classical education would not fit one for anything practical and that knowledge of Latin and Greek would not be of much use in a diplomatic or consular service career, where they would suppose that living languages were indispensable.

I would not call myself a good linguist, although I seem to have acquired the reputation of being one. It is true that I speak, write and read Russian, Serbo-Croat, Czech, Slovak, German, French, Norwegian and Swedish, that I read Italian and Slovene without difficulty and that I could once read Hungarian, Flemish, Spanish and Portuguese reasonably well. It is also true that I have no difficulty in construing Polish, Bulgarian, Ukrainian or Lusatian Serb if I hear it spoken (in the case of the last you would have to go far to hear someone speaking it), or see it written, and that Romanian has no terrors for me. I once had a conversation with a Turkish military attaché in a sham Turkish made up of the Turkish words in Serbian. When I speak of a linguist, however, I mean someone who speaks a language perfectly, and I should be more than glad if I could speak any one foreign language as perfectly as many foreign colleagues of mine do. If we compare, shall we say, a Swedish diplomat with a British one, the former has all the linguistic advantages. He is sure to be fluent in English, French, German and his own language, and it is quite possible that he will have acquired another language in the course of his career. British diplomats can generally speak French alone and sometimes indifferent French at that, although through having served in various posts they may often have acquired another language such as Spanish or perhaps Arabic. This is not to say that we do not have our orientalists, our 'old China hands' or our Russian specialists. But specialists they most of them are. The only modern language I was taught properly at school was French. Otherwise I was self-taught and, while I believe that a knowledge of modern languages is vital to a diplomat, this can be acquired *en route.* A classical education is still as much an asset for high administrative posts as it always has been. Nor do I think it necessary for an entrant to the Foreign Service to have studied politics as a university subject, because diplomacy does not develop according to the laws they teach in politics departments any more than recent Russian history has developed according to Marxist principles. On the other hand, some grounding in economics and business methods seems to me most desirable.

Once I was in the Foreign Service, I was struck by the fact that hardly any of the career members knew anything about economics and that only those of them who had been trained as Consuls were really business-like. The administration in our missions abroad appeared terribly amateurish and inefficient, mainly because no one had had any kind of business training whatsoever. Of course, when I joined, I had had no training either. But I found that I did a lot of things in a business-like way by instinct, whereas many of my colleagues seemed to lack that instinct.

Another thing I was told – when as a student I was thinking of going in for the Foreign Service – was that it was essential to spend six months in France and another six in Germany in order to be able to pass the language part of the exams. I was badly off as a boy, since my father had retired from the Navy on a very small pension, and when he died my mother had a widow's pension of literally £90 a year! There was therefore no question at all of my being able to spend six months in France and six months in Germany at that time. There was no one to pay for it: grants, scholarships and fellowships which provide these facilities today simply did not exist. It was, I think, chiefly on these grounds that I completely abandoned the idea of sitting for the Civil Service examinations and went in for schoolmastering – not as a permanent occupation, but as a preparatory step for something political. Subsequent experience taught me that what I had been told about the need to study abroad was also utter nonsense as far as the Diplomatic Service was concerned. If the colleagues with whom I was to rub shoulders had in fact spent a year abroad before taking their entry examinations, they had remarkably little to show for it. Without any of the advantages that money and perhaps birth and position had given my colleagues, I hoped that I was at least a match for them in the ability to speak and understand foreign languages. At the same time, having had five years experience at a foreign court and another five years at British Legations in Scandinavia, I had undoubtedly gleaned some knowledge of diplomacy as well.

◇ For my temporary employment I asked for a Foreign Service posting – the kind of posting which is open to people who are not regular members of the Service – and while I was negotiating this the Foreign Office was still considering whether I was suitable for permanent establishment as a regular member of the Service.

First replies from the Foreign Office were not encouraging. Later, I was offered the post of Press Attaché at Sofia. I had no wish to be a Press Attaché and did not even know whether I would be good at doing the job. In London they naturally assumed that because I was running a Press Reading Bureau, my obvious employment would be that of Press Attaché. The main function of a Press Attaché is publicity (in fact, propaganda). I had not had experience of this even in Oslo, nor was it anything that I felt particularly qualified to do. I hated propaganda, especially now that the war would soon be over. What I was interested in was diplomacy and the study of political developments abroad.

The trouble was that the straight diplomatic posts were not normally given to people who were temporaries, and until the decision was taken about my acceptability for establishment in the Diplomatic Service I should have to content myself with a Press Attaché job. But to go to Sofia! Stockholm had been very important, but would be much less so after the war. If I were to leave and go to a Slav country, why should I have to go to the smallest and, at that time, least significant one? Moreover, to someone who had spent five years in Yugoslavia and had grown to love the Serbs, it was curious (though not surprising) news that the Foreign Office should be thinking of sending him to Bulgaria! Serbs and Bulgarians have never got on particularly well together throughout their history and anyone popular with the Serbs might well be regarded with some reserve by the Bulgars. I felt I must try and get a more active posting.

It was no good asking for Moscow. The post had been filled. When it had been decided to appoint our first Press Attaché there my name had come up for consideration among others, but I was in Stockholm and it was difficult for me to press my claims. I did find out that Mr. (afterwards Sir) Kenneth Grubb, then Controller of the Ministry of Information, had had my name in mind as a possibility. There were certain people in the Ministry in England, however, who were 'cornering' Anglo-Russian relations, and I was not one of the fraternity. Someone else was appointed. But when his tour of duty eventually came to an end, they would have to look for a successor. I went to London and spoke personally to Grubb. He was not unsympathetic but seemed undecided. At the same time I was hesitant about pressing him too hard. Conditions might turn out to be very difficult in Moscow for my wife and family.

And then my thoughts turned to Prague. During my time in Stockholm I had grown very interested in Czech and in the Czechs, and I thought that Prague would be a nice change after Belgrade. In any case, it would scarcely be possible for me to go back to Belgrade itself, for already in Yugoslavia there were the makings of a strong Stalinist dictatorship which would certainly be anti-British, and my past connections would obviously put me 'out of court'. Czechoslovakia, on the other hand, would, it was hoped, be restored as a democratic republic. It was a Western state with much that bound it to England and France. It would be a rewarding place to work in. But the main feature about it which attracted me was that it was more of a cultural centre than Belgrade: it possessed one of the loveliest cities in Europe and had wonderful music. So I transferred my efforts to trying to obtain the post of Press Attaché in Prague.

Some time later, I heard from London that there were a large number of applicants and that I should have to come over to England, stand in the queue and be seen by the future Ambassador in Prague, Mr. (Sir) Philip Nichols. I travelled over for the interview. My numerous rivals included the *Times* correspondent, Godfrey Lias. But I was chosen. Maybe it was because Nichols had been Head of the Southern Department when the Yugoslav *coup d'état* took place in 1941 and he remembered how he had seriously considered sending me to Belgrade and attaching me to the young King. Anyhow, my association with King Peter had probably helped me again. It was a pattern which was to be closely followed on other selection bodies. When I came up before a Civil Service Commissioners' Board to be examined on whether I was suitable for eventual establishment in the Foreign Service, the Chairman of the Board and some of its members questioned me most of the time about my experiences as tutor to a King. Did they do their work of selection badly? I am not sure. It is true that they were more interested in hearing about my experiences as a King's tutor than gauging my suitability as a future diplomat. But the job I held for five years in Belgrade required more personal diplomacy than any post I occupied afterwards in the Service.

◇ I was to go to Prague, then, as Press Attaché and in January 1945 I left Stockholm for Britain to be briefed for my new assignment. It was sad leaving Sweden. I had become much attached to Stockholm and for my wife it had become a second home. But much as I loved Scandinavia, which was one of the pleasantest parts of the world to live in, I had no doubt that it would now be the Slav and Central European countries on which the political interest of the world would be focused. And I still had a burning desire to immerse myself in their languages and cultures. I had not forgotten my five years in Yugoslavia and was impatiently awaiting further initiation into Slav enchantment.

ACKNOWLEDGMENTS

◇ The events I describe in this book took place between thirty and forty years ago. To fill the gaps in my knowledge of them and the blanks in my memory I have drawn on information contained in contemporary official documents and memoirs written by some of the main actors in the events, although unfortunately it has not usually been possible for me to talk to them in person. A notable exception were the discussions I was privileged to have in recent years with H.R.H. Prince Paul, the former Prince Regent of Yugoslavia. I should like to express my deep gratitude to him for so patiently allowing me to question him for so long, and to H.R.H. Princess Olga for graciously permitting me to reproduce an entry from her diary on the day of the Belgrade *coup*. Prince Paul's remarkably clear memory, which spans so wide a field of foreign relations and in personal matters goes back nearly eighty years, combined with his acute intelligence and scholarly knowledge made this a particularly precious and rewarding experience.

In my researches on all three of the countries I describe I have drawn extensively on Foreign Office documents. Transcripts of Crown-copyright records in the Public Record Office appear by permission of the Controller of H.M. Stationery Office. In the case of Norway I should like to acknowledge my debt to Sir L. Woodward's admirable book *British Foreign Policy in the Second World War*. I should like to thank the Swedish government for kindly giving me permission to look into the files of their Foreign Ministry for the war years, which constituted an important source of material for my main chapter on Sweden. I am also much indebted to Mr. Erik Boheman's very human and fair-minded book *På Vakt*, Mr. Gunnar Hägglöf's witty memoirs *Samtida Vittne*, and Countess Amelie Posse's *Åtskilligt kan nu Sägas*.

I should like especially to place on record my very warm gratitude to Dr. Wilhelm Carlgren of the Swedish Foreign Ministry for the kind personal help and advice he gave me, and the benefit I had from studying his book, *Svensk Utenrikspolitik 1939–45*. Needless to say, the responsibility for all my assumptions, opinions and theories on the events discussed is entirely my own.

Finally, I should like to acknowledge a further debt – to my old friend and colleague from our Embassy in Prague, Mr. Albert Harrington, whom I was so happy (and so fortunate) to find again in the Public Record Office.

INDEX

The plate references are asterisked